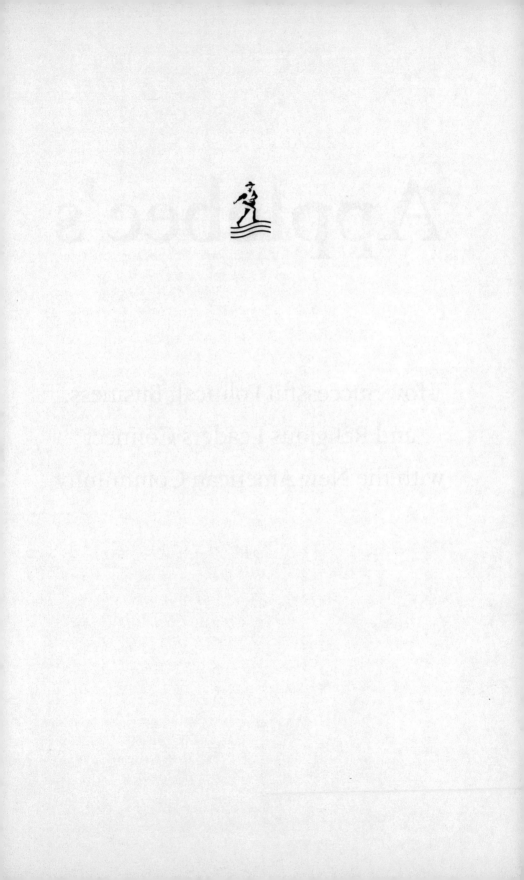

# Applebee's

How Successful Political, Business,
and Religious Leaders Connect
with the New American Community

# America

Douglas B. Sosnik,
Matthew J. Dowd
and Ron Fournier

*Simon & Schuster*
New York London Toronto Sydney

SIMON & SCHUSTER
Rockefeller Center
1230 Avenue of the Americas
New York, NY 10020

For information about special discounts for bulk purchases,
please contact Simon & Schuster Special Sales at
1-800-456-6798 or business@simonandschuster.com

Book design by Ellen R. Sasahara

Manufactured in the United States of America

10  9  8  7  6  5  4  3  2  1

Library of Congress Cataloging-in-Publication Data

Sosnik, Douglas B.
    Applebee's America : how successful political, business, and religious
leaders connect with the new American community / Douglas B. Sosnik,
Matthew J. Dowd, and Ron Fournier.
    Dowd, Matthew J.
    Fournier, Ron.
        p.   cm.
Includes bibliographical references and index.
1. Leadership—United States.   2. Leadership—United States—Case
studies.   3. Organizational change—United States.   4. Business enterprises—
United States.   5. United States—Politics and government.   6. United States—
Civilization.   I. Title.
HD57.7.S693   2006
658.4'092—dc22                                              2006047298

ISBN-13: 978-0-7432-8718-0
ISBN-10:      0-7432-8718-5

To the true loves of my life: my mother, Marge, and father, Robert, my wife, M. Fabiana, and my wonderful children, Christopher, Phillip, and Nicole, whom we are expecting this fall.

—Douglas B. Sosnik

I dedicate this book to my four children: Daniel, Benjamin, Jacob, and Josephine. You are the light in my eyes, you touch my soul and you are who bring God's hope and Grace to our world. And I want to give credit to my mom and pop, and my ten brothers and sisters who helped and help me remember where I came from, respect the opinions of everyone, and to not take myself too seriously.

—Matthew J. Dowd

To my wife, Lori, and our three children, Holly, Abby, and Tyler; you shine brighter for me than "the fiery passion of a thousand suns." And to our extended families in Michigan and Florida whose love and support erase the miles between us.

—Ron Fournier

# Contents

# Authors' Note

---

W E'RE ASKED ALL THE TIME, "What is Applebee's America?" The answer is that it's what you want it to be: a town, a neighborhood, a job, an Internet site, a church or club or cause, a place of business, or any place that evokes a sense of community, a feeling that *I belong here*. It is your way of life.

Our journey to "Applebee's America" began more than three years ago and resulted in a unique partnership between a Democratic strategist and former adviser to President Clinton (Doug Sosnik), a Republican strategist and adviser to President Bush (Matthew Dowd), and a nonpartisan political writer (Ron Fournier). In an era of polarization, we found huge common ground despite our political differences. We wrote this book in the third person because we shared the workload and agreed on every conclusion and opinion.

It's a long story about how the three of us got together, but suffice it to say that it was Sosnik's idea to write the book, Fournier's idea to recruit Dowd, and Dowd's idea to incorporate the groundbreaking connecting strategies he helped pioneer during the Bush campaign in 2004. The research for this book actually began in 2003, when Fournier got into the habit of conducting voter interviews at Applebee's. The restaurant chain is ubiquitous in the nation's fast-growing exurbs and caters to middle-class families—the perfect setting and cast for a book about how to connect with a fast-changing American community.

Much of the book takes place in exurban Detroit because Fournier was born and raised in the city, Dowd was born in Detroit and raised in the nearby suburbs, and Sosnik worked in Michigan, spending quite a bit of time in Howell and surrounding Livingston County. For us, Livingston County is a slice of "Applebee's America," a friendly, familiar community filled with the type of people whom we wanted to know more about. That was our motivation for writing this book: to discover the strategies and characteristics that help political, business, and religious leaders succeed. It turns out they have more in common than not, perhaps because they are appealing to the same people: folks like you.

We learned about Applebee's culture of community when we visited Lloyd Hill and his team in Overland Park, Kansas. We met Rick Warren, the megachurch maven whose marketing and organizational genius is easily translated into politics and business. We drew on our collective political experiences, of course, and interviewed dozens of experts, including a few associates (Howard Schultz is a friend and client of Sosnik, and Dick DeVos is a friend and client of Dowd). Most important, we spoke to dozens of ordinary people whose stories reminded us that America is a collection of communities—some as traditional as prayer groups and neighborhood associations, and others more groundbreaking, such as a globe-spanning Internet video game, a "house party" for 20,000 Republicans, or a megachurch's motorcycling club. It was through these and other examples of people coming together—these bastions of belonging far outside Washington, D.C.—where we found "Applebee's America," a restless people in an era of change.

The Authors, February 2006

*Introduction*

# Stormy Present

*In times of change, learners inherit the Earth, while the learned find themselves beautifully equipped to deal with a world that no longer exists.*

—American social philosopher ERIC HOFFER

*It is not the strongest of the species that survive, nor the most intelligent, but rather the one most responsive to change.*

—CHARLES DARWIN

WILLIAM JEFFERSON CLINTON breezed to reelection in 1996 just two years after his presidency hit the rocks with his health care reforms a bust, his relevancy in doubt, and voters so leery of his leadership that they gave Republicans control of Congress for the first time in forty years.

George Walker Bush won reelection in 2004 even though a majority of Americans questioned his rationale for invading Iraq, fretted about the economy, felt the nation was headed in the wrong direction and favored Democrat John Kerry on education, health care, jobs, Social Security, and most other policies.

Lloyd Hill helped build Applebee's International into the world's largest casual dining chain despite his lack of experience in the restaurant business, middling reviews of the chain's food, and the challenges of running a "neighborhood grill and bar" in 1,700 neighborhoods.

Rick Warren preached to 21,000 worshipers each week, inspired countless megachurch copycats, and wrote the best-selling hardcover in U.S. history just two decades after starting his southern California ministry with no money, no church, no members, and no home.

Each case makes you wonder: *How did that happen?* The answers are in this book, which goes behind the scenes of political campaigns, corporate boardrooms, and church services to reveal how these and other leaders succeed in an era of intense transition. Whether your product is a candidate, a hamburger, or the word of God, the challenge is the same: How do you connect with a fast-changing public and get them to buy what you're selling?

But this book is not just about America's successful leaders. It's also about the people they lead. Anxious witnesses to terrorism, technological revolutions, and globalization, Americans are making seismic changes in the ways they live, work, and play—and those choices ultimately determine how they vote, what they buy, and how they spend their Sunday mornings. People are adjusting their lifestyles for many reasons, chief among them their insatiable hunger for community, connection, and a higher purpose in life. Presidents Bush and Clinton, and Hill and Warren, figured that out, one of the many things they have in common.

We'll draw lessons from the successes of these and other *Great Connectors* that you can apply to your next election campaign, your business or your church. It starts with their ability to touch people at a gut level by projecting basic American values that seem lacking in today's leaders and missing from the day-to-day experiences of life— among them: empathy and optimism; strength and decisiveness; authenticity, faith, and a sense of community, belonging, and purpose. Some people would call these traits, but that term is too small for such an important concept. Hair color is a trait. Authenticity and community are values.

Values are what Americans want to see in a candidate, corporation, or church *before* they're even willing to consider their policies and products. The choices people make about politics, consumer goods, and religion are driven by emotions rather than by intellect. That's why we call President Bush's tenacity, President Clinton's empathy, and the sense of community and purpose of Hill and Warren *Gut Values*. Hill wasn't just selling burgers. The presidents weren't just peddling policies. Warren wasn't just pitching the word of God. They were making *Gut Values Connections*.

With rare exceptions, Gut Values Connections don't just happen. They are built. Chapters 1 to 3 (starting with politics, then turning to businesses and megachurches) explore the common routes taken by Presidents Bush and Clinton, and Hill and Warren, to establish Gut Values Connections and the new tools and technologies they have used to communicate them. First, they adapted to a changing public in ways that existing political, corporate, and religious institutions had not. Second, they found and targeted their audiences through strategies that predict voting/buying/church habits based on people's lifestyle choices. Who are their friends? Where do they get their information? Who do they turn to for advice? What are their hobbies? What magazines do they read? Where do they live? What car do they drive? Where and how do they shop? What do they do for vacation? What angers them? What makes them happy? What do they do for a living? These and thousands of other lifestyle questions form a vast constellation of data points that Presidents Bush and Clinton, and Hill and Warren, used to make and maintain Gut Values Connections. Each man had his own name for what Bush's team called "microtargeting." We give this critical tool a new name—*LifeTargeting*—because the strategy tracks people based on their lifestyles. We also reveal new details about how Presidents Bush and Clinton, and Hill and Warren used the targeting strategy. Third, they said the right things to the right people in the right ways. Great Connectors use every available communications channel and new technology to push out their messages. We'll share their marketing strategies, including one that is as old as mankind and more powerful than ever.

## GREAT CHANGE

We use the second part of the book to delve deeper into the intense societal changes that are forcing political, business, and religious leaders to adapt or perish. Change is a key word here—rapid, bone-jarring change. Consider what we've seen in just one generation:

- Women flooding the workforce, reshaping the American family
- Vast immigration, migration, and exurban sprawl
- The rise of a global economy
- The dawning of the infotechnology era
- The worldwide war against terrorism

In chapter 4, we'll explain how this crush of events has changed Americans. Tired of chasing careers and cash, many Americans entered the twenty-first century determined to rebalance their priorities and find a higher meaning in their existences. The September 11, 2001, attacks intensified these feelings. People spent more time with family and friends, took longer vacations, and sought jobs with flexible hours. They spent more time praying and volunteering.

The meaning of life changed in America, or at least the meanings of money and success changed. The first years of the twenty-first century saw a rise in the number of people who said cash could do more than bring them pleasure; it could help them contribute to society, leave something to their heirs, or otherwise help their children. A growing number of Americans told pollsters that being a good parent or spouse defined success for them. GfK, a leading market research and consulting firm that has tracked public attitudes for decades in its Roper Reports consumer trends research, called this era of transformation a "recentering" of the American public. "Whatever" became "whatever matters." And "getting by" wasn't good enough when "getting a life" was possible. The "Me Generation" has given way to the era of "us."

Yet life continues to grow more complicated. Global competition is forcing jobs overseas and cutting salaries, pensions, and other benefits that had defined the twentieth-century middle class, producing the first generation of Americans who fear their children will fair worse than they did. The dot-com bust wiped out the savings of middle-class Americans who had finally thought they were getting ahead. No longer are Americans' perception of the health of the economy and their consumer confidence driven by macro factors like the unemployment rate, the inflation rate, and Gross Domestic Product growth. They have become untethered to those factors as they change jobs multiple times and worry about pensions and health care. The coarsening of popular culture has fueled the belief of many people, particularly parents, that their values are out of sync with the elite. New technologies both improve and complicate the way Americans live.

"Life is changing too damn fast," Cindy Moran told us one day at an Applebee's restaurant in Howell, Michigan. A single mother of two, Moran was one of the dozens of people we interviewed for this book to gauge the mood of the country. "It's not easy being the kind of mother I want to be," she said, carving a high-calorie path through a bowl of spinach dip while her daughter begged for more, "not with life stuck on fast-forward."

Buffeted by change, people like Moran crave the comfort of community. They want to know their neighbors and meet people like themselves no matter where they live. They want to help improve their neighborhoods and their country. They want to belong. Chapter 5 explores how Americans are redefining the meaning of community and finding new ways to connect in an Internet-fueled expansion of civic engagement that political, business, and religious leaders are just learning to exploit. Building communities on the Internet is a potent new trend.

People continue to lose faith in politicians, corporate executives, religious leaders, and the media, all of whom used to be society's public opinion leaders. In this age of skepticism and media diversification, Americans are turning to people they know for advice and direction. We call these new opinion leaders *Navigators*: they're otherwise average Americans who help their family, friends, neighbors, and coworkers navigate the swift currents of change.

Twentieth-century technologies gave rise to the television era, and for five decades mass media had an outsized influence on the American public. New technologies are breeding niche media—cable TV, podcasting, wireless messaging, etc.—and returning us to a pre-TV environment in which word-of-mouth communication is the most credible and efficient way to transmit a message. With their large social networks, Navigators rule the word-of-mouth world. In chapter 6 we tell you who the Navigators are and why they're so important to political, business, and church marketers.

Americans are not just changing how they live. Many are changing *where* they live, and the implications are enormous for would-be Great Connectors. Chapter 7 explores the impact of an increasingly self-polarizing society. The mobility, technology, and relative affluence we enjoy allow us to pick up stakes and move to communities of like-minded people. And so we see middle-class minorities and immigrants moving from cities to inner-ring suburbs; suburban white families to new exurbs; and young singles and empty nesters circling back to cities, where they're gentrifying decayed neighborhoods. Ironically, as the nation is becoming increasingly multiracial, the American people seem to be seeking more homogeneity in their lifestyle choices. It's as if life were a pickup basketball game and Americans are choosing teams. Actually, they're bigger than teams; they're tribes.

In the final chapter, we sum up and look to the future. How will the country change in the next few years? How will the next generation of Great Connectors be created? Chapter 8 profiles "Generation 9/11," led by the young men and women who were in high school or college when terrorists struck New York and Washington. They are generally more civic-minded, politically active, and optimistic about the nation's future than Americans in general. Indeed, they put their baby-boomer parents to shame and remind us in more ways than one of the so-called Greatest Generation, men and women who came of age during World War II. A college student today has more in common with his or her grandparents than parents. These future leaders are off to a promising start. Their attitudes about diversity, social mobility, women in leadership, technology, institutions, and spirituality portend big change for the next wave of Great Connectors.

Any leader hoping to draw lessons from this book should start first by jettisoning any preconceived notions about how to connect with voters, consumers, and churchgoers, ignoring conventional wisdom and the false assumptions of pundits. This book debunks their many myths. Our findings include:

**Myth 1:** A company's product, a candidate's policies, or a pastor's sermons are the main appeal for most people.
**Reality:** People are looking first for a Gut Values Connection.

**Myth 2:** September 11, 2001, changed Americans.
**Reality:** The attacks did hasten change, but Americans had been transforming their values and lifestyles since the mid-1990s.

**Myth 3:** Technology has created a more disconnected nation.
**Reality:** Americans are using new technologies to build new forms of community and civic engagement.

**Myth 4:** The glut of information has made people more independent and less reliant on one another.
**Reality:** The Information Age and fragmented media have caused people to turn more often to peers for advice, giving rise to Navigators.

**Myth 5:** A vast majority of megachurch worshipers are antigay, antiabortion conservative Republicans.
**Reality:** Few megachurches are politically active because they don't want to turn off a single potential customer. A surprisingly large portion of megachurch worshipers are Democrats and independents.

**Myth 6:** The electorate is divided into Republican "red states" and Democratic "blue states."
**Reality:** Americans are highly mobile and self-polarizing, so it makes more sense to categorize them by their lifestyle choices rather than arbitrary geographic boundaries. We call them *Red Tribes*, *Blue Tribes*, and *Tipping Tribes*.

**Myth 7:** Republicans have a lock on exurban America, as shown by the fact that because Bush won 96 out of 100 of the fast-growing counties in 2004.
**Reality:** Democrats can win exurbia because voters in these new, fast-growing areas are driven by their lifestyle choices and values, not partisanship.

**Myth 8:** Americans slavishly vote their self-interest.
**Reality:** Their idea of self-interest is more selfless than most politicians realize. Voters will turn to a candidate who reflects their Gut Values over one who sides with them on policies.

**Myth 9:** The best indicator of how a person will vote is his voting history or views on abortion, taxes, and other issues.
**Reality:** The key to predicting how a person will vote (or shop and worship, for that matter) is his or her lifestyle choices. To borrow and bastardize a phrase from President Clinton's 1992 campaign—It's the Lifestyles, Stupid.

Is all this change good or bad for America? The truth is, we don't know. But we do know it's inevitable. It is no time to ignore the lessons of success from Presidents Bush and Clinton, and Hill and Warren— four imperfect men who nonetheless understood the value of community, connections, and purpose in this new social order. Great eras of change seem to occur about every seven or eight decades (a long life span) and follow a war or crises. In this post-9/11 world, the nation's leaders should pay heed to the words of Abraham Lincoln, who called on his generation to have the courage and foresight to change. "The dogmas of the quiet past are inadequate to the stormy present," Lincoln said. "The occasion is piled high with difficulty, and we must rise with the occasion. As our case is new, so we must think anew, and act anew."

This book will help twenty-first-century American leaders think anew about the people they serve. We hope the people they serve will find comfort in knowing that there are new ways to connect, create community, and navigate change.

# PART I

# Great Connectors

# 1

## POLITICS:
## Values Trump the Economy

*His 1840 campaign plan divided the party organization into three levels of command. The county captain was to "procure from the poll-books a separate list for each precinct" of everyone who had previously voted the Whig slate. The list would then be divided by each precinct captain "into sections of 10 who reside most convenient to each other." The captain of each section would then be responsible to "see each man of his section face to face and procure his pledge . . . [to] vote as early on the day as possible."*

— DORIS KEARNS GOODWIN, *Team of Rivals:*
*The Political Genius of Abraham Lincoln*

I N 2000, the nation was at peace, the economy was booming, and President Clinton's approval rating stood at 62 percent. The odds were stacked against Texas Governor George W. Bush in his bid to defeat Clinton's vice president, Al Gore. One day at Bush headquarters in Austin, Texas, his media adviser, Mark McKinnon, blurted out a perfectly facetious campaign slogan: "Everything's going great. Time for a change." It became a running joke inside the Bush team.

Four years later, the nation was mired in an unpopular war, the economy was slumping, and President Bush's approval rating had dipped to 46 percent. No president had ever been reelected with such a low number. This time, his strategist Matthew Dowd put a sardonic twist on McKinnon's line: "Everything sucks. Stay the course" was the 2004 rallying cry.

President Bush twice defied conventional wisdom and won national elections. We're going to tell you how. But we're not going to stop there. We're also going to explain how President Clinton battled back from political irrelevancy to win reelection in 1996. Despite their different ideologies, these two men had strikingly similar approaches to making and maintaining Gut Values Connections.

First, they recognized changes in the political marketplace and adapted. For President Clinton, that required expanding his appeal to "swing voters" (independent-minded folks who bounce between the parties) after being elected with just 43 percent of the vote in 1992. For President Bush, it was the determination that there were not enough swing voters to make a difference in 2004 and that his reelection hopes hinged on finding passive and inactive Republicans.

Second, both presidents blended cutting-edge polling and consumer research strategies to target potential voters based on how they live. A

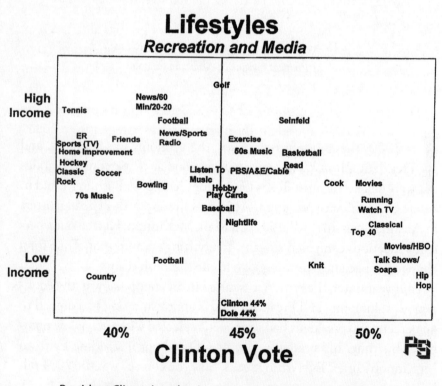

# Lifestyles
## *Recreation and Media*

# Clinton Vote

President Clinton's reelection team predicted political behavior based on a person's recreation and media habits.

voter who played tennis and watched *ER* was pegged by President Clinton's team as a supporter of his Republican opponent, Bob Dole. Another who watched basketball and public television was considered a Democrat. If the Clinton plan had been the equivalent of LifeTargeting 1.0, President Bush's advisers created LifeTargeting 4.0—a quantum leap that allowed them to track millions of voters based on their confidential consumer histories. If you're a voter living in one of the sixteen states that determined the 2004 election, the Bush team had your name on a spreadsheet with your hobbies and habits, vices and virtues, favorite foods, sports, and vacation venues, and many other facts of your life.

Presidents Bush and Clinton also found new ways to talk to people. For the Clinton team, that meant identifying where the swing voters lived and basing presidential travel and paid advertising decisions on their whereabouts. President Bush's advisers devised a formula that estimated how many Republicans watched every show on TV. They also revolutionized word-of-mouth marketing for politics and the use of Navigators—society's new opinion leaders helping Americans navigate what Lincoln called the "stormy present." Both presidents were innovators in the use of niche TV and radio ads.

Though wildly successful in 1996, President Clinton's playbook was out of date by 2004. President Bush's reelection strategies were breakthrough two years ago, but they will be stale by the next presidential election. Great Connectors like Presidents Bush and Clinton adapt to the times.

They also realize that tactics do not win elections. Gut Values do. Cutting-edge strategies are useful only when they help a candidate make his or her values resonate with the public. For all their faults (and they had their share), Presidents Bush and Clinton knew that their challenge was in appealing to voters' hearts, not their heads. We heard this countless times: "Sure, he had sex with an intern and lied about it, *but he cares about me and is working hard on my behalf*." And this: "The Iraq war stinks and his other policies aren't so hot, *but at least I know where he stands*."

Even as the war in Iraq grew unpopular in 2004, President Bush's unapologetic antiterrorism policies seemed to most voters to reflect strength and principled leadership—two Gut Values that kept him afloat until mid-2005, when he lost touch with the values that had gotten him reelected. Even after lying to the public about his affair with a White House intern, President Clinton never lost his image as an empathetic, hardworking leader—the foundation of his Gut Values Connection.

Both presidents understood that the so-called values debate runs deeper than abortion, gay rights, and other social issues that are too often the focus of the political elite in Washington. Voters don't pick presidents based on their positions on a laundry list of policies. If they did, President Bush wouldn't have stood a chance against Al Gore in 2000 or John Kerry in 2004. Rather, policies and issues are mere prisms through which voters take the true measure of a candidate: Does he share my values?

For those Democratic leaders, including Kerry himself, who whined and wondered why people "voted against their self-interests" in 2004, here's your answer: the voters' overriding interest is to elect leaders who reflect their values even when, as in 2004, the Gut Values candidate (Bush) fared poorly in polls on the economy, health care, Social Security, the war in Iraq, and other top issues. These are not selfish times. Americans are not selfish people. A quarter century ago, Ronald Reagan asked, "Are you better off today than you were four years ago?" That was an effective question in 1980, but more relevant ones today would be: Is your *country* better off? Is your *family* better off? How about your *community*? Voters are looking for leaders to speak to those questions—those Gut Values.

Today, two Gut Values dominate the political landscape. Success will come to any leader who appeals to the public's desire for *community* and *authenticity*. President Bush's team knitted existing social networks into a political operation that fed on people's desire to be part of something, anything—preferably a cause greater than themselves. Democratic presidential candidate Howard Dean created communities on the Internet and exploited them in 2004, a topic for chapter 5.

Authenticity is a valued commodity in the political marketplace because Americans have been subjected to years of failure, scandal, and butt-covering by institutions that are suppose to help them prosper.

From the Vietnam War, Watergate, Iran-contra, and President Clinton's impeachment to runaway deficits, soaring health care costs, and Hurricane Katrina, voters have been fed a steady diet of corruption and incompetence in government. Business scandals at the turn of the millennium soured the public on corporate America. The unseemly excesses of TV evangelism, the Catholic Church's sex abuse scandals, and wrongdoing at several charitable organizations challenged the public's faith in private institutions.

Tired of the lies and half-truths, people are more jaded than ever. They're also better educated and better informed than in the past, which helps them spot a phony. Americans don't expect their leaders to be perfect, but they want them to be perfectly frank: to acknowledge their mistakes, promise to fix the problem, and then *actually fix it*. This we learned from President Bush in 2005: when a politician loses his credibility, voters start to question his other values and eventually start looking at his policies differently. In politics, this can be doom.

To explore the shifting political landscape fully, we'll keep taking you back to a table at an Applebee's restaurant in exurban Detroit, where two middle-class women named Debbie Palos and Lynn Jensen explained how their political inclinations changed after they became mothers and moved to a Republican-dominated exurb.

When you get done with this chapter, you'll see that while the playing field has tilted toward the GOP in recent years, neither party has cornered the market on "Applebee's America."

---

### Swing Voters

HOWELL, Mich.—Debbie Palos is a prochoice nurse and the daughter of a Teamster who cast her first two presidential ballots for Clinton. Her friend and neighbor Lynn Jensen supports abortion rights, opposes privatization of Social Security, and thinks President Clinton was the last president "who gave a hoot about the middle class."

They're lifelong Democrats, just like their parents. Economically, the Hartland, Michigan, women and their families fared better in the 1990s than they have so far in this decade. Both opposed the war in Iraq.

Yet they both voted for President Bush in 2004.

"I didn't like doing it, but the other guy was too radical for me," says Jensen, a thirty-three-year-old mother of two. She scoops a spoonful of rice from her plate into the mouth of her fourteen-month-old daughter, Ryan.

Across the polished wood table at their local Applebee's, Palos picks at a steak salad, enjoying lunch with Jensen while her nine-year-old boy and six-year-old girl are in school.

"I just don't think much of Democrats anymore," says Palos. "Besides, I may not agree with President Bush on everything, but at least I know he's doing what he thinks is right."

# PRESIDENT CLINTON

## Adapting

Doug Sosnik was summoned to the Oval Office for a job interview. Actually, it was more of an introduction. Clinton's adviser Harold Ickes had already assured Sosnik that he had it wired and Sosnik would be White House political director after a perfunctory meeting with President Clinton.

"Take a seat," President Clinton said to Sosnik, who fell into a yellow-striped sofa across from the young leader. It was February 1995. Just three months earlier, voters had signaled their frustration with President Clinton by abruptly ending the Democratic Party's forty-year reign over Congress. The president already was considered a lame duck, not that he ever saw it that way.

"I'm really looking forward to the campaign," President Clinton told Sosnik, jumping excitedly into a conversation about the 1996 presidential race. He said he expected to win reelection, a prediction that caught Sosnik off guard. Suppressing a smile, Sosnik replied, "Me, too." The new White House political director walked from the Oval Office wondering why President Clinton was looking forward to a campaign that few thought he could win.

Sosnik was not the only Clinton adviser worried about the president's chances. Shortly after Sosnik took the job, the pollster Mark Penn completed a confidential survey for President Clinton that suggested that 65 percent of Americans would not consider voting for the incumbent in 1996. It was not just that these people were saying they didn't like the president or didn't approve of his performance. *They were determined to never, ever vote for him.* Talk about tough political terrain.

The lowest point of Clinton's presidency was yet to come. It was two months later, on the night of April 18, 1995, when the White House press corps filed into the elegant East Room for a prime-time news conference. Past presidents had made these events must-see TV. John F. Kennedy had kept reporters at bay with sharp humor. Richard Nixon had scowled at questioners over Watergate. Former actor Ronald Reagan had charmed the nation even as he muffed policy details. But in April 1995 there was little interest in a White House news conference.

President Clinton was overshadowed in Washington by the bombastic leader of the GOP revolution, House Speaker Newt Gingrich. The networks had just given Gingrich airtime to address the nation on the hundredth day of the new Congress, a remarkable show of deference for a House speaker. By contrast, just one of the three major networks, CBS, agreed to broadcast President Clinton's news conference, and its ratings were less than half those of *Frasier* on NBC and *Home Improvement* on ABC.

Making matters worse, President Clinton admitted in that April 18 news conference how far he had fallen. A reporter asked whether he worried about "making sure your voice will be heard" if no one was covering his words. President Clinton replied, "The Constitution gives me relevance. The power of our ideas gives me relevance. The record we have built up over the last two years and the things we're trying to do to implement it give it relevance. The president is relevant here, especially an activist president—and the fact that I'm willing to work with Republicans." When the president of the United States plaintively argues his relevancy, it's time to ditch plans for a second term and start working on the presidential library.

"If he would have taken voters on face value, they would never re-elect him because so many voters said that they were unalterably opposed to his election," Penn said a decade later. "We were at low tide."

The tide began to rise the day after the disastrous April news conference, when domestic terrorists bombed the Alfred P. Murrah Federal Building in Oklahoma City. The bombing was for President Clinton what September 11 would be for President Bush—a national tragedy that cried out for leadership. Both men seized the moment. But, as at the Bush White House, nothing was left to chance by the politically astute Clinton administration. With the advice of the hard-nosed political operative Harold Ickes, the mercurial consultant Dick Morris, and the pollster Penn, the Clinton team assembled four tools for reelection:

- Comprehensive polling of the political attitudes, lifestyles, values, and personality traits of voters. Nothing like it had ever been done before.
- A formula for determining where to advertise and where to schedule presidential trips to maximize the campaign's appeal to swing voters.
- Development of bite-sized policies they knew would appeal to swing voters, noncontroversial and cheap initiatives such as supporting school uniforms, and giving cell phones to neighborhood watch programs.
- A contingency LifeTargeting plan that, though never fully implemented, foreshadowed what President Bush's team would do in 2004 by mixing political and consumer data on potential voters.

### Swing Is and Swing IIs

In 1992, then–Arkansas Governor Bill Clinton defeated President George H. W. Bush while getting just 43 percent of the vote. That means nearly six of every ten voters *wanted somebody else to be president.* Thirty-eight percent backed the incumbent president, and the independent Ross Perot received two of every ten votes.

Penn's 1995 surveys showed that only 28 percent of the public was committed to President Clinton and another 7 percent might consider voting for him. Without a thriving third-party candidate in the race (a diminished Perot would earn about 8 percent of the vote in 1996), Pres-

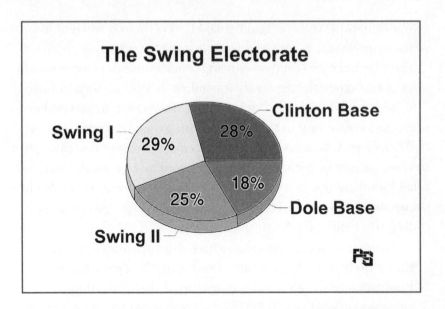

## The Swing Electorate

Clinton Base — 28%

Swing I — 29%

18%

25%

Dole Base

Swing II

President Clinton's team told him that he would win reelection if he could secure 60 percent of Swing I and 30 percent of Swing II voters.

ident Clinton needed a much stronger plurality to win reelection. The breakthrough was realizing that the voters who had helped him climb from 35 percent to 36 percent in the polls would be much different from those who lifted him from 48 percent to 49 percent. President Clinton's team needed to figure out who those voters were, what motivated them, and how best to communicate with them.

Through standard polling (Penn eventually logged more than 100,000 interviews), personality tests, and analysis of voter lifestyles and values, Penn broke President Clinton's target audience into two groups: Swing I and Swing II. A memo written by Penn's team for President Clinton at the time explained them this way:

Swing I voters are less concerned with partisan politics and more interested in family-oriented middle-class programs. These voters remain supportive of many progressive causes, but their first priority are programs that will help them feel safe physically and financially. This group has personal priorities and wants to solve them before delving into environmental regulations (which it wants more of) and abortion rights. Many of these voters hurt from the cost of health care and want insurance companies to cover them between jobs and pre-existing conditions; this group wanted guaranteed health care for their families. A raise in the minimum wage would benefit this group most. To protect their families, Swing I voters want to fight crime utilizing the carrot and the stick. Their liberal-moderate values tell them crime prevention through social programs, including apprenticeships and Domestic Service and jobs, are the best solutions, but their support for more death penalty provisions and harsher penalties for illegal gun possession show they will not tolerate violent crime. . . .

Swing II voters are disgusted with Beltway politics that have ignored their struggling middle class needs. A perfect example is how they direct their anger towards illegal aliens who they feel receive undeserved benefits. Their position is not based on a racial problem but more as a matter of survival since they feel they are competing for scarce federal resources. They also support the death penalty for a wide range of criminals who have been coddled by a system that cares more about a criminal's rights than that of the victims. One indication of their anti-Washington fervor is their support for term limits. . . . On social issues, this group's moderate-conservative composition has a low tolerance for a progressive agenda. These people . . . identify with traditional values that match their middle American culture. Overall, this group shows little inclination to support President Clinton and is a primary target of the Republican or independent candidate.

For every three swing voters President Clinton won over, his advisers estimated that two would be Swing I and one would be Swing II. While those in the second group believed in many Democratic policies, they didn't believe that Clinton had what it took to be president. He looked weak and unaccomplished and was utterly lacking in a Gut Values Connection. "They have to see that you are willing to draw lines and make choices," Penn told the president, "because they believe that they're not going to get a better education or improved health care if you don't."

## Targeting

The Clinton team broke the electorate into nine distinct groups of voters who had similar tastes in politics. Three of the groups were part of President Clinton's base: *Economic Liberals* (9 percent of the electorate), *Social Liberals* (10 percent), and *International Liberals* (7 percent), according to a campaign memo. Another group of voters backed President Clinton in 1992 but were wavering in the 1996 campaign. These so-called *President Clinton Voters* made up 9 percent of the electorate and were likely to be in the Swing I category.

There were three groups that generally fell into the Swing II cate-

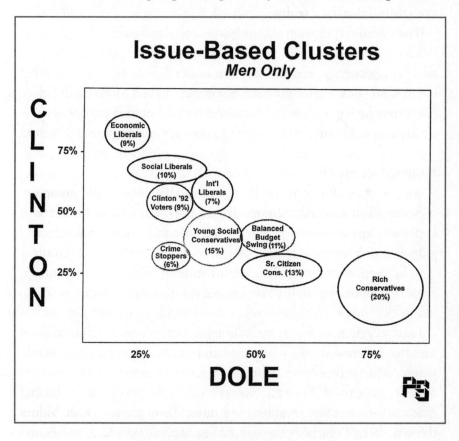

**Issue-Based Clusters**
*Men Only*

C
L
I
N
T
O
N

75% — Economic Liberals (9%)

Social Liberals (10%)

Int'l Liberals (7%)

50% — Clinton '92 Voters (9%)

Young Social Conservatives (15%)

Balanced Budget Swing (11%)

Crime Stoppers (6%)

25% — Sr. Citizen Cons. (13%)

Rich Conservatives (20%)

25%        50%        75%

**DOLE**

The 1996 electorate divided into nine clusters,
with those in the middle up for grabs.

gory: *Balanced Budget Swing Voters* (11 percent), *Crime Stoppers* (6 percent), and *Young Social Conservatives* (15 percent).

Republican candidate Dole's base consisted of *Senior Citizen Conservatives* (13 percent) and *Rich Conservatives* (20 percent).

The Clinton team produced a chart labeled "Issue-Based Clusters" that plotted all nine groups according to their likelihood of backing President Clinton or Dole. Falling to the far left were Economic Liberals and Social Liberals and to the far right Rich Conservatives. Smack dab in the political middle were Crime Stoppers, Young Social Conservatives, and Balanced Budget Swing Voters, a visual reminder of which voters mattered most. "We figured out who those (Swing I and Swing II) voters were, everything from their sports, vacations, and lifestyles," Penn said.

The Clinton campaign also indexed voters' values based on their attitudes toward homosexuals, sex before marriage, pornography, the sanctity of marriage, and the importance of religion, as well as their belief in God. The higher they scored on the "Values Matrix," the more likely they were to vote Republican. Penn said that the matrix was a better indicator of voting behavior than a person's income, age, or religion.

### Hearts, Not Heads

Based on a modified Myers-Briggs personality test given to scores of voters, Penn divided the electorate into four sets of basic traits: extroversion–introversion; sensing–intuition; thinking–feeling; and judging–perceiving.

"The purpose of this analysis is to determine if President Clinton appeals to certain personality types and if it is possible to better relate to the rest of the people," Penn wrote in a confidential campaign memo. "In many cases, people may actually agree with President Clinton on issues but are turned off by his communication style." In other words, voters judge Clinton with their guts, not their heads.

Penn continued, "In fact, voters that share the same personality characteristics as the president are more likely to support him, and those with opposing personalities are less likely to vote for him." Penn's analysis showed that President Clinton was doing well among voters who acted on intuition and feeling but not well among "sensing, thinking, and judging" swing voters.

# Issues Motivating Key Voter Groups
## % Much More Likely to Vote For Clinton
### Swing I Voters

| Possible Candidate Positions | Much More Likely |
|---|---|
| Insurance companies taking over more of health care. We need laws to prevent them from denying coverage based on preexisting conditions and to allow people to keep coverage when changing jobs | 65 |
| Raise minimum wage from $4.25 to $5.00 | 63 |
| Crime prevention is answer - Midnight basketball & job training | 62 |
| Support ban on smoking advertising aimed at kids | 61 |
| Need programs to help people take care of aged parents | 61 |
| Need guaranteed health care for all | 60 |
| Need commitment to guaranteed health care for all | 60 |
| Support complete ban on assault rifles | 58 |
| If Japan blocks trade, need to take strong corresponding action | 56 |
| Medicare, Social Security - Can slow rate of growth but no cuts | 55 |
| Cut aid to Russia if they sell nuclear reactor to Iran | 55 |
| Strengthen maternity and paternity leave laws | 55 |
| Commitment to gun control with stiff sentence to reduce crime | 54 |
| Balance budget in 10 years - cut waste, bureaucracy, spending 1.1 trillion - slow growth of Medicare by reducing health costs - don't cut education | 52 |
| Make low inflation, especially for food prices, a priority | 50 |

This chart showed President Clinton how much more likely he would be to earn a person's vote by taking certain positions.

The next challenge was to determine what issues appealed to each personality type. Campaign surveys found that "sensing voters" liked limited affirmative action, a higher minimum wage, and lower inflation. "Thinking" voters favored cutting able-bodied people off welfare after two years. "Judgment" voters wanted stiff sentences for crimes.

President Clinton dutifully embraced those and other policies, some of which were derided by critics as bite-sized, or "small-bore," initiatives because they seemed almost too puny for presidential action. But those policies spoke to people's concerns. They showed that President Clinton *could draw lines and make choices*. He pivoted off both parties, fighting GOP budget cuts and angering liberals by signing welfare reform, a "triangulation" strategy crafted by Morris, who would resign under pressure during President Clinton's nominating convention due to a sex scandal.

While President Bush would later use LifeTargeting to sharpen his message and strengthen his get-out-the-vote operation, President Clinton used a primitive form of it to shape his message *and policies*. Clinton's speechwriter Don Baer said that was how the president connected. "For most voters what's important is not some big health care reform bill or some long list of policies, it's *just me. Right now. My life*. Help *us* out a little bit." He said President Clinton had been a success because he had done "all of the small things he promised and half of the big."

In other words, the Democrat promised real, concrete changes that would affect a voter's everyday life and could easily be implemented. This is what we mean by giving voters a sense of authenticity—or, as Baer put it, "Doing things in a way that actually delivers goods to the customer, the voter."

**First Steps**

Throughout the 1996 campaign, the telephone numbers of every person polled by President Clinton's team were turned over to Claritas, a private marketing firm that marries demographic and lifestyle data to help companies target customers. The firm assigned each telephone number to one of its fifty-five PRIZM Clusters—from *Blue Blood Estates* and *Kids & Cul-de-Sacs* to *God's Country*.

Penn said that with additional polling he could have predicted the political attitudes of people—in units as small as a few blocks—based on their lifestyle choices. But the plan was never implemented because Clinton was so far ahead of Dole by mid-1996 that he didn't need the extra help, Penn said. The $10 million price tag might have had something to do with it.

Four years later, President Bush would have no shortage of money and the technology would allow his team to track and target *individual voters*, not just their neighborhoods.

## Communicating

Now that it had identified President Clinton's targeted voters and knew which issues and values appealed to them, his team had to figure out how best to communicate with them.

It started with a formula that measured the cost of advertising to Swing I and Swing II voters. This first-of-its-kind formula determined how many swing voters were in each TV market in the battleground states (the dozen or so states where President Clinton and Dole were competitive). In the Jacksonville, Florida, TV market, for example, the campaign identified 16,476 Swing I and Swing II voters, using the polling and focus groups. Then they divided that number by the price of ad time in the market to determine the cost-per-swing-voter in Jacksonville.

The rule of thumb was to buy ads in markets that had a low price per swing voter. In markets where the price was too high per Swing I or Swing II voter, President Clinton would travel there to exploit the power of the bully pulpit.

Clinton was the first candidate to realize the value of targeting TV ads to the most important markets rather than carpet bombing the nation with ads, wasting money in states that were overwhelmingly Democratic or Republican and therefore unswayable by advertising. The Clinton team used its data on swing voters to aim other forms of communication at them, using the power of the White House to create local TV, radio, and print coverage of the president's activities.

Though innovative at the time, the communication strategies seem quaint compared to what you'll read about President Bush and his cost-per-Republican-voter formulas.

President Clinton was the master of niche and nontraditional media. Immediately following his laughably boring speech at the 1988 Democratic convention, the then–Arkansas governor salvaged his national standing with a self-depreciating, saxophone-playing appearance on *The Tonight Show with Johnny Carson*. In his 1992 campaign, President Clinton reached young voters by playing the saxophone on Arsenio Hall's show. Once in the White House, he famously acknowledged his preference for boxers over briefs in an MTV town hall meeting. His communication team opened the North Lawn and White House driveway for talk-radio hosts to broadcast live from the White House in 1993 and 1994. For President Clinton and his advisers, the essential thing was to find the right voters (Swing I and Swing II) and talk to them in the right way. That meant staying alert for the emergence of new communication channels and inserting President Clinton into them.

## Connecting: It's Values, Stupid

While Gut Values Connections in general are enduring, specific values rise and fall in significance as the national environment changes. In the aftermath of Watergate, integrity was the Gut Value of people's choice and the one that President Carter projected in his 1976 election. The Iran hostage crisis and tensions with the Soviet Union made 1980 (like 2004) ripe for a leader such as President Reagan, who promised strong leadership.

In 1992, voters wanted a candidate who cared about their travails as an emerging global economy wreaked havoc on their lives. Candidate Clinton felt their pain. When a strategist posted an "It's the Economy, Stupid" sign in the Clinton campaign headquarters, he had it only half right. The campaign wasn't merely about the economy. It was about the Gut Values Connection the candidate made when he vowed to work every day, "until the last dog dies," to improve people's economic condition. It was a visceral appeal based on empathy, not policy. "Values trump the economy," the Arkansas governor told his staff, according to his adviser Paul Begala.

Begala now believes that Democrats have become "too bloodless," focused on lists of policies and how those issues rank in polls. "We're spending too much time staring at voters behind one-way glass windows" in focus groups "and not enough time connecting with them based on their values—on the traits they want out of their leaders, a gut-level feel, not some poll-tested policy," Begala said in 2005.

Two former Clinton White House advisers, William A. Galston and Elaine Kamarck, wrote in their report *The Politics of Polarization* that Democrats must forge a "bond of trust" with voters based on the Gut Values we discuss in this book. They cited a Pew Research Center poll suggesting that 27 percent of respondents had chosen "moral values" as the principal determinant of their vote in 2004. Gay marriage and abortion topped the list of moral values issues, but "candidate qualities" was close behind. "This more nuanced and personally driven view of the 'moral values' debate should remind us that selecting a president is a deeply personal transaction between candidates and the electorate," Galston and Kamarck wrote. ". . . In the public mind morality has as much to do with the personal integrity of the presidential candidates as it does with their stance on hot-button social issues. . . . Having logged many presidential campaigns between us, the authors can attest to the fact that Democrats are likely to spend days on health care plans and minutes on character issues (Republican campaigns do not often make such mistakes)."

## Community and Anxieties

President Clinton built community with his words. He had a way of convincing people that they were all in this together—that no matter how bad things might be, they would get better if Americans rallied as one. A big reason for his early success was his knack for seeing change coming before most and putting words to voters' pangs of anxiety. As governor of Arkansas in the 1980s, he constantly warned of "massive changes in the world economy" that would impact people's lives. As a presidential candidate in 1991 and 1992, he talked about the nation "standing at the threshold of a new millennium" and called himself "an instrument of change."

During his first two years in the White House, his aides were puzzled as to why President Clinton was not getting credit for the rebounding economy. They discovered in focus groups that every time a member of the Clinton administration spoke of economic problems, it reinforced voters' anxieties about the future and drove down the president's approval rating. President Clinton was the worst offender, often telling audiences that the new economy would require Americans to change jobs a half-dozen or so times in their lifetimes. "He was trying to explain the challenges ahead but really was scaring the hell out of people," said the speechwriter Don Baer.

A new rule was put into place at the White House: stop bad-mouthing the economy. Aides tweaked the president's stump speech to talk about how much opportunity the new economy offered for hard-working Americans under his leadership. President Clinton started urging voters to join with him and "build a bridge to the twenty-first century." The slogan was mocked by critics, but it spoke to people's concerns and their desire to do something constructive *together*. It was an optimistic message crafted out of necessity.

"Because the information age is so dramatically changing the way we work, the way we live, the way we relate to each other and the rest of the world, the next generation of Americans is literally going to have more opportunities to live out their dreams than any generation in American history," President Clinton told a Denver audience in July 1996. Still, in the same speech, you could hear the loquacious Clinton fighting his old habits: "The young people that are in this audience today, within a matter of 10 years, will be doing jobs that have not even been invented yet. Some of them have not been conceived yet. So this is going to be a very exciting time, full of enormous opportunity. But as is inevitable in the human condition, it will also have some very stiff challenges."

## A Fragile Connection

At the start of President Clinton's reelection campaign, both Swing I and Swing II voters supported Democratic policies in 1995, yet most were saying they would never vote for President Clinton "because they really didn't know what he stood for," Penn said. He had damaged his Gut Values Connection by stumbling out of the gate early in his first term with liberal policies and a string of political failures that made voters wonder whether he had lost touch with their values. He seemed to be fighting for everything *but them*—and looking ineffective while doing it.

With the Oklahoma City bombing, the budget fight with House Speaker Newt Gingrich that led to a government shutdown, and the poll-tested "bite-sized" agenda he outlined in the 1996 State of the Union address, President Clinton convinced many Americans that he was fighting for them again. He won reelection with 49 percent of their votes in 1996 (he got 65 percent of the Swing Is and 35 percent of the Swing IIs).

Two years later, President Clinton lied to the public about his affair with Monica Lewinsky. He survived impeachment, fighting to preserve his empathy-based Gut Values Connection by telling voters he'd get up each day worried about them. The Lewinsky scandal hurt the Democratic Party (Swing II voters were especially angry at the president), but Gore still had huge advantages: a strong economy, experience, and

Clinton's still solid job approval rating. But the vice president failed to make a Gut Values Connection. To many voters, he seemed aloof, disingenuous, and unprincipled. Bush, then the Texas governor, took advantage of the values vacuum, vowing to restore honor and dignity to the White House. President Clinton and Gore had to share the blame for giving Bush the chance to connect.

Again we quote Galston and Kamarck, who said the Clinton scandal "left a lasting moral stain on Democrats" that can be wiped clean only by candidates who display strength, integrity, and empathy. "Candidates who say only what they think others want to hear cannot display strength. Candidates who shift positions on what should be matters of conviction can not pass the integrity test. And candidates who are far removed from the lives and feelings of average families will have a hard time understanding the daily challenges these families face, or credibly conveying care and concern about them."

---

### Anxious Americans

HOWELL, Mich.—Palos's father immigrated from Mexico in 1953 and found a job at Kroger, a grocery store chain, where he was a proud member of the Teamsters Union. Her mother, an insurance specialist at a Detroit-area hospital, grew up on the city's west side. They met in a Detroit library, where she worked and he was studying.

The family lived in Dearborn, an inner-ring suburb filled with white, middle-class families during most of Palos's childhood. By the time she graduated from the University of Michigan and moved to Livingston County in 1998 to raise her family, Dearborn had changed dramatically, becoming one of the nation's largest Arab-American communities.

The promise of a bigger home and safer streets drew Palos to what she calls "the boonies." Gesturing out the restaurant window toward the bumper-to-bumper traffic and rows of big-box stores on Grand River Road, she says, "None of this was out here then. That's why I moved out here. It was two lanes and quiet. Look at it now."

She and Jensen kibitz about a series of neighborhood break-ins.

"We moved out here to get away from the city," Palos says with a sigh. "But it's scary even out here now."

Jensen's journey to exurbia is less typical. She grew up in Caro, a small town in northern Michigan, graduated from the University of Michigan in 1994, and moved to Royal Oak, about two miles from Detroit's northern border. In 1996, she and her husband moved to fast-growing Brighton, Michigan, nearly sixty miles from Detroit. The move put them halfway between each other's work, giving them both a long commute: Jensen worked as a civil engineer in Lansing, while her husband, also an engineer, was based in Detroit.

She now stays at home with their children, despite the strain that it puts on a household budget built for two incomes. Most of her friends work outside the home, a fact that only adds to her sense of isolation in exurbia. "This is going to sound silly, but I wish things were like they were when we were growing up," Jensen says.

"I know what you mean," replies Palos.

"I wish I could go back in time. We had stable lives. Mom could stay home, and we could afford it. Life was slower. God, I'm sounding like my parents—all nostalgic for the old days. But it's true: there wasn't trouble then like there is today. Take my kids—they're growing up too fast. My daughter is only five, and she knows too much."

"They don't let them be children as long in school, testing them all the time, pushing them in sports," says Palos.

"And the sex, the violence," adds Jensen. "Can you believe what they could see on TV if you're not careful?"

As they wrestle with their anxieties, you hear the first inklings of why Jensen voted Republican for the first time in 2004, why Palos left the Democratic Party four years before that, and why their stories reflect the shifting landscape of American politics.

## PRESIDENT BUSH

### Adapting

Matthew Dowd was chewing on an unlit cigar, staring in disbelief at the numbers on his computer screen in Austin, Texas. It was a winter day, shortly after the Supreme Court settled the election recount in George W. Bush's favor. Dowd had stayed behind in January 2001 after most of his colleagues headed to Washington with the president-elect to claim their narrow victory. Gore had won the popular vote but lost Florida, and thus the presidency, by a mere 537 votes. Both sides had run a traditional-style campaign, focusing on independent-minded swing voters while doing as little as possible to keep their most fervent supporters happy. There was no reason to think 2004 would be different.

Until Dowd started chewing over the numbers.

It was well known that people who identified themselves as independents divided almost evenly between President Bush and Gore. Digging deeper, Dowd discovered that 75 percent of the self-described independents who backed President Bush also voted GOP in down-ballot races. The same percentage of independents who backed Gore cast down-the-line Democratic ballots.

That left only 7 percent of the electorate who not only called themselves independents but also voted like independents. His head spinning from the implications, Dowd turned to even older exit polls and did the same math. The trend was unmistakable: one in four voters was a ticket splitter in 1984, falling to 16 percent in 1988, to 15 percent the year President Clinton was elected the first time, and to 10 percent in 1996.

The percentage of consistently Republican and Democratic voters had increased every election cycle. For now, it didn't matter to Dowd whether self-polarizing people were motivated by partisan issues (the answer is no) or emotional connections such as the desire to be part of a political community (the answer is yes). He just knew that politics had changed.

Dowd banged out an e-mail to the longtime Bush strategist Karl Rove, asking for a meeting in Washington: *It's time for a different strategy.* Dowd, a former Democrat who had recently converted to the GOP, wrote that it didn't make sense to focus 75 percent of a campaign's resources on finding, targeting, and communicating with a declining number of swing voters, as had been done in 2000. Shouldn't the bulk of time and money be spent targeting passive and inactive Republican voters? *We must adapt,* he said.

A few days later, Dowd walked into Rove's office on the second floor of the White House with a simple bar graph showing the growth of the

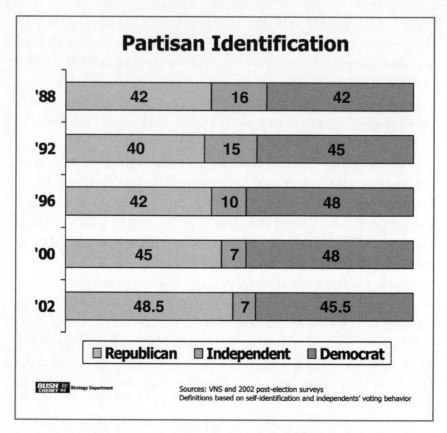

**Partisan Identification**

| Year | Republican | Independent | Democrat |
|------|-----------|-------------|----------|
| '88  | 42        | 16          | 42       |
| '92  | 40        | 15          | 45       |
| '96  | 42        | 10          | 48       |
| '00  | 45        | 7           | 48       |
| '02  | 48.5      | 7           | 45.5     |

□ **Republican**   ■ **Independent**   ■ **Democrat**

BUSH CHENEY '04 Strategy Department

Sources: VNS and 2002 post-election surveys
Definitions based on self-identification and independents' voting behavior

Matthew Dowd crunched some numbers in early 2001
and determined that the percentage of truly independent voters had
been falling steadily, prompting a big shift in GOP strategy.

GOP base and the decline of swing voters. Rove instantly recognized the significance of the numbers. "Really?" he said, grabbing the sheet from Dowd's hands, his voice rising with excitement. "Man, this is a fundamental change."

**More Changes**

Suddenly, instead of looking for new ways to identify and persuade swing voters, Rove and Bush's campaign manager, Ken Mehlman, were obsessed with finding new Republican voters. In the months to come, a team of GOP strategists headed by Dowd would make two other discoveries that reshaped their strategies for 2004:

- Only 15 percent of Republican-leaning people lived in precincts that were heavily Republican (65 percent or higher). Most of the rest were rarely targeted by GOP campaigns. *That had to change*. Many passive and inactive Republicans were living in the fast-growing new exurbs, which the Bush team made a focal point of the campaign.
- The heaviest TV watchers tend to be Democrats. President Bush's team couldn't change that, but they could figure out how to target their ad money to broadcast and cable shows favored by potential Bush voters.

President Bush's strategists realized the deck was stacked against them. They had to find and motivate new GOP voters, and that meant new strategies. Dowd had one in mind: targeting people based on their lifestyles rather than just their voting histories and their policy views.

## "Don't Know What You'd Call Us"

HOWELL, Mich.—Jensen and Palos have a difficult time categorizing themselves politically. Like most voters, they spend little time thinking about politics and less time talking about it.

On this day, gentle prodding reveals that both women are still coming to terms with their recent turn to the GOP. Their allegiances to the Republican Party are fragile and still forming but will cement in due course unless the Democrats give them reason to pause.

Jensen and Palos say Kerry is too liberal, but they struggle to name a position of his that led them to that conclusion. They are certain about one thing: the Democratic senator is a waffler, and indecision is dangerous when the nation is at war.

"I don't think Kerry was too consistent," Jensen says.

They oppose the war in Iraq but say they respect President Bush for doing what he thought was best for the country. They gave the president high marks for the war on terrorism, which they called the single most important issue of the election.

Other than the character of the candidates and perhaps terrorism, it's hard to find an issue that motivates either woman.

They believe women have a right to abortion, despite their personal opposition to the procedure. They don't have strong feelings about President Bush's tax cuts.

They would ban gay marriage but say the issue had no role in their decision for president. "It's not something that gets me bent out of shape," said Palos.

They support prayer in schools. "That's where I'm more conservative," says Jensen. She attends church regularly, Palos less so.

The women backed a Republican bankruptcy bill making it harder for debt-ridden Americans to wipe out their debts. "People should pay what they owe. I do," Palos says.

"But that doesn't make us Republicans," Jensen says. "I don't know what you'd call us."

## Targeting

President Bush's advisers knew what to call Palos and Jensen: *Terrorism Moderates*.

The Bush team also knew the size of their mortgages, their favorite vacation spots, magazines, music, sporting activities, and virtually every other lifestyle checkpoint that money can buy. Without ever talking to Palos or Jensen, the Bush team knew how they had voted in past elections and could predict with 90 percent certainty how they would vote in 2004. They knew what issues angered them (Democrats' plans to weaken the USA PATRIOT Act) and what messages would get the women to the polls (President Bush would keep them and their children safe).

It was all in a 157-page book titled *Michigan MicroTactics: The Party Model*, a highly confidential 2003 report compiled under Dowd's direction by Alex Gage of TargetPoint Consulting in Alexandria, Virginia. It compared the political and lifestyle habits of Palos and Jensen with those of every other voter in the state, then lumped them in with people exhibiting similar sociopolitical DNA.

Despite the small steps with LifeTargeting taken by the Clinton team in 1996, Kerry and his fellow Democrats had nothing like it. Here's the step-by-step rundown on how the Bush team did it.

### Voter Lists

They began with the Republican National Committee's list of Michigan's 6 million registered voters: their names, ages, addresses, and voting histories. Over the years, the list had been enhanced by any additional political information the RNC could buy or collect. If, for example, Palos or Jensen belonged to an antiabortion group, there would be a notation in their file. Democrats started with the same voter registration list and made note of such things as union memberships and abortion rights supporters. For years, this was as close as any party got to LifeTargeting.

### Consumer Histories

President Bush's team sent the RNC list to a data-mining firm called Axciom, which has the largest collection of consumer data in the United States. Axciom buys customer information from credit card companies, cruise lines, airlines, retail stores, and scores of other places where people do business. It sells it to other businesses, which mine it for potential new customers. If Palos subscribed to a wine magazine, gambled at casinos, or collected stamps, Axciom had a record of it. If Jensen liked taking cruises, purchased dog food, or bought golf equipment, Axciom knew that, too.

### Master List

Axciom cross-referenced the Bush team's voter list against its own list of Michigan consumers and found a 95 percent match. It had consumer histories on about 5.7 million of the 6 million registered voters in Michigan. The Bush team did not have access to the raw consumer data, but it had all it needed: a list from Axciom showing the stage in life (age, marital status, number of children, etc.) and lifestyles (hunter, biker, home renter, SUV owner, level of religious interest) of each voter, drawn from a menu of more than four hundred separate categories. Palos and Jensen were on this list.

### Polling

The Bush team called 5,000 people from the Axciom list and asked them a series of questions to gauge their political behavior and attitudes. Did they back Bush or Kerry? Who did they support in past elections? Their views on abortion, school choice, and other ideological issues were recorded. To find out what issues might motivate them to vote, the Bush team asked a series of questions about their "anger points": How angry are you that Democrats are trying to repeal tax cuts? Does legalized abortion make you angry? Pornography on the Internet? Gay marriage?

Remember, the Bush team's goal was to find passive and inactive Republican voters.

### Political/Lifestyle DNA

Bush's team ran the polled voters' answers through a sophisticated computer program and grouped the 5,000 voters into thirty-four segments, each consisting of people who shared political and lifestyle traits; think of them as a virtual community. Then every other voter— nearly 6 million in all—was assigned to one of the thirty-four segments that fit *based on the lifestyle and political habits he or she shared* with those surveyed and already placed in groups.

This is how the computer identified 101,200 politically moderate, middle-class voters whose No. 1 issue was terrorism. They were roughly in the same stage of life and had similar lifestyles. Though they were more likely to come from union households and therefore sure to be targeted by Kerry, most of them supported Bush's reelection. The Bush team labeled them Terrorism Moderates.

Gage compared the process to identifying a DNA strand. Palos, Jensen, and the other Terrorism Moderates had similar political/social genetics. If John Doe earned $150,000, drove a Porsche, subscribed to a golf magazine, paid National Rifle Association dues, *and told a Bush pollster* he was a pro–tax cut conservative who backed President Bush's war again terrorism, the Bush team figured that anybody with similar lifestyle tastes would hold similar political views.

Nearly every time a person takes out a loan, uses a credit card, makes an Internet transaction, books a flight, or conducts any of hundreds of

## The Michigan MicroTargeting Segments

| Segment | Segment Name | Segment Size | GOP Base | Committed GWB |
|---|---|---|---|---|
| 1 | Religious Conservative Republicans | 51,308 | 92% | 94% |
| 2 | Tax Cut Conservative Republicans | 111,676 | 79% | 90% |
| 3 | Flag & Family Republicans | 54,659 | 79% | 83% |
| 4 | Anti-Porn, Anti-Terrorism Republicans | 160,131 | 75% | 88% |
| 5 | Terrorism & Tax Cut Conservatives | 56,804 | 72% | 78% |
| 6 | Younger & Average Republicans | 93,210 | 62% | 80% |
| 7 | Archie in the Bunker | 144,261 | 60% | 71% |
| 8 | Religious Weak Republicans | 69,733 | 58% | 75% |
| 9 | Mellow Bush Supporters | 123,076 | 58% | 79% |
| 10 | Tax & Terrorism Moderates | 85,147 | 54% | 66% |
| 11 | Social Conservative Weak Republicans | 183,526 | 54% | 70% |
| 12 | Schoolhouse & Tax Cut Weak Republicans | 96,429 | 51% | 69% |
| 13 | Secular Average Voters | 120,302 | 49% | 62% |
| 14 | Terrorism Moderates | 101,200 | 47% | 62% |
| 15 | Younger Cultural Liberals | 225,652 | 44% | 63% |
| 16 | More Social Conservative Weak Republicans | 66,659 | 44% | 75% |
| 17 | Middle Aged Female Weak Republicans | 95,246 | 43% | 58% |
| 18 | Turned Off Weak Republicans | 126,740 | 41% | 58% |
| 19 | Older Conservatives, Traditional and Tax Cuts | 59,988 | 39% | 66% |
| 20 | Education Independents | 400,549 | 34% | 51% |
| 21 | Religious Independents | 101,689 | 34% | 57% |
| 22 | Younger Secular Independents | 684,580 | 34% | 58% |
| 23 | Younger Motivated Independents | 138,758 | 33% | 50% |
| 24 | Unmotivated (Mostly) Female Independents | 142,481 | 31% | 60% |
| 25 | Younger Secular Independents II | 237,231 | 30% | 52% |
| 26 | Middle Aged Moderate Democrats | 47,226 | 27% | 47% |
| 27 | Terrorism and Health Care Democrats | 89,785 | 25% | 39% |
| 28 | Wageable Weak Democrats | 516,261 | 21% | 43% |
| 29 | Traditional Marriage Democrats | 124,974 | 18% | 30% |
| 30 | Available Independents | 236,346 | 16% | 51% |
| 31 | Last Chance for Votes | 129,087 | 16% | 31% |

The cover page of the Michigan targeting book shows
the size of each segment, the percentage of staunch Republicans
in each category, and the percentage of those committed to
voting for President Bush's reelection. "A Few Stranded Good Guys"
and two other segments are listed on the second page.

other business transactions, he or she leaves a data trail. The average consumer travels through life trailed by thousands of clues to future buying and voting habits, a veritable gold mine for any organization with the money and motivation to solve the mysteries of his or her political attitudes.

The Bush team's LifeTargeting program was able to predict with 80 to 90 percent certainty whether a person would vote Republican, according to postelection surveys conducted by the Bush team. Under the old tactics, campaigns couldn't predict voting behavior with even 60 percent certainty.

Much of corporate America and the megachurch industry embraced LifeTargeting years ago, but political leaders inexplicably resisted. Strategists for businesses and churches understood that people's foremost priority is deciding where and how they'll live and work; and those lifestyle choices are the predicate for every other decision people make—including how they shop, worship, and vote.

To those political strategists who still doubt the merits of LifeTargeting, we wonder why you would spend millions of dollars to track a person's voting history, political affiliations, survey responses, and other imperfect predictors of future political activity yet turn your back on an information-rich new consumer data resource. Consider an average twenty-six-year-old single Virginia man who has voted Democratic in three straight elections, including for Kerry in 2004. Imagine that sometime before the 2008 election, that same man turns thirty, gets married, has two children, buys a van, moves to the exurbs, and joins a megachurch—all changes that make him, statistically, much more likely to vote Republican. Will his past voting history be the best indicator of his 2008 vote? Or will his lifestyle choices be the best guide? The answer is that you must know both, and failing to take advantage of lifestyle data available to twenty-first-century campaign strategists borders on political malpractice.

## Micro-Michigan

The Bush campaign's *Michigan MicroTactics* book ranked the voter groups from the most pro-Bush group to the most anti-Bush group.

The description of each group included an extensive analysis of voters who fell into that category—their demographics and their views on hot-button issues such as terrorism, gay marriage, birth control education in public schools, taxes, the influence of the religious right in politics, the cost of health care, and tort reform.

The group most in favor of President Bush was called *Religious Conservative Republicans*, 51,308 voters who were most angry about pornography on the Internet and most supportive of the ban on partial birth abortions. The Bush team now had their names, mailing addresses, e-mail addresses, and phone numbers, along with an analysis on what messages were most likely to get them to vote. That influenced where they sent their campaign mail and what the fliers said.

There were other advantages. Campaign organizers could have supporters from one of their LifeTargeting groups call like-minded people and ask them to get involved. A voter from Warren, Michigan, who fit into the group called *Flag and Family Republicans* would get calls from other Flag and Family Republicans from Michigan. This is how the Bush team used Navigators, real-people opinion leaders who have more credibility in an age of skepticism and media fragmentation (see chapter 6). More than at any time in recent history, Americans are more likely to be influenced by other people than by traditional advertising, studies show. That's why campaign volunteers who happened to be *Mellow Bush Supporters* and *Religious Independents* were used by the Bush team to reach outside the GOP base and court moderates.

The worst-performing group for President Bush was called *A Few Stranded Good Guys*, a sardonic title for 69,681 voters who opposed affirmative action and gun control but were otherwise big-government Democrats. Bush could ignore them.

Terrorism Moderates was segment 14, sandwiched between hardline Republicans and liberal Democrats.

"Sounds like me," Palos said.

## Selling Karl Rove: A History of LifeTargeting

It almost didn't happen. Though LifeTargeting has been done by churches and businesses for years, politicians have long been skeptical of it. Even Karl Rove, Bush's sharp-minded political strategist, needed to be convinced by Dowd and others.

Let's start this little history in Texas, where the president and his top political advisers got their start. Rove said it's where the seeds of the 2004 LifeTargeting plan were planted.

In every election since 1978, Texas Republicans have made hundreds of thousands of telephone calls to voters, seeking to find and motivate potential backers. "So all of our mind-sets were 'Hey, this is how politics is normally done.' What we found when we got on the national stage is that this was just not the case," Rove said. "The idea that you'd have a couple of phone banks in a congressional district was unheard of, particularly on the GOP side of the aisle."

But the Texas system described by Rove was at best a rudimentary form of LifeTargeting. Phone banking from voter registration lists doesn't account for people with unlisted numbers. Even worse, the operations usually focused on people living in GOP areas, missing thousands of potential Republicans who live in swing or Democratic areas.

While working on a Missouri campaign in the mid-1980s, Rove had a hand in a phone bank operation that asked voters their views on hot-button issues. That was a step forward, but the process still had major limits.

By the end of the decade, some political campaigns were purchasing limited amounts of consumer data and overlaying that against information gathered from state voter files and through phone banking. That was a major breakthrough. Still, it took eight years of technological advancement and prodding from Dowd for President Bush to take political LifeTargeting to the next level.

"This has been bubbling around for a while," Rove said. "It's just that there has never been as much data as we were able to collect this time. There's just an explosion of data—an exponential increase each year in the amount of information that is available on a household."

The information revolution that Rove talked about arrived just in time for Bush's advisers. Coming off their narrow victory in 2000, they were desperate enough to try new things. In the spring of 2003, Rove gave Dowd the OK to test the LifeTargeting system in Pennsylvania and report back to him and Mehlman.

Dowd made his case in a PowerPoint presentation at the campaign's headquarters in Arlington, Virginia, where a handful of aides gathered around a shiny faux-wood conference table. They included Dowd and his deputies Sara Taylor and Mike Shannon, as well as the political director Terry Nelson and his aide Coddy Johnson.

Distracted as usual, Rove flipped through a stack of paperwork while Dowd got things started. Mehlman paced the room, a habit that reflected his well-known and intense nervous energy. A laptop sat in the middle of the conference table, hooked to a projector that displayed Dowd's slides on a white screen.

The first slide had five words in white letters on a purple background: "Standard Precinct Targeting versus Micro-Targeting." Rove's eyes didn't move from his paperwork.

The second slide said that 20.6 million voters lived in precincts dominated by Republicans while 26.1 million lived in Democratic-dominated precincts. "Advantage: Democrats (5.5 million voters)."

The third slide made the same point: 24 percent of all voters in the 2000 election had come from Democratic precincts, while only 19 percent had come from Republican bastions. "Advantage: Democrats (5 percent)."

That one got Rove's attention.

He was looking at the screen when the next two slides pointed out similar Democratic advantages. In Pennsylvania alone, 1.4 million voters lived in precincts that were heavily Democratic, an astounding 855,000 more than the number of voters who lived in heavily GOP precincts.

The next few slides pointed to a huge new pot of potential Bush voters: conservative-minded people who had not been targeted in the past. In fifteen battleground states, there were some 5 million "suspect Republicans" (likely to vote GOP if properly motivated), 6.7 million "unreliable Republicans" (people who like the GOP brand but are infrequent voters), and 2 million "registration targets" (likely Republicans who are not registered to vote).

The last slide sealed the deal. It said that traditional targeting based on voting histories and political habits would reach 1.8 million unreliable Republicans in fifteen crucial states while LifeTargeting would reach 11.7 million.

Rove was sold. Before leaving the room, he approved the $3 million LifeTargeting plan.

**Micro-nation**

The Bush team eventually conducted LifeTargeting campaigns in the sixteen states they knew were critical to President Bush's reelection. The names and ideological tenor of the groupings varied from state to state, just as the lifestyles of voters do.

"This was like a dream come true," said Terry Nelson, flipping

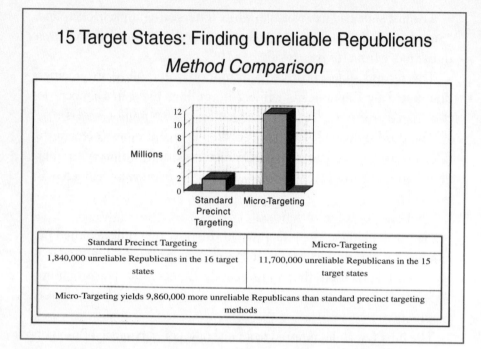

## 15 Target States: Finding Unreliable Republicans
### *Method Comparison*

| Standard Precinct Targeting | Micro-Targeting |
| :---: | :---: |
| 1,840,000 unreliable Republicans in the 16 target states | 11,700,000 unreliable Republicans in the 15 target states |
| Micro-Targeting yields 9,860,000 more unreliable Republicans than standard precinct targeting methods | |

Dowd's slide showing Karl Rove how many voters could be found through LifeTargeting as opposed to traditional methods.

through the LifeTargeting analysis of Ohio's 7 million registered voters. As the Bush campaign's national political director, Nelson was a greedy consumer of the LifeTargeting data. He turned to the back of the book and ran his finger down a chart that ranked voters from 1 to 10 based on their likelihood of showing up on Election Day (10 being the most reliable voters, 1 being the most suspect). Taking a pen out of his pocket, Nelson drew a line around a series of numbers representing Republican-leaning Ohio residents who tended not to vote. "That's where we focused our volunteers," he said. "We focused on people we thought were inclined to vote for the president if we touched them in the right way."

The chart gave Nelson access to remarkably specific information about the people he needed to touch. For example, there were 20,000 *Tax Cut Conservative Republicans* in Ohio who had spotty voting histories. He had their names and addresses, and he knew what they liked and didn't like about politics. Working from the LifeTargeting books,

Nelson's team would have volunteers whose views fit with Tax Cut Conservative Republicans call or visit the unreliable voters in that group.

"That decision was not without controversy," Nelson said. In the past, volunteers had been used to contact only reliable GOP voters. "People wanted to know why we were changing the way we did things. We changed because the way we looked at the electorate had changed."

The LifeTargeting books shaped what was said during those telephone calls and written in direct mail to voters. In Ohio, for example, there was a group of voters called *Young Unreliable Pro–President Bush Independents* who had a favorable view of President Bush's education policy. Those voters would get mail about his No Child Left Behind legislation. *Anti-Porn Women* in Ohio heard about President Bush's proposal to restrict access to pornography in libraries. It was not unusual for a voter targeted by the Bush campaign to receive fifty or sixty separate pieces of mail before Election Day.

The Bush team, which tested and measured just about every action it took, ran the LifeTargeting system through the wringer during and after the election. "We have no doubt it worked," Nelson said, pointing to Florida as a case study. In 2000, after Florida determined the election, Republicans looked back and found that they had targeted 33 percent of the people who had eventually voted for Bush. In 2004, they managed to contact 84 percent of eventual Bush voters. In Iowa, 92 percent of eventual Bush voters were targeted in 2004, up from 50 percent four years earlier.

Democrats, meanwhile, fought the first twenty-first-century campaign with tactics mired in the twentieth century. Kerry's advisers managed to combine traditional voter list information with some consumer data from an Axciom competitor, a process that helped them identify undecided and Kerry voters. But the system was barely functional, and, unlike Bush, they had no idea what made these voters tick. Kerry's team failed to do the polling and analysis required to segment the electorate into like-minded groups and determine what issues angered or excited them.

This was inexcusable. The strategies behind LifeTargeting had been used in many business and megachurches for years and had even been explored for use in the Clinton reelection campaign in 1996. "We had several long phone calls and endless meetings where we talked about the idea of layering messaging on top of our targeting like Bush did, but nothing ever came of it," said a Democratic analyst who worked for Kerry during the primary and general election campaigns. "It's kind of the nature of the Democratic Party to talk about what we need to do—and talk and talk and talk—and not do it."

Even after the 2004 election, there has been precious little activity among Democrats to institutionalize a long-term national LifeTargeting program like the one at the Republican National Committee. Instead, the Democratic National Committee has inexplicably decentralized the compilation of LifeTargeting data by allowing each state to control it. Frustrated by the DNC's position, a group of well-connected Democrats led by former Clinton adviser Ickes is attempting to raise millions of dollars to start a private LifeTargeting firm. It would be a huge asset should Senator Hillary Clinton run for the presidency in 2008.

In 2005, Democratic Governor Tim Kaine's successful campaign in Virginia gambled on an ambitious LifeTargeting program that combined voter lists, private-sector consumer data, and 10,000 interviews (twice the number the Bush campaign conducted in the biggest states). Kaine's team divided the electorate into several like-minded segments, including 150,000 Democrats who voted in presidential races but who rarely, if ever, bothered with statewide races. These so-called *Federal Democrats* were scattered throughout the state, many in heavily GOP precincts, and thus were unlikely to have been targeted by past Democratic campaigns. Kaine's strategists knew who they were, where they lived, and what messages would motivate them to vote.

Kaine's campaign manager, Mike Henry, said that the modeling program had helped Kaine find and win over Democrats in exurban precincts that had voted Bush in 2004. "We found Democrats who had never been touched before," he said.

## A Way of Life

HOWELL, Mich.—Palos and Jensen say they're getting used to the idea of being Republican, though the Democratic Party is still after their hearts, minds, and votes.

"Are you kidding me? My mailbox was jammed all year," Jensen says shortly after the 2004 election.

"Mine, too," says Palos.

Both women received mail from Kerry late in the campaign, which makes sense, given their voting histories. It's harder to figure how President Bush and other Republican campaigns found them for the first time.

Jensen says it might be because somebody in her church group was a big Bush backer and perhaps put her name on a campaign list. Palos says she voted for President Bush in 2000 "and maybe now they have got my number."

Or it could be that they both know the Livingston County clerk, who, like most politicians in their fast-growing community, is a Republican. "She had me sign something, a ballot petition or something at some point," says Palos. "I support her because I know her and like her."

Both women also voted for their GOP congressman. This is the Democrats' greatest fear: voting Republican becoming a habit in the fastest-growing parts of the country.

"It's hard not to like Republicans in Hartland," Jensen says of her hometown in Michigan, "because everybody out here seems to be Republican. All of Hartland is Republican."

Says Palos, "It's become a way of life."

## Communicating

With Republican-leaning voters such as Palos and Jensen opposed to gay marriage, why did the President Bush campaign broadcast 473 commercials on a sitcom celebrating gay life in New York?

"I've got the answer right here," said Will Feltus, the head of research at National Media in Alexandria, Virginia, who was directed by Dowd to help Bush get a bigger bang for his advertising buck. He flipped to a

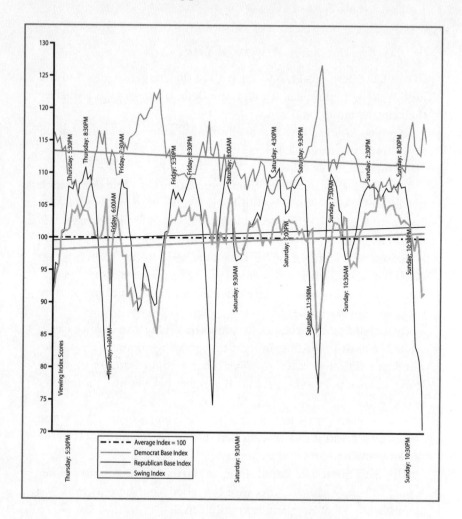

**Democrats watch TV more than Republicans,**
**though the gap narrows on weekends.**

spreadsheet prepared for Dowd that ranked the partisan audiences of network and cable TV shows.

As you might expect, the sitcom *Will & Grace* had a disproportionately Democratic audience among voters 55 years and older. However, among voters between 18 and 34, the show was incredibly popular with Republican and swing voters. Running a finger down a dense column of figures, Feltus said that *Will & Grace* was especially strong among young GOP women.

To hell with conventional wisdom, he said; "These numbers don't lie."

Neither do these findings that Feltus gave to Dowd:

- Nationally, Democratic voters were 14 percent more likely on average to be watching television than Republican voters.
- Cable audiences skewed Republican by about 4 percentage points. Network audiences skewed Democratic by 14 to 37 points.
- The gap between Democratic and Republican voters narrowed by about 5 percentage points during weekend network broadcasts.

President Bush's advisers didn't know why Democrats watched more TV overall or why Republicans picked up the slack on the weekends. They didn't care. What mattered to them was who watched what TV shows when. Now they had their answers, and many of them flew in the face of conventional wisdom (for example, political operatives had long assumed that GOP voters were out and about on the weekends). In a January 2003 report to Rove, Mehlman, and the rest of President Bush's reelection team, Dowd and Feltus argued for a complete overhaul of ad-buying strategies to get President Bush's message to more Republicans and at a lower cost.

### Eureka Moment

In early 2001, about the same time Dowd was having his eureka moment about base voters, Feltus stumbled into his innovation for measuring the partisan makeup of TV viewers. He was sitting in a meeting at an Internet start-up with several people, including Bob Cohen of Scarborough Research. Cohen's firm surveys 200,000 adults per year for more than eight hundred measures of demographics, consumer behavior, and lifestyle interests.

Bored by the meeting, Feltus thumbed through the Scarborough questionnaire. A tingle went down his spine when he spotted three questions buried in the thick packet:

Are you registered to vote?
What party do you belong to?
How often do you vote?

"Excuse me, Bob?" Feltus said. "What do you do with these questions?"

"I don't do anything with them, really. We put them in just because I'm interested in politics," Cohen said, adding that he had hoped local media outlets would use the results to sell advertising time to political campaigns.

"I have a better idea," Feltus said.

## The Formula

Feltus and his National Media team took Nielsen's data on television-viewing habits and cross-referenced them with the Scarborough surveys of viewing habits, political allegiances, and lifestyle preferences. It was the tool Dowd had been pushing for.

Some of the findings had limited practical implications. Porsche owners tend to be Republican, while Volvo owners tilt Democratic. Jaguar owners are the most likely to vote, Hyundai drivers among the least likely. Dr Pepper is the only sugared soft drink that has a GOP-leaning consumer base.

It's anybody's guess as to why Democrats favor Volvos and why Republicans prefer diet drinks, but at least Feltus had figured out their lifestyle preferences. His other findings were more useful to President Bush's aides trying to find Republican voters on the expanding spectrum of TV channels. He developed a formula that measured GOP viewers and found that:

- The gap between Democratic and Republican viewing habits was narrowest during prime time, early evening, and early morning. The gap was largest during the daytime and late-night hours, when Democrats tended to watch much more TV. Those Republicans who tended to watch late-night TV preferred Jay Leno over David Letterman.
- NASCAR, college football, college basketball, and hockey skewed Republican. NFL viewers tended to be Republican, but pro football had a lower rate of GOP viewership than college football.
- Heavier viewers of television were more likely to vote.

- Swing voters watched less television than Republicans, but they tended to watch when Republicans were watching.
- Speedvision was the most GOP-leaning cable channel, followed by Outdoor Life Network, Great American Country, and Country Music TV, all in what National Media called the "Good Ol' Boy" factor group.
- Sports channels (the Golf Channel, ESPN) and "learning" formats such as the History Channel also tilted Republican. Among the news channel entries, Fox News Channel, MSNBC, CNBC, and the Weather Channel were favored by Republicans, but CNN leaned Democratic.
- Republican and Democratic television usage varied from market to market, often without a discernable reason. Roanoke, Virginia, Atlanta, and Salt Lake City, Utah, three areas considered strongly Republican, were among the markets with the highest percentage of Democratic viewers.

Feltus applied his formula to every network and cable TV show airing in battleground states. *Jag* and *Navy NCIS* had heavy Republican audiences.

*NYPD Blue* was popular with Republican and swing-voting men but not women. *The West Wing* leaned Democratic. *The Simpsons* was popular with Republican men, while *Gilmore Girls* was favored by GOP women.

On the radio, Feltus found that the best way to reach Republican men was on pop, classic rock, and sports stations. Country music stations, long thought to have solidly Republican audiences, drew nearly as many Democratic as GOP voters.

Religious-oriented radio was the best way to reach women, along with adult contemporary formats.

The Scarborough data even allowed National Media to rank newspapers by the partisanship of their readership.

Another National Media analysis ranked Pittsburgh tourist attractions by the partisanship of people who use the facilities. The Phipps Conservatory, for example, is popular with Republicans, a factoid that might help a grassroots organizer who's looking to get petitions signed.

In 2005, the Kaine gubernatorial campaign considered buying Nielsen's data to determine what shows Virginia Democrats tended to watch. Henry had the same problem in Virginia that Dowd had nationally: fewer of his candidate's voters watched TV, in general, than the opposition's supporters. In the end, Kaine could not afford the expensive Nielsen project.

### Cable and Other Niches

The networks no longer rule. In a watershed development for political and business marketing, cable TV surpassed broadcast networks in audience size in 2001.

The Bush team realized that it could get more for its ad money by reducing the proportion of its budget spent on broadcast television and diverting resources to niche cable channels and radio, where it could be targeted more precisely to GOP viewers.

While business advertisers have aired ads on cable TV for years, political campaigns have tried to reach the widest possible audiences with broadcast TV. Caught in the old way of thinking, Kerry virtually ignored cable TV and radio in his advertising strategy, remarkable omissions in an age of media fragmentation. The decision gave President Bush's advertising team a way to narrow the traditional Democratic advantage on TV.

In Cleveland, a key market in the campaign, a National Media study showed that buying only broadcast TV would put President Bush at a huge disadvantage because Democratic viewership was 25 percent higher. Adding targeted radio narrowed the Democrats' advantage to 16 percent. A targeted campaign on broadcast TV, radio, and network cable closed the gap to 8 percentage points. The Bush campaign went so far as to air ads on the internal TV feeds at public gyms in Ohio.

"Anybody who's in the business of persuading the public, which is corporate America and political America, must now share their message in a way that not only reaches people based on how they get their information but also reaches people in a way they like to get information," said campaign manager Mehlman. "The person who gets their information on the Web and the person who gets information from TV are two very different people."

He knows as well as anybody that Internet-savvy people tend to be younger, and their influence is growing each year. Mehlman promised after the 2004 election to push new frontiers as RNC chairman, offering podcasting of presidential speeches and conservative talk shows on the RNC Web site.

In 2006, Mehlman launched "My GOP," a Web site allowing Republicans to create personal Web sites that keep track of their political activity—everything from the number of people they register to vote to the amount of money they raise. The highly interactive site was designed to allow people to create their own ads and podcasts that they could e-mail to friends. Mehlman said the idea is to give Navigators more tools to communicate the party's message. "Gone are the days where politics is a passive business where we from Washington or some state capital dictate what information people are going to get and what activities they'll do on behalf of the party," Mehlman said. "Now we're helping people give *us* our marching orders and navigate the flood of information out there."

For any enterprise trying to get a message to the public, the days of single-outlet communications are over. In 2008, chances are that broadcast TV, radio, national cable, and even local cable won't be enough. Cutting-edge campaigns will have to look for smaller and smaller niches.

## Connecting: Iraq as a Value, Community as an Asset

### Iraq

President Bush couldn't sell the Iraq war strictly on its merits. It was an unpopular war by the time the 2004 reelection campaign rolled around, with the death toll climbing; his initial justification for invading Iraq, Saddam Hussein's weapons of mass destruction, had turned out to be unfounded; and the insurgency was stronger than the public had been told to expect.

So he used the war to project a Gut Value. To the dismay of Democrats, who claimed there was no connection, Bush said the Iraq war was part of the global war on terrorism, thus playing to the public's fear and patriotism. He made his difference of opinion with the majority of Americans an asset—a sign of strong and principled leadership.

"Even when we don't agree, you know what I believe and where I stand," Bush said at his 2004 nominating convention. Watching the convention from her suburban Chicago home, Bonnie Kohn rubbed the goose bumps out of her arms after that line. A Democratic-leaning voter, she had been on the fence in the 2004 presidential race. "I decided right then and there that even though I couldn't put my finger on it, there was something about that guy that made me feel safer. Something gut level about him made me trust him. He had me thinking we were all in this together," she said months later. Polls suggest that there were many more like Kohn who opposed the war but voted for Bush because they thought he had the Gut Values to keep them safe.

Bush amplified his Gut Values Connection by insisting that Kerry was everything he himself was not—a waffler on the war who had no core values. Though the president's team oversimplified and exaggerated Kerry's positions, the Democrat didn't help himself by shifting his views on Iraq and suffocating his explanations in nuance. Kerry famously said he had voted both for an Iraq war spending bill and against it—a statement that was defensible to voters who cared about the byzantine legislative process and horrifying to the 99.9 percent of voters who did not.

## Community

Terry Nelson will never be confused with Bruce Springsteen, but the Bush campaign's political director once got rock-star treatment. It was at a breakfast for top Republican volunteers attending the president's second inauguration. "I mean, they couldn't get enough of me," said Nelson, a shy Iowa-bred operative with floppy brown hair. He wasn't bragging. A year later, he was still stunned by the reception, which taught him something about the power of political communities in the Internet age. "They had all gotten e-mails from me during the campaign. They all knew who I was. I can't tell you how many of them came up to me and said, 'Your campaign really meant something to me.' And campaigns don't really mean anything to people unless there is a real personal connection. It's not ideology that motivated these people, it's because we made a connection and they became part of a community."

A certain esprit de corps is common among campaign staffs, bound together by long hours, cold pizza, and a common cause fulfilled or forsaken on Election Day. What makes twenty-first-century campaigns different are technologies that allow old hands like Nelson to reach beyond the headquarters' four walls and create that sense of community with millions of campaign volunteers.

The method was particularly effective where the bulk of President Bush's voters live—in isolated rural areas and the fast-growing exurbs. In the newest suburbs, people tend to be busy raising families and working long hours to pay their mortgages in neighborhoods filled with people from somewhere else. The desire to form friendships and build communities was enormous, and President Bush's advisers felt that Republicans would benefit by feeding that hunger. Typically, they had a number to support their theory: if a person was contacted in person, he or she was four times more likely to vote, internal polling showed.

A favorite tool of the Bush campaign was the so-called house party, an age-old political tactic taken to a new level by the technologically savvy campaign. Here's how it worked: Volunteers were urged to invite their friends to their homes for a Bush-themed party, sometimes organized around a major event such as a debate or the president's convention speech. The campaign would provide fliers, information packets, and computer tools to help bring people together. For every party, a computer program automatically e-invited Bush volunteers who lived near the host. With a few keystrokes, guests could RSVP and get directions to the party. Scores of parties would be connected together by teleconference calls, usually with President Bush, First Lady Laura Bush, or some other dignitary, who would thank the volunteers for their help. On one night alone, 130,000 people tapped into the house party network.

"If you're talking to people who are like you and like the things you do, you're more likely to take their advice and vote—maybe even vote for President Bush," Nelson said.

In addition to house parties, which tapped into neighborhood ties, Bush advisers plumbed scores of other social networks. They collected membership lists: of hunting clubs, Boy Scouts, Little Leagues, neighborhood associations, and, most significantly, churches. Nelson estimated they collected 2 million names of churchgoers, checking each one against his or her state's voter registration rolls. Those who were not registered were sent a form to do so. Those who were registered had another piece of lifestyle data plugged into the campaign's database. The practice drew howls of protest from critics, some of whom accused the Republicans of blurring the line between church and state, but to the Bush team church rolls were simply social networks too large to ignore.

The Bush campaign collected the names and e-mail addresses of 7 million volunteers and supporters. With the power of new technologies, the campaign was able to keep in touch with each volunteer, urging him or her to talk to friends, coworkers, and neighbors about President Bush. Just as megachurch pastors urge worshipers to recruit the "unchurched," the Bush machine prodded supporters to court the "un-Bushed"—and trained them how to do so.

"As people sort of began to move in their own communities and networks, it became clear that one way you could affect people who were prospects for us was by talking to their friends in their networks," Rove said. "Whether it was 'I worship with him. I live in the same neighborhood. We work in the same place. We share the same interests'—all of those things were susceptible to organization and focus."

Tapping into these networks also gives political campaigns access to a new kind of opinion leader—the firemen, pharmacists, PTA presidents, and others who qualify as Navigators. Dowd recognized the potential when he gave Rove and Mehlman copies of *The Influentials* shortly after the 2000 election. The book, written by Roper executives Jon Berry and Ed Keller, makes a convincing case that one of every ten Americans tells the other nine what to buy, how to vote, and where to eat.

Eventually, the campaign had a list of more than 2 million people identified as Navigators, based on their willingness to write letters to help recruit Bush backers. They used that list to communicate deep into communities. For example, before President Bush visited Detroit, the campaign notified the 52,000 Michigan Navigators and asked them to invite friends to the event or write letters to the editor praising President Bush after the appearance. This sort of word-of-mouth or buzz marketing is new to politics but should be more common, as we'll explain in chapter 6.

"One lesson for me from this campaign is you can have a lot of people talking about [LifeTargeting] or some other new election tool, but you can't just rely on that," Nelson said. "You have to have person-to-person contact and personal volunteers to make things really happen."

The same goes for governing. As President Bush sought to relaunch his troubled presidency in January 2006, Mehlman urged volunteers to throw house parties the night of the State of the Union address. "A house party is a great way to carry the president's message into your community, while having fun with friends old and new," Mehlman wrote in an e-mail to 15 million Republican activists and supporters.

### Bush's Frayed Connection

In the summer of 2005, the Gut Values Connection between Bush and many voters was frayed. In August, images of the president riding his bike in Crawford, Texas, joshing with the cyclist Lance Armstrong, and bragging about his heart rate clashed with grim news from Iraq, antiwar vigils outside his ranch, and soaring gas prices. When he refused to meet with the peace activist Cindy Sheehan, whose soldier son had been killed in Iraq, many voters saw that not just as a snub of the so-called Peace Mom but also as a refusal to acknowledge their own simmering concerns on Iraq. To many Americans, the president looked disconnected from their anxious reality, even arrogant.

People started looking at President Bush's politics and policies through a skeptic's prism. Things worsened when the sluggish response to Hurricane Katrina brought into focus the public's loss of faith in government, anxieties about the war, and concerns about their president. It gave evidence to the uneasy feelings they had started to get in August: *Bush just doesn't get it, does he?*

Bush waited two days to cut short his Texas vacation and return to Washington. On the flight back, he looked down on the ravaged Gulf Coast from a window in Air Force One, an image that struck some Americans as imperial and insensitive. It was another two days before he visited the Gulf Coast. From the start, President Bush reflexively echoed his advisers' things-are-okay spin. Americans didn't buy it. They were glued to their TV sets, watching the government's response play out in slow motion. They heard President Bush praise "Brownie," the hapless FEMA Director Michael Brown. It took President Bush several days to criticize the response led by the Federal Emergency Management Agency, and even then he appeared reluctant to do so. It took nearly two weeks for him to take personal responsibility. By then it was too late. In anxious times, the public demands buck-stops-here accountability. Had he immediately declared the response as lacking, taken responsibility, and demanded action, the political damage might have been mitigated.

It was quite a reversal for a leader whose actions after September 11, 2001, could not have been more in line with public sentiment. President Bush seemed jolted at first by the attacks, staying away from Washington for hours before delivering a grim-faced address to the nation that night. He choked up in the Oval Office two days later and won favor at week's end with Americans when he stood atop a charred New York City fire truck alongside a fireman and vowed vengeance. Over four horrific days, President Bush reflected the emotions of Americans: stomach-churning shock, then grief, and finally angry defiance.

After Katrina, polls showed steep declines in the number of voters who trusted President Bush, considered him a strong leader, valued his judgment in a crisis, and approved of his overall job performance. Six in ten voters wanted him to cut back on spending on Iraq to help pay for relief and recovery from Katrina.

Bush's credibility took another hit when Vice President Dick Cheney's chief of staff, I. Lewis "Scooter" Libby, was charged with covering up his role in leaking the name of the CIA operative Valerie Plame to journalists. Rove also came under scrutiny for talking to journalists about Plame. The president's approval ratings were still falling a year after his reelection, with voters raising doubts about the Bush administration's use of prewar intelligence. The percentage of voters who trusted him plummeted. The political free fall touched off an internal struggle in the White House. Bush's communications advisers Dan Bartlett and Nicolle Wallace urged the president to be more candid with the public about the administration's misjudgments on Iraq and the problems that lay ahead. Older advisers, including Rove, insisted that the president not give an inch to his critics. In the end, their boss

## Gut Instinct

HOWELL, Mich.—More than a year after the election, Palos still struggled to answer the question "Why did I vote for Bush?"

"I don't know."

When we reinterviewed her in December 2005, Palos said she didn't regret having cast her vote for the president, despite her growing opposition to the war in Iraq, the lousy Michigan economy, and a vague sense that the country is "kind of in the dumps."

She was disappointed with the president. He hadn't performed well after Katrina, "and this war hasn't exactly turned out as he promised." Yet there was something about him that still struck a chord.

"It's just the whole measure of the man," she said. "When I voted for Clinton, I did it on gut instinct. I look at a person, and I try to see through their eyes to their values.

"Who knows if I know everything on policy," she added, "but I can get a sense of who a person is."

split the difference and gave a series of speeches that both struck a more humble tone and lambasted Democratic war critics. Predictably, President Bush's approval numbers climbed a bit after he took some accountability, but his Gut Values Connection had already been damaged. Once a Gut Value is lost, it's almost impossible to get it back.

## *Beyond the Horizon*

### WHAT TO LOOK FOR IN POLITICS

### Tipping Tribes: The Disenchanted Middle

It's time to bust another myth. Conventional wisdom suggests that 2004 was the first of what will be a series of "base elections," with both parties catering only to their core voters. Supposedly, there is no longer a vital American middle.

Wrong.

It's true, as Dowd found, that just 7 percent of voters in 2000 were ticket splitters (people who cast ballots for both Republicans and Democrats) and the number dropped to 6 percent in 2004. But a closer look at the numbers reveals a much higher percentage of voters—as much as 35 percent—who don't feel at home in either party. According to 2004 exit polls:

- 35 percent of voters were small-government, fewer-services conservative Republicans.
- 30 percent were big-government, more-services liberal or moderate Democrats.
- The remaining 35 percent were a muttlike mixture. They identified themselves as big-government Republicans, small-government Democrats, and big- and small-government independents. By casting all-Republican or all-Democratic votes in 2004, these people created the false impression that the U.S. electorate is permanently polarized.

What really happened? With no other alternative, these voters reluctantly cast their lot with either the Red Tribe or Blue Tribe, choosing sides based on which seemed to be closest to their values at the time. But they were actually part of the vast Tipping Tribe—frustrated, disenchanted voters who could easily be persuaded to switch sides in the next election. This is one way the craving for connection and community manifests itself in politics; people want to be part of a team, so they choose sides even when neither party truly suits their needs. More than ever, Americans make their choices based on the recommendation or by the example of friends, family, coworkers, or neighbors. They want to *belong* and *be involved* so badly that they're willing to forgive the imperfections of their "tribe" and its leader.

It stands to reason that when these voters switch allegiances, they'll do so in big chunks, dragging their like-minded communities with them. This is what happened in the 2005 Virginia governor's race. Exurban voters peeled away from the Republican Party when the Democratic candidate, Tim Kaine, spoke to their values (more on this in chapter 7).

Because both parties are captive to their most extreme voters, the twentieth-century political playbook required candidates to "run toward their base" in the primaries and "run toward the center" in the general election. From this election forward, voters will be too well informed (thanks to technology) and too cynical (thanks to bitter experience) to be easily gamed. This applies particularly to well-known candidates such as Democratic Senator Hillary Rodham Clinton of New York, whose best course would be to frankly acknowledge any differences with voters and carry that disagreement as a badge of honor. As Bush did on Iraq in 2004, the trick is to portray unpopular decisions as a sign of strong, principled leadership. Candidates who fudge or fuzzy their positions are setting themselves up for failure. The same rule applies to mistakes. The old playbook is to never admit error or give ground to opponents. The new rule is to be accountable; Bush learned this the hard way in 2005. Voters don't expect candidates to be perfect. But they do demand that they be honest and straight-shooting. It's the era of spine, not spin.

In "The Politics of Polarization," Democrats Galston and Kamarck point out that the percentage of self-identified liberals (21 percent), conservatives (34 percent), and moderates (45 percent) in 2004 was about the same as it was thirty years ago. "Our politics is more polarized than the people themselves," they wrote. "Thus, a system of polarized parties does not provide a natural home for the plurality of Americans who define themselves as moderates. Indeed, it leaves them feeling frustrated, unrepresented, and alienated from public life."

This could lead to sudden and vast shifts in the U.S. electorate—perhaps a third-party movement, as we saw in 1992, or even a more permanent realignment. Regardless of how it plays out, this we know: more than a third of voters are frustrated by politics as usual and could be galvanized by a candidate—Republican, Democrat, or whatever—who strikes them as authentic and rallies Americans behind a cause greater than themselves.

## Gut Values Issues: Health Care, the Environment, and Service

Certain issues are poised to become platforms for displaying a candidate's Gut Values, including health care, the environment, and community service. Health care costs have been increasing at three or four times the rate of inflation, a crisis that cries out for bipartisan solutions. The Democratic-controlled Massachusetts legislature passed a bill in the spring of 2006 that requires all residents to obtain health insurance much as they would car insurance, with the state subsidizing premiums for the poor and middle class. Republican governor Mitt Romney, a potential presidential candidate, said the plan reflected his emphasis on both compassion and personal responsibility—two potent Gut Values. The environment is increasingly becoming a lifestyle issue—a matter of clean and safe water, beaches, and parks for most people. Republicans don't talk about the environment. And Democrats talk about it in the wrong way. On global warming, for example, Democrats should discuss how climate changes affect people's lives rather than focusing on emission targets, treaties, and other abstract nuances. Both parties are missing the boat.

Finally, service may be the ultimate Gut Values issue. Americans have a unique history of forming voluntary associations and taking action to help others, from Franklin D. Roosevelt's Civilian Conservation Corps and John F. Kennedy's Peace Corps to Bill Clinton's AmeriCorps and the USA Freedom Corps created by George Bush. "The next candidate who can awaken citizens further to think more of others than themselves and to devote themselves to causes that promote the public interest will tie into a deeply seated gut value that transcends party and reaches across the political divide to find any citizen," said a former USA Freedom Corps director, John Bridgeland.

## Navigating the Stormy Present
# How to Be a Great Connector

1. **Make and Maintain a Gut Values Connection.** Voters felt President Bush was a strong and decisive leader. They felt President Clinton cared about them and would work hard on their behalf. Both presidents fell out of favor when they were not true to their Gut Values, proving that authenticity matters in this era of spine, not spin.

2. **Adapt.** President Clinton realized he needed to change his message and methods to appeal to Swing Is and Swing IIs. Eight years later, President Bush determined that there were no longer enough swing voters to make a difference and that he had to find new Republican voters.

3. **LifeTarget.** President Clinton barely scratched the surface of the potential to find and motivate voters based on their lifestyles. President Bush took it to a new level in 2004.

4. **Talk Smart.** Both presidents broke new ground in niche and local advertising, constantly looking for ways to communicate to their voters through the channels those voters used to get information.

5. **Find Navigators.** President Bush's campaign identified more than 2 million people who could influence how their friends, family members, and associates make political decisions.

# 2

# BUSINESS:
## Selling Community

*Understanding the demographics of your community is important, but understanding the culture of your community is even more important.*

—PASTOR RICK WARREN of Saddleback Church,
on the business of religion

*There's something evangelistic about what we do.*

—Applebee's CEO, LLOYD HILL, on the religion of business

WHAT'S WITH THESE POLL NUMBERS? That's the question blurry-eyed strategist Dave Goebel tried to answer as he tapped at his keyboard and pulled up the next slide—one with the white outlines of a rectangle against a deep-blue background. The rectangle was divided into four sections, each pocked by a handful of red dots. Each dot represented an issue of importance cited most frequently by the 20,000 Americans in a poll Goebel was using to determine why opponents were cutting into his lead. The strategist pointed to the box on the upper right and said, "Our people."

Bottom left: "Theirs."

Bottom right: "Neutral. They don't care."

Finally, he pointed to the top left box. "These are the swing voters. This is what's up for grabs."

Goebel may talk in terms of "partisans" and "targeting" and "lifestyle segmentation," but he is not a political consultant. This is not the Clinton White House or the Bush White House. It is Hill's House—the exurban Overland Park, Kansas, headquarters of Applebee's International, run by Lloyd Hill.

Goebel is Hill's number two and likely successor as Applebee's CEO. The two restaurant executives have a major problem on their hands. The world's largest casual dining chain, while hugely successful and growing, had experienced an unexpected sales slump in 2005. Hill's team hoped to use the data on Goebel's computer to get the company back on track. "The idea is to really understand the customer well enough that we can get an expanded number of them to vote for us with their wallets," said Phil Crimmins, another member of Applebee's close-knit leadership team.

The ability of Applebee's or any other company to succeed in fast-changing times—to get people to *vote with their wallets*—hinges on its efforts to make and maintain Gut Values Connections. Projecting a sense of community and purpose means more to Applebee's bottom line than does the quality of its food. Of course, the food is important—the product is always important, in politics or business—but Hill knows where his proverbial bread is buttered. "We're not in the food business serving people. We're in the people business serving food," Hill said, sounding a bit like Starbucks founder Howard Schultz, another Great Connector.

Despite its size, Applebee's markets its restaurants as the place for people to gather with coworkers, friends, and family—a neighborhood grill and bar in more than 1,700 neighborhoods. Hill also has tried to make the workplace inspirational, inviting employees to join a great cause—"changing the world one guest at a time" by making customers walk out of Applebee's restaurants happier than when they came in. In their book *Built to Last*, Jim Collins and Jerry I. Porras talk of "Big Hairy Audacious Goals." For Hill, the purpose behind his audacity is to create a culture of community at Applebee's.

Throughout America, and particularly in the exurban areas where Applebee's made its name, there is a huge market for community. Virtually everybody is new and a stranger. People are busy raising families, building careers, and making mortgage payments. There are little time and few places to make friends. People's lives revolve around home and the workplace. Hill wants his chain to be their Third Place, another phrase coined by Schultz at Starbucks.

Applebee's and Starbucks share surprisingly simple values. The coffee giant has more than seven thousand locations in the United States, but has built a community-conscious brand and neighborly feel that defies logic: How can something so big feel so small? Schultz sounds like Hill when he addresses that question. "We are not a coffee company," he told shareholders in February 2006. "We are a people company." One would think that if Applebee's is a corporate soul of fast-growing Republican-leaning exurbia, Starbucks would be the heart of hip, urban Democratic neighborhoods. The fact is that while Applebee's and Starbucks have different geneses, they're guided by the same Gut Values principle that allows them to grow big while feeling small, extending their reach far outside their geographic comfort zones. Today, Applebee's highest-revenue restaurant is in Democratic Manhattan. A Starbucks in Des Moines, Iowa, is a hangout for Republican campaign workers.

Any company worth its salt tries to forge a Gut Values Connection. Apple Computer marketed its own "technology lifestyle," creating a culture of kinship around its technosystems. JetBlue created a loyal following by using the latest technology (satellite TV) to get customers on their planes and then made them feel at home with a community of happy, motivated employees. Hobby Lobby, Chick-fil-A, and Alaska Airlines are among the growing number of corporations injecting faith into the secular marketplace. Whether including scripture in their advertising or marketing directly through churches, the idea is to show voters that the company shares their values. "It's a way of saying 'We know what you're about and respect it,' " said Bob Buford, a businessman-turned-church-adviser.

Successful business leaders forge Gut Values Connections with approaches that Presidents Bush and Clinton would recognize. To varying degrees, winning corporations adapt to changing markets, LifeTarget potential customers, and talk to people through the communication channels that fit their lifestyles. A few examples:

- *Adapt:* Just as Applebee's hitched its fast-growth wagon to the rise of exurbia twenty years ago, Home Depot realized that the typical hardware store was a males-only environment and began marketing to women. Some companies shift gears out of desperate necessity, including the once-floundering McDonald's and Apple Computer.

- *LifeTarget:* Applebee's queried thousands of people about sixty-three different reasons why they chose to eat at its restaurants or a competitor's, then grouped the respondents into thirteen like-minded clusters (not unlike President Bush's LifeTargeting). Harrah's casino has built a database of 25 million customers, their demographics, and their gambling habits.

- *Communicate:* Successful companies pitch a lifestyle rather than just a product, and their channels of communication are as varied as the public's. Applebee's carefully targets its advertising, and uses its community ties to build word-of-mouth buzz from the moment a parcel of land is bought for a future restaurant. Starbucks, the Gap, and many other corporations identify people in communities who influence the opinions of their friends and neighbors, then get company products in the hands of those Navigators.

While Applebee's is our central focus, we'll point to other thriving companies to explain how these tactics help communicate a firm's Gut Values brand. We'll also take you to Applebee's tables across the country to illustrate why Gut Values Connections mean more to the bottom line than the food itself—just as the values of Presidents Bush and Clinton trumped their policies. And you'll get a glimpse behind the scenes at Applebee's headquarters, where executives acknowledged that their food may not be the company's strongest suit. They're not just selling food, said one Applebee's franchisee, "we're selling a connection."

That's a lesson for anybody selling anything—a hamburger, a candidate, or eternal life. It's the connection that counts. Applebee's success illustrates the value of forging an emotional bond with customers. Its troubles in 2005 underscore the dangers of taking a Gut Values Connection for granted.

## The Business of People

KANSAS CITY, Mo.—George Heier is sipping a cup of coffee at his usual table, between the bar and the bathrooms and within sight of the front door. "I like to see my friends coming in," he says.

At eighty-three, George has lost many of his oldest friends, but he makes new ones here all the time. On the beam above his table, next to a lithograph of Elvis Presley, is a picture of George and his wife, Helen, celebrating their fifty-fifth wedding anniversary at this same Applebee's.

When he didn't show up for lunch recently, the restaurant's general manager asked a colleague to call Heier's house. "You know what it means to have somebody check up on me?" Heier says, holding his arms out as if to embrace the entire restaurant. "I love these folks."

When he moved into this neighborhood in the late 1960s, it was located on the flat and empty fringes of Kansas City. "Hell, there were cattle roaming just up the road a bit," Heier says. Over time, the area's population exploded, and the Heiers had a network of friends and acquaintances—along with places like Applebee's to keep them connected to the community. Now he's living farther away from the city, with his son and daughter-in-law, in a new suburb filled with strangers.

Even the politics is unfamiliar in his new hometown, Blue Springs, Missouri. "Hell, they're all Republicans out there," he says with a laugh. The Roosevelt Democrat and veteran of D-Day opposed the war in Iraq and President Bush's domestic policies yet voted with the majority in his new community. "I backed Bush because I liked him, and even though I didn't support what he stood for, at least I knew he stood for something."

"I was born and raised a Democrat," he says, "but life changes, and so do politics."

The restaurant's general manager, Keith Leonard, stops by and says hello. He's the guy who threw the anniversary party, complete with cake, songs, and the photo that is now hanging above their heads. The frozen smiles of George, Helen, and Elvis warm the room. "They're good people," Leonard says of the Heiers, "and we're taught from the day we join this company to take care of our customers, especially our regulars."

A stranger from out of town notices the anniversary photo. Where's your wife? The smile slips from Heier's face as he nods at his visitor. "You're sitting in Helen's chair." She died of cancer in 2000, the old man says. "We were married for fifty-eight years, four months, and four days. This is our table. This is our place."

## ADAPTING: BUILDING AND PROTECTING A BRAND

It's been a meteoric rise for Applebee's since November 1980, when Bill and T. J. Palmer opened T.J. Applebee's Rx for Edibles & Elixirs in Atlanta. The Palmers envisioned a restaurant that would provide full service, consistently good food, reasonable prices, and quality service in a neighborhood setting. They opened a second Applebee's in Atlanta in 1982 and sold the concept to W. R. Grace & Co. a year later, hoping the conglomerate could take Applebee's nationwide.

W. R. Grace & Co., founded in 1854 to trade in bat guano and bird droppings, is a corporate behemoth. A global trader in fabric, fertilizer, machinery, and other products, Grace diversified after World War II to dabble in everything from sporting goods to tacos. Needless to say, a small Atlanta-based restaurant chain with a funky name was never high on Grace's list of priorities. That may be why the company was eager to deal when Abe Gustin came calling.

The Alabama-bred son of a bakery foreman and part-time Bible salesman was operating seventeen Taco Bell restaurants, most of them in the Dallas–Fort Worth area. He wanted to keep expanding, but the chain wouldn't allow him to do so. It did let him explore a new, non-competing concept and suggested two possibilities: the Grace-owned Applebee's and a low-calorie hamburger concept called D'Lites.

"Man, I really liked the D'Lites concept," Gustin said years later in that wistful voice multimillionaires use when they recall the dead-end road never traveled. "D'Lites had a better facility, and it was all-around more attractive at the time. But I kept thinking to myself, 'As soon as McDonald's or Wendy's introduces a low-fat burger, they'll turn out our lights.'" Although Houlihan's, TGI Friday's, Bennigan's, and Red Lobster seemed to have a stranglehold on the casual dining market, Gustin liked the Applebee's culture and price levels. He and five other partners put up $15,000 apiece for a franchise agreement.

Gustin's colleagues quickly grew worried that the growth of antialcohol organizations such as Mothers Against Drunk Driving would cut into Applebee's valuable bar business, and they plotted behind Gustin's back to sell the fledgling concept back to Grace. Gustin caught a whiff of the plans and bought his partners out for their original investment. To this day, he won't let his old partners forget their multimillion-dollar gaffe. "Whenever one of them is lined up over a short putt, I clear my throat a bit and say, 'Hey, Bill, do you realize that $15,000 stock you sold me is now worth $98 million?' "

In 1988, Gustin and a new partner, John Hamra, purchased the rights to the Applebee's concept from Grace, named the company Applebee's International, and took it public in 1989. They controlled fifty-four restaurants. Within a decade of the Gustin-Hamra purchase, Applebee's became the first casual dining chain with one thousand restaurants.

It didn't take company executives long to realize that their neighborhood grill concept was a perfect fit for the disconnected people who were moving to exurbia. The company's core customers were the middle-class city dwellers and suburbanites who had sacrificed convenience and short commutes for bigger homes, lower taxes, better schools, and safer streets. While anxious to leave their fast-changing neighborhoods, they were nostalgic for the sense of community that had buoyed their childhood—memories of close-knit neighbors raising families together, playing together, worshiping together, and, after church on Sunday, waving hello to one another at the local diner. Applebee's rushed into that void.

Starbucks stumbled into the same opportunity in urban settings after the thirty-four-year-old Howard Schultz took over the tiny chain in 1987. He actually merged it with an even tinier group of Italian-style cafés called Il Giornale. "We were filling a void in people's lives. The regulars learned to pronounce the name Il Giornale (*il jor-nahl'-ee*), and even took pride in the way they said it, as if they were part of a club," Schultz wrote later in a book about the rise of Starbucks called *Pour Your Heart into It*. Schultz had not anticipated the market for a Third

Place, but quickly adapted, building larger stores with more seating and room for jazz bands.

The desire for atmosphere and camaraderie was most intense among people in their twenties who had grown up with no safe place to hang out other than shopping malls, Schultz told us in 2006. As young adults, some found bars too noisy and threatening for companionship. So they hung out in cafés and coffee bars. Other trends of the 1990s helped Starbucks, including the growing number of people who worked from home and used coffee shops as a second office. It helped that the Internet was becoming a part of the culture at the same time that Schultz was making Starbucks part of it, too. Wireless access to the Internet helped make coffee shops a Third Place. "We have evolved and taken advantage of changes in the way people work and how they live in their homes, and, most of all, the fact that people are very hungry for human contact," Schultz told us. "I think it's a new phenomenon. I think if you kind of get underneath the rise in technology and the way people use personal electronic devices, it has become a secular way in which people act and that has led to people's desires to have some degree of human contact during the day, and Starbucks has definitely benefited from that."

Applebee's also kept pace with societal shifts. The chain beefed up its curbside pickup service after noticing that people wanted to eat at home more frequently, especially after the September 11, 2001, attacks awakened the nation's nesting instincts. With TV and radio ads aimed at busy commuters, pickup sales soared.

The trendsetting chain rode a generational wave to the top of the industry, catering to baby boomers who were raised on fast food and grew health conscious in their middle years, bored with burgers and fries, and endowed with enough time and money to enjoy casual dining. Many Applebee's franchisees and corporate leaders made their first fortunes in the fast-food industry before following baby boomers into the realm of casual dining.

Throughout the restaurant business, the changes people make are forcing companies to change, too. The next time you grab a quick burger and fries at McDonald's, notice how the busiest part of the restaurant is not the dining room, as it was for the first generation of fast-food eaters. It's the parking lot. The long lines of cars queued up at multiple takeout windows are a sign of the times: busy baby boomers want to eat and run (about 70 percent of fast food is eaten outside restaurants), so fast-food chains learned to accommodate.

Gustin retired as CEO in December 1997, giving way to Hill with 960 restaurants under the Applebee's name. With 1,732 restaurants in the United States at the end of 2005, Applebee's had nearly as many sites as its two closest competitors combined (Chili's with 1,021 and Ruby Tuesday with 805). Applebee's also has 72 franchise restaurants overseas.

After opening at least a hundred restaurants a year for thirteen straight years, including 2005, Applebee's plans to expand to at least 3,000 units in the United States and another 1,000 overseas. "The trick is to feel small. And you do that by making your place part of the community," Hill said, checking himself. "No, you *make your place a community*."

## When Bad Things Happen to Good Companies

They vowed it would never happen, but Applebee's executive team got a bit cocky. "I think there was a little too much comfort and complacency," Hill said. "While we kept saying 'Don't pay attention to press clippings,' maybe we did." Other chains had narrowed the Gut Values gap.

When sales slumped in 2005, the stunned Applebee's team concluded that their competitors had so effectively copied the company's food and atmosphere concepts that people could no longer differentiate one casual dining chain from another. They commissioned Goebel's segmentation study—the first survey in four years and the first ever to go beyond Applebee's customers and question people who frequent the competition.

In hindsight, Hill said it was a mistake to focus exclusively for so long on the shifting demands of Applebee's customers. "We had a mantra: get close to the guests, and they will tell you what you need to know. But what I learned is that you have to also get close to the people who are not your guests and find out about those people who tried you and didn't like you," Hill said.

The other change Applebee's made was to increase dramatically the frequency of its surveys. Instead of feasting for four years off a single segmentation study (which had been the case for years), Applebee's now surveys the same 10,000 casual diners via the Internet to track their behavior throughout the year, as the economy and marketplace shifts.

"Everything is just so dynamic now. It changes constantly," Goebel said. "We can't put the kind of distance between the time we really reach out to people and figure out what's making them tick."

The 2005 study revealed that Applebee's regular customers were pinching pennies because of the sluggish U.S. economy. Generally speaking, these are people with incomes of less than $50,000 a year who visit their local Applebee's five or six times a month. It wasn't that they ate at Applebee's competitors. They simply didn't eat out as much, and when they did, they ate and drank less than usual. "They said, 'I still love you, but I've got a problem with my pocketbook. I can't pay my mortgage. I'm staying home,' " Goebel said.

It was a different story with higher-income families. The 2005 study revealed that people earning more than $75,000 were choosing Chili's, TGI Friday's, Ruby Tuesday, and smaller local chains because of the quality of the food or a craving for a specific menu item. Hill's team discovered, for example, that the typical family man still enjoyed Applebee's low-priced steak when he ate with the wife and kids, but when he went out alone with his wife, he wanted a better cut of steak.

The study made it clear why sales had slumped in 2005: some customers couldn't differentiate Applebee's from its competitors, especially in exurbia; other customers appreciated the difference in atmosphere but liked the other guys' food better; and their most loyal customers couldn't afford to eat out as much. Armed with a better sense of casual diners' tastes and shifting lifestyles, Hill and his team began in 2005 to adjust.

Before we dig deeper into Applebee's Gut Values challenge, let's be clear that the Kansas company is not the only quality corporation that understands the importance of adapting to a changing public. McDonald's suffered a 50 percent drop in profits from 2000 to 2002 before realizing that a generation of customers raised on fast food now wanted healthier fare. Apple Computer posted five straight quarters of losses in late 1995 and 1996 before cofounder Steve Jobs returned to the company in 1997 and started selling Apple as a lifestyle rather than just another computer company. The rest of the chapter will highlight how these and other companies forged Gut Values Connections by identifying with people's fast-changing lifestyles.

## "It Wasn't Just a Restaurant"

INDIANAPOLIS, Ind.—Rick Cole loved his "Coronatinis"—a Corona beer, frosted glass, and three olives. He also loved his wife of thirty-three years, Wanda, and the Applebee's Neighborhood Grill & Bar on State Street in Greenfield, Indiana.

Whenever he could, Rick spent time with all three.

So it was that once a week Rick, an elementary school principal, and Wanda, an elementary school teacher, drove twenty miles from their Indianapolis home to the Applebee's run by Jeff Luebbe. They passed other Applebee's and several casual dining competitors to get to Luebbe's place. "The idea at first was to put some distance between us and our students, God bless them," Wanda says with a laugh. "But then the place started feeling like a second home, so we kept making the drive."

They had their favorite table, a round wooden one inside at the bar area where Wanda, Rick, and his chilled Corona became regulars. Rick didn't like the limes normally served with Corona, so he'd ask for olives—"a poor man's martini." One day they pulled into the lot, and the Applebee's staff realized there were no olives. No olives! A waitress met the Coles at the door, apologized, and bolted across the street to a grocery store. Rick had his Coronatini.

In June 2004, he retired. Wanda kept working, but the Coles visited Applebee's two or three times a week. "Rick liked to have a Coronatini after a hard day's work," said Luebbe, the restaurant's general manager. "He really liked a Coronatini after retiring."

Rick died unexpectedly of a heart attack on January 1, 2005. Wanda made a list of friends whom she wanted notified. Jeff's name was on it.

Wanda and her sons decided that family and friends could meet for lunch at Applebee's between the funeral and burial. "We knew Rick would have loved it," she said.

When she arrived at the restaurant, the place was packed. "I went over to our table, the one Rick and I always sat at. There were two huge baskets of flowers, one from Jeff and the other from the staff," Wanda said. "And on our table—on all the tables—were dishes of olives."

Months later, memories of the gathering still brought tears to

Wanda's eyes. "They ran out of Corona that day," she said, "and Jeff ran out to the store and brought some back. He wasn't just a manager, he was a friend. It wasn't just a restaurant, it was our place to be when we weren't at home or school."

## TARGETING: FOCUS GROUPS, POLLS, POLICIES

"I've got a problem with the mango," says Pat.

It's a steamy August evening, and ten women from Wayne, New Jersey, are hunched over plates of grilled citrus salad in an air-conditioned room.

"Tell me about the mango," says the only man in the room. He's taking notes. "Should I kill the mango?"

"No."

"No."

"No."

Three women reply in sequence as Pat grimaces at her plate of mango-slathered salad.

A Thanksgiving dinner dispute? Nope. It's just another focus group for Applebee's—this one to test potential Weight Watchers menu items. It was part of a lengthy and expensive research project the company conducted to decide whether to partner with Weight Watchers and, if so, how to sell the partnership to consumers. Political operatives do the same thing to decide whether to push a new policy and, if so, how to sell it to voters.

The project got off to an unscientific start. The sister of an Applebee's executive, Lou Kaucic, herself a member of Weight Watchers, came up with the idea. Kaucic brought it to other corporate leaders, who commissioned industry surveys on healthy food that found that:

- Sixty-five percent of U.S. adults are overweight, and nearly three fourths are watching their weight or dieting.
- The Weight Watchers brand is recognized by 97 percent of women in the United States.

- Weight Watchers and Applebee's had several shared traits, including neighborhood locations, franchised organization, and community involvement, and both businesses have social elements.
- In most families, women hold a "veto" on dining choices, and they often use it to avoid diet-busting food.

The next step was to test, through online surveys, forty-six potential menu items with 392 Weight Watchers members and 262 Weight Watchers team leaders. Contacted through the Weight Watchers database of e-mail addresses, the respondents were shown a written description of each item and asked whether or not they would make a special trip for it. The items that scored the highest were tested again, this time in focus groups.

Eight focus groups were conducted with Weight Watchers members and leaders, including the one in Wayne, New Jersey. In addition, focus groups were conducted with health-conscious people, mostly women, who were not members of Weight Watchers. The goal: to find the most popular food and learn how to market it. Applebee's knew from its research that the campaign would have two distinct target audiences, both of them dominated by females: the 13 million current and former Weight Watchers members; and the 56 million so-called Health Seekers, people who watch their weight but don't belong to Weight Watchers. Much of the marketing money would be aimed at Health Seekers.

Finding a message that appealed to both audiences proved difficult. At a focus group in Providence, Rhode Island, nine Health Seekers were asked what kind of people belong to Weight Watchers.

"Middle-aged," one woman replied.

"People struggling lifelong," said another.

"I just feel it's people who need structure," said a third.

None of the women thought they needed Weight Watchers, though they had plenty of reasons why others might. An Applebee's analysis said that Weight Watchers would bring credibility to the chain's health-conscious menu, but Health Seekers might be turned off if the company were not careful about how the new menu was described. The analysis put it this way:

Eating healthy has now become part of their lifestyle . . . it is not a fad or a diet. They feel proud that they are doing something good for themselves so there is no need to focus on the problem; they get it, just focus on the solution. Therefore, our copy should avoid:

- Words that (suggest) diet: "light," "fit"
- Overeating words: "hearty," "filling"
- Language that does not make them feel positive: "guilt-free"

So now Applebee's had a handle on its market. First, the chain needed to get families through its doors by avoiding the veto cast by dieting women. Secondly, the best way to do that was to sell the Weight Watchers menu as a healthy choice rather than as diet food. Applebee's marketing team got to work.

## Targeting Customers—Yours and Theirs

Harrah's casino leaves little to chance. CEO Gary Loveman, a former Harvard Business School professor, has built a massive customer database that allows Harrah's to target and market to its customers. Harrah's knows all customers' age, sex, zip code, and other demographics, as well as how much they bet and win when they play in the casino. It's LifeTargeting Vegas-style.

The key to tracking its customers are the so-called loyalty cards that Harrah's customers use at slot machines. Every dollar they spend adds points to the card that can be redeemed for prizes. Through the card's magnetic strips, Harrah's keeps track of its customers' betting habits. The program also tells Harrah's officials which gamblers are motivated by cash prizes and which would prefer a free hotel room. When a gambler's wagers fall off, he or she might get a call from Harrah's offering a free meal, a show ticket, or a cash voucher.

Harrah's VIP hosts are required to call at least 240 customers each month and divide their lists into behavior groups: "upsides," who have the potential to increase their gaming at Harrah's; "past dues," who haven't visited a Harrah's casino for some time; and "new to me" gamblers who will get a cold call. Harrah's next step will be to give hand-held computers to the VIP hosts so every contact with a customer could be downloaded into the database, according to an April 2005 *Business Life* article. "There's no question that other industries can learn from us," Loveman told *Business Life*. "Not just in loyalty programs, but in the process of taking a level of mathematical sophistication to prob-lems that have big profitability consequences."

Applebee's executives are far behind those of Harrah's and other companies in customer tracking. But they're getting better. The 2005 segmentation study ranked sixty-three attributes that customers said caused them to choose one restaurant over another—from "Great place to go with the family" and "On the way to where I was going" to "Crav-ing a favorite menu item" and "Great value for the food."

Those sixty-three attributes were broken into six categories: food, service, price value, experience, convenience, and atmosphere. On the chart made by Goebel that we described in the opening of this chapter, each red dot represented a reason why customers chose a particular restaurant ("Craving a menu item," etc.). The attributes in the top right box were Applebee's strengths; bottom left favored the com-petitors; bottom right didn't make a difference; and top left were wavering—the ones Goebel cheekily called "swing voters."

The constellation of red dots showed that people who craved a fa-vorite menu item or put a premium on the quality of the food tended to go somewhere other than Applebee's. They cast their vote for the other guy. Applebee's was favored by customers whose top concerns were value, convenience, and a social or family-friendly atmosphere.

If this were a political campaign, the question would be whether a candidate who is losing on the big issue (food) can still win the race. After reading in chapter 1 about President Bush and the Iraq war, you already know the answer.

"You can ask a consumer about a political issue or a restaurant attrib-ute and they'll speak to it as far as they know, but what counts are the in-tangibles, which are always hard to articulate," Goebel said. In other words, it's all about Gut Values Connections. He said a restaurant can succeed when the competition's food scores higher if people otherwise like the feel of the place—in Applebee's case, that it's a great place to bring the family, meet friends, and get that sense of belonging. Goebel said it's not unlike President Bush getting reelected despite Kerry's policies (his "food") faring better in polls. Of course, if the food is truly awful, that would affect a customer's view of the overall dining experience.

Just as Bush separated voters by like-minded segments, Hill and his team wanted to group casual diners based on the lifestyle choices that motivated their restaurant selections. From the 20,000 interviews, the survey identified thirteen separate "occasions" that brought casual diners to any restaurant. Of those thirteen occasions, *only one had to do with the quality of the food*. That segment (called "My Favorite Food") consisted of people who chose a restaurant mainly because it had their favorite menu item. But the "My Favorite Food" people spend less than a third as much money as those looking for a good spot to take their families out to eat—Applebee's strong suit. Applebee's was also favored by customers seeking a social outing and value.

Specifically, the Applebee's study identified four occasions that held the greatest potential for the chain:

**Family night.** This was one of the largest occasions and a huge contributor to Applebee's bottom line. Improving the "family experience" could help Applebee's increase its sales by tens of millions of dollars, the study said. Improving the food would bolster the "family experience," the study found.

**The convenience of a bar-and-grill setting.** Applebee's was doing well in this category, which skewed to singles and medium to high incomes.

**Healthy food.** Customers who came to Applebee's for perceived health and fresh food tended to be older women with high incomes, which played well with the company's partnership with Weight Watchers.

**High-energy social occasions among groups of friends.** People who came to Applebee's for this type of occasion tended to be younger than the average customer and single. Their income exceeded $75,000.

The segmentation study told Hill and his team that they could expand their customer base (Applebee's version of a political base) with food that would appeal to upper-middle-income families and new restaurant designs that would help distinguish Applebee's from other casual dining chains. They had less control over their most regular customers, who typically earn less than $50,000 a year and visit Applebee's five or six times a month. About one fifth of Applebee's customers are regulars, and they account for nearly half of its sales. Hill couldn't improve the economy for them, but he did insist that affordable meals stay on the menu even as pricier items are added to attract rising-income families.

"We can leverage our muscle and buying power to maintain the opening price point [low-priced menu items] with good value and good quality and also recognize that we have to cater to people whose palates are becoming more sophisticated," Goebel said. "These are people who are looking for a strip steak on Friday night but will load up the kids on Tuesday and want the sirloin." Beginning in 2006, Applebee's added items such as fancier sandwiches and contemporary breads, soups, and dressings along with spicier, more sophisticated entrées such as roasted garlic and Asiago chicken. The menu still includes the lower-priced favorites such as riblets and oriental chicken salad.

Crimmins, the senior vice president of development, said that one thing Applebee's will do with data from the study is determine how to redesign restaurant exteriors to stand out from the mind-numbing sameness of exurbia. "We're still the neighborhood grill and bar, but the concept is changing. The neighborhoods all look the same no matter where you go in the country—box stores and busy intersections," Crimmins said. "People are getting tired of that. So how do we relate as a unique neighborhood and business place. How can we contribute to changing the look of exurban neighborhoods?"

After a weak year for the bottom line, Hill's team opened 2006 with a rebound in sales. They had not lost their Gut Values Connection. Their challenge now is to adapt to the lifestyle changes of their customers without losing the culture of community that made Applebee's special.

When this book went to print, the full extent of the chain's rebranding plans was still in the works. Whether the chain reframes its TV advertising to focus on families or begins courting bar-hopping young Navigators with word-of-mouth buzz marketing, company executives say it's safe to assume that the primary appeal will go beyond just the food. True, the segmentation study found that improving the menu would enhance the "family experience," but that's no different than a politician using policies to enhance his Gut Values Connection. Just as the bottom line in politics is not policies, there's more to the restaurant industry than food. It's about making the connection. The key to Applebee's future is no different from the key to its past success—the promise of comfort, community, and connection in a neighborhood restaurant, a Gut Value repeated in 1,732 neighborhoods—and counting.

## Integrity Pays

OVERLAND PARK, Kans.—Lloyd Hill is prowling the stage at Applebee's headquarters. "For you to lead people where they normally don't go, they must trust you implicitly. And trust is based on integrity, isn't it?" Hundreds of heads nod. The general managers of Applebee's restaurants have heard Hill's pitch many times since he joined the company in 1994.

He runs his hands through his silver-gray hair, which curls up at the nape of his neck, a bit long for a sixty-one-year-old approaching retirement. "It may cause you a revenue shortfall. It might cause you to lose someone who you thought was one of your best people, but I tell you that in the long term integrity is one of the only things you can guarantee yourself, and one of the only things you can guarantee others. You cannot presume to lead without integrity."

In this age of corporate crime and corner cutting, Hill's speech might sound like cynical spin. He is, after all, a multimillionaire who literally swims with sharks, a ladder climber in four separate industries before he got into the restaurant business. Judge for yourself, but keep in mind that the annual meeting of restaurant managers was closed to the media (we were given a videotape of the April 2005 meeting). If Hill was simply posturing, it was a lot of effort for an exclusive audience.

"Do you have a vision for the people in your restaurant? Have you helped them get a vision for their lives? Do they have something beside the paycheck? Do they have some sort of vision for the restaurant and some sort of vision for greatness for themselves?" Hill asks.

If you're still skeptical about his motives, that's understandable. The bottom line for Hill is the bottom line. Applebee's revenues surpassed $1 billion in 2004, and its CEO has made as much as $10 million annually in salary, bonuses, and stock options. But what sets Hill and his company apart is the way he goes about making profits.

"We all want to be something bigger than just individuals," says a firm and folksy Hill. "We want to be part of a great team, some world record-setting team." Hill believes that great leaders—whether businessmen seeking customers, politicians targeting voters, or preachers saving souls—appeal to people's desires to be a part of something greater than themselves.

Now he's taking three steps toward the foot of the stage, pointing to his heart. "If we're going to get people to believe in our vision and if we're going to engage them, we have to genuinely care for them. You have to make one of the most difficult investments you'll ever be asked to make. It's not a financial investment, it's an emotional investment. You've got to make an emotional investment in people, make an emotional connection with them. You've got to create a positive, caring atmosphere in a restaurant that people can't wait to get to and don't want to leave."

## COMMUNICATING: MARKETING A LIFESTYLE

Applebee's and Weight Watchers launched their partnership in May 2004 with national and local advertising and merchandising. Applebee's used incentives and bulletins to tell Weight Watchers leaders about the new menu, knowing these were classic Navigators whose opinions mattered to members of the diet program. In a cross-marketing scheme, Weight Watchers advertised Applebee's at its meetings and Applebee's touted Weight Watchers at its restaurants. Weight Watchers announced the partnership in e-mails to nearly 5 million current or recent Weight Watchers members. That list was chock full of women who talk to other women about dieting.

National TV ads were used to launch the campaign, with an emphasis on early morning and daytime spots popular with women. For pinprick targeting that would have made the Bush campaign blush, Applebee's geared the ads toward consumers' lifestyles and bought time on several cable networks geared toward women, including TV Land, Lifetime, and the Food Network.

Radio ads were placed because they reach "women at home, at work, in the car, at the gym, etc.," according to an Applebee's memo. In a hopeful aside, the memo suggested getting radio DJs to sample the menu live. "DJ could 'talk up' new healthy and tasty menu or have sampling remotes."

A series of ads was prepared for women's magazines such as *Better Homes and Gardens* and *Ladies' Home Journal*. An ad titled "For Nine Months You Ate for Two. Now, Eat for You," ran in parenting magazines for ten weeks.

The one spot aimed at men ran for ten weeks in *Men's Health* magazine. "Goodbye, Love Handles," read a headline superimposed over a Tortilla Chicken Melt. "Hello, Love Machine."

The marketing plan was based on company polling and focus groups that showed a growing number of health-conscious Americans who were too busy to cook at home every night but wanted quality food when they ate out.

Beyond the new Weight Watchers program, Applebee's spent a total of $150 million on advertising in 2004, about $90 million of it on national campaigns. In 2005, the total jumped to $160 million, with $120 million set aside for national ads. A considerable percentage of the money paid for emotional spots playing up Applebee's culture of community. One ad, based on a true story, showed a small-town Applebee's restaurant closing on a rainy night as local TV news reported the local high school football team's big loss. On cue, the team bus pulled into the parking lot, and the community-minded Applebee's employees reopened the restaurant for their local heroes. Another sentimental ad showed a local basketball coach being surprised with a plaque in his honor hanging in his neighborhood Applebee's.

Indeed, the company does go out of its way when a store opens to contact high schools, civic clubs, chambers of commerce, and newspapers in search of "local heroes." Usually fireman, coaches, high school athletes, and the like, these Navigators' pictures are prominently displayed on the restaurant's walls. Hill says the practice gives each restaurant a local flavor. It has an added benefit: the local heroes program puts Applebee's employees into early contact with the community's quiet leaders. It's not quite as scientific as the Bush team's outreach to Navigators, but the local heroes program helps Applebee's produce early word-of-mouth buzz. In the 1990s, Starbucks would prepare to open a new site by assembling a list of people who could serve as local "ambassadors." Each would get a two-drink coupon with a note inviting them to "Share Starbucks" with a pal. The company held tastings with local reporters, food critics, chefs, and owners of fancy restaurants.

As we explain in chapter 6, word-of-mouth marketing is on the rise because people are losing faith in traditional opinion leaders, the media, and advertising. They're turning to one another for advice on what to buy and where to shop and for various other lifestyle cues. Enthusiastic customers "are the power behind our word-of-mouth strategy," said Schultz of Starbucks. Living proof that the connection matters more than tactics, Schultz eschews national advertising, polling, and even LifeTargeting. "We do research, but I would be embarrassed to say how little. It's laughable," he said.

"One of the benefits of our business is we get to interact with 40 million customers a week. We know what they're drinking, buying, and how they feel about the stores because that's the business we're in and we talk to them every day," Schultz said. Even the long-running program to get Starbucks products into the hands of Navigators is small by modern standards, he said.

"We recognize that there are people of influence, and we try to provide them with knowledge about the company and things of that nature—not to the degree of a political campaign or a larger consumer product company," Schultz said. "But we have targeted people in the past."

Schultz conceded that his company may not be taking full advantage of the growing power of word-of-mouth marketing and Navigators. "We have never lived in a time where there is such a fracturing of trust

and such cynicism in which public institutions and things we're suppose to trust have let us down. As a result, we all have everyday people
in our lives who hold great influence over us," he said. "These are people you can't buy, which is what makes them valuable, and that speaks
to the strength of our company. The quality and strength of our brand
grew exactly that way—organically and with great authenticity, not
thirty-second promotional campaigns."

## From Applebee's to Apple

After its profits slump, McDonald's brought James Cantalupo, the former head of McDonald's International, out of retirement to jump-start
the company. Under Cantalupo, the company broadened the restaurant's appeal to people who cared more about healthy, quality food.
McDonald's made the change without losing its base customers (Presidents Bush and Clinton could sympathize) who just wanted a quick
hamburger and fries. The company's new marketing strategy, termed
"Rolling Energy," focused on younger customers with a new slogan
("I'm lovin' it"), pop star endorsements, and a partnership with MTV.
McDonald's introduced Go Active! meals to improve its health image
and published the caloric content of its meals. Company profits and
stock prices soared.

Under Steve Jobs, Apple's advertising urged Americans to join a
technology revolution that revolved around users' digital lifestyles.
The "Switchers" campaign used "come to Apple" testimonials in which
Mac users explained how Apple products had made them more produc-
tive and creative people. Apple billed itself as a lifestyle change, rather
than just a switch in personal technology. The subtext was clear: When
you join the Apple community, you're a smart person who has seen the
light—not like the misled mass of PC users. The company flourished,
introducing the ubiquitous iPod in 2001 and a video iPod four years
later.

Just as Applebee's appealed to baby boomers' changing eating habits,
Home Depot took advantage of generational and lifestyle shifts among
hardware buyers. Recognizing the growing influence of women in
American life, the company began selling hardware not as individual
items but as home-building or lifestyle improvements. "Instead of dis-

---

### Changing the World

OVERLAND PARK, Kans.—Wearing an open-necked shirt and khaki slacks, the uniform of a megachurch pastor, Hill continues his sermon to company executives.

"I'm not telling you this because we want everybody to be warm and happy and feeling good. I mean, I'm not the warmest, fuzziest guy you're ever going to meet," Hill says with a sly smile. "I'm a pretty results-oriented individual, but the way you get those results in our business is with people, right? Technology plays a role, but it's the people. The better you can fully engage people, the better results you'll get. So I'm telling you this because it's good business."

Hill pauses now, letting the words settle into the crowd. Then he closes with a thought about Applebee's most successful managers because, like a good politician or preacher, Hill wants to give his people a purpose—a grand goal.

"They build connections with their guests. They build connections with their community, and I tell you, these people—these leaders—are making a difference in the lives of their associates. They're making a difference in the lives of their guests and in their neighborhoods," the CEO says. "They're changing the world one guest at a time."

---

playing a box of bathroom faucets, stores now show the whole tub, complete with shower curtains and towel," wrote Paco Underhill in his book *Why We Buy*, which explored how retailers woo buyers.

## CONNECTING: A VALUES-DRIVEN BRAND

Surely, a sense of common decency drove the Applebee's staff to treat George Heier and Wanda Cole well. But so did their training. From the hourly wage cooks to the wealthiest franchisees, it's understood that the Applebee's team is not in just the business of cuisine; it's in the business of community. Their task is to make Gut Values Connections with people who are hungry for belonging. Ed Doherty, one of the company's most successful franchisees, said that's the only way Applebee's can distinguish itself from fast-rising competition. "Our food is not that different from Ruby Tuesdays or Chili's, but we're making a connection with people," he said. "We're selling a connection."

Schultz said Starbucks created "a comfortable, sociable gathering spot away from the home and work, like an extension of the front porch. People connect with Starbucks because they relate to what we stand for. It's more than great coffee. It's the romance of the coffee experience, the feeling of warmth and community people get in Starbucks stores." That tone is set by Starbucks baristas, who happily thump and clang coffee-making gadgets while shouting out orders in a Starbuckian language that gives regulars a sense of belonging—*I'm around enough to know what they're saying!* The connection is no different in the thirty-six other countries where Starbucks has set up shop. "There is a need and a desire for a sense of community, a need for human contact," Schultz said. "There is a real hunger for community worldwide. People want to be with people of like-minded values. And at a time of our lives when there is such a fracture of trust and confidence, people have started to rely on Starbucks as a place that they can be a part of."

You get the same feeling at an Applebee's, where happy young servers hang around the bar after doting on customers all day. At both Applebee's and Starbucks, the "red" and "blue" of corporate America, Hill and Schultz and their teams have instilled a deep, cultural commitment to Gut Values.

"Unfortunately, in our society—especially in business schools and in politics—we've lost the intuitive feel. The word I would use is 'touch,' " Schultz said. "We're a high-touch company, and we value that. We value the relationships we make with our customers. People don't want to respond to marketing programs or advertising programs. In the world today, you want to create emotional connections with people that are based on authenticity and trust—not thirty-second ads."

Let's look at three ways in which Hill and Schultz do it.

### 1. They Hire and Retain Great Connectors

Applebee's has brought a bit of science to the task of finding employees willing to give customers what they want: a friendly encounter. All applicants are required to take a psychological test to determine whether they have the drive and personality to serve customers. The test asks 150 yes-or-no questions such as "Are there times when your future looks dark?" and "Are you so shy it bothers you?"

Hill said the goal is simple: "We're looking to see whether you love your mother," he said. "Think about it; if you don't like your mother, then you have some baggage we don't want to deal with."

A fifteen-page booklet tells store managers how to conduct interviews, complete with questions designed to uncover an applicant's best and worst personality traits. Under the heading of "composure," managers are instructed to ask applicants to describe the last time they had a conflict with a fellow employee. The "teamwork" section suggests that applicants be asked to describe the last time they disagreed with the feedback from a supervisor.

Rather than calculating a restaurant's success and the general manager's bonuses solely on profits, Applebee's also measures the satisfaction of guests (through telephone surveys) and the happiness of employees (through retention rates). The company adopted a "mixed management" approach developed by the legendary General Electric CEO Jack Welch. Under the system, employees are evaluated twice annually and assigned a rating: in the top 20 percent, the middle 60 percent, or the bottom 20 percent. Managers are rewarded based on how well they retain the top 80 percent and not penalized when a bottom-20 performer departs the company. In fact, managers are taught to encourage poor performers to improve quickly or leave. To win employees' loyalty, managers can give out small raises; award workers "Applebucks" points toward prizes such as radios and DVD players; or distribute special pins. Managers are encouraged to be flexible with employees' schedules, especially when it comes to family or school time.

Applebee's wages are competitive with the rest of the industry, which is to say that nobody is going to get rich serving Oriental Chicken Salads and Riblets. But the company credits the retention system with helping to reduce the annual turnover among hourly workers at company-owned restaurants by almost half in four years, from 146 percent in 2000 to 83 percent in 2005. We talked to dozens of Applebee's employees across the country, both on and off the record, and found a constant thread of esprit de corps. "This is going to sound corny, but I like working with quality people, which I do, and being around good people, which is what I'd call my customers," said Erin Kinjorski, a twenty-one-year-old waitress in Howell, Michigan. "I like being a part of this team. On my best days, I feel like I'm doing more than just serving food. I'm being a friend." We heard this time and time again, like an echo of Hill's bottom line: *changing the world one guest at a time.*

Companies like Applebee's and Starbucks spend weeks recruiting employees before opening new locations. Schultz said he decided to provide better pay and benefits than his competition because they attract and keep top-notch staff. "That led to a tremendous level of trust and confidence and enthusiasm in the company," Schultz said. "They recognized that they would be a part of something in which everybody shares in the success, not just a few executives. That served as a model for our unique culture."

*2. They Create the Right Ambience*

Applebee's is constantly changing its interior designs to fit the community and keep pace with changing tastes. But there are certain basics that give the restaurants a warm, welcoming feel. One is the open design that lets customers see one another from across the restaurant, gazing beyond the low-slung center bar to the knickknacks on the walls—pictures of sports and movie stars, antique sporting gear, and, of course, "local heroes." At Applebee's, there are certain rules that must be followed: hold the door open for incoming guests, greet every customer, thank guests for coming, and ask them to return. Regular guests can expect to have their table waiting for them.

While Applebee's décor tends to be middle-class nostalgia with a local flavor, Starbucks strives for a hipper look. Its creative team designs artwork that celebrates each city's heritage, such as a likeness of Paul Revere in Boston. "Every Starbucks store is carefully designed to enhance the quality of everything the customers see, touch, hear, smell, or taste," Schultz said. Aroma is a big selling point. Even non–coffee drinkers love the smell of java brewing. Starbucks banned smoking long before it became fashionable because coffee beans absorb odors. Employees are asked not to wear perfume or cologne. "We want you to smell the coffee only." Classical and jazz music are a signature Starbucks sound, though more contemporary music is also now part of the ambiance.

### 3. They Support Community Values

Applebee's aggressively integrates itself into the neighborhoods where it operates. Each restaurant has a healthy budget for community services and charities. Each franchisee can adapt as much as 40 percent of its menu to local tastes. Doherty and a few other franchisees have scrapped the pop culture icons and fill their walls with local pictures to give their restaurants an intensely hometown feel, an idea that company officials said might become more widespread.

Starbucks gets involved in local and global causes, with an emphasis on supporting AIDS programs, children's causes, and the environment. Schultz said that this is a key to feeling small while growing big. "It is probably more an art than a science, but at the end of the day it's about being as relevant as possible to the local communities," he said. "It's not a matter of issuing a press release and giving somebody a check. It's involvement. It's engagement." Like Applebee's, Starbucks gives its store managers community service budgets and autonomy in using them.

"None of this is a silver bullet," Schultz said. "It's part of an overall approach. There is no marketing plan or prescription. You can't prescribe engagement. You can't teach a sense of community. It has to be done by the people working in the area who know that it's part of the culture of their company."

## *Beyond the Horizon*
### HOW TO CONNECT IN THE FUTURE

Leadership Succession:
*The Last Great Act of a Great Connector*

Organizations that thrive under charismatic leaders such as Presidents Bush and Clinton, and Hill and Warren, risk a falloff when the Great Connector departs the scene. It's a major concern in the megachurch industry, built largely by a generation of baby-boomer preachers who are now nearing retirement. At Applebee's, Hill, sixty-two, took the first step in 2006 to carry out a long-planned succession strategy: he gave Goebel day-to-day control of Applebee's, with plans to nominate him for CEO later in the year. Hill said that ceding power had not been easy, but a smooth succession will protect the culture of community that he helped create with his mentor and predecessor, Gustin. "It's about the future and heart and emotion—and believing that what you leave behind is a better judge of your performance than what happens while you are there." This is the one element missing from President Bush's portfolio as a Great Connector. We wonder about his political succession plan: Who does he want to see be the next president?

## The Amway Way

Long before Applebee's and Starbucks stumbled into the community-building market, there was a Michigan-based company that thrived on the power of networking. Amway urged people to sell its goods to families, friends, and neighbors—and to recruit them to become sellers, too. President Bush's campaign manager, Ken Mehlman, compared his zeal for tapping into existing social networks to the Amway model.

"Amway never went knocking on doors, which is the great myth," said a former Amway president, Dick DeVos. "We were always about relationship selling. Bring a product you like to the people you know, and some of them may choose to do the same. We were filling a need, not just for the product, but to be a part of something bigger than themselves," he said.

As a Great Connector, DeVos is a three-way threat—a man familiar with our busy intersection of politics, business, and religion. A businessman first, DeVos, a Republican, entered the 2006 race for governor of Michigan, a Rust Belt state struggling mightily in the transition to an information- and technology-based society. He was also a member of the board of the Willow Creek Association, the influential church consulting group spotlighted in the next chapter. DeVos hosts "small-group" sessions out of his home for a prominent western Michigan

megachurch, part of a phenomenon that is the focus of our next chapter. The small group system creates nodes of community where none
had existed and is a potent form of social networking that some experts
believe has replaced the labor movement as the nation's No. 1 organizing force.

Like other companies featured in this chapter, Amway adapted to a
dramatically changing public. Under DeVos, the company repositioned
itself through technology advances by moving much of its U.S. sales systems online, preserving a Michigan manufacturing base while, unlike
other companies, eliminating white-collar management jobs and not
blue-collar line jobs. "We thrived by building communities," he said.

## Maintaining the Connection

We're not suggesting that Applebee's and the other companies featured
in this chapter are perfect. Far from it; they are just as prone to flaws and
failures as successful politicians or church leaders. But the best in business acknowledge their vulnerabilities and move quickly to address
them, openly and honestly. Applebee's received plaudits from investors
and analysts for Hill's candid assessment of the company's sales slump
in 2005. (*Institutional Investor* put Hill and Chief Financial Officer
Steve Lumpkin on its cover for a story praising their lack of "spin.")

As it grows, Applebee's faces an obvious dilemma: How can it be
both big *and* local? It's an oxymoron of corporate proportions: How can
a fast-growing chain of more than 1,700 restaurants be a neighborhood
establishment? Company executives believe their community-based
strategies will keep Applebee's true to its brand.

Right now, Applebee's and other large chains control just 37 percent
of the casual dining market. As that percentage rises, Applebee's could
face the same public relations problems that Wal-Mart is battling. The retail giant, one of the greatest corporate innovators of its time, is
facing a challenge to its Gut Values Connection as critics challenge Wal-
Mart's salaries, health care benefits, commitment to U.S.-made products,
impact on local businesses, and compliance with child-labor laws. Goebel
feels that Wal-Mart's battle against Target may take on a Bush-versus-
Kerry quality. "Wal-Mart may win the policy vote—prices—but Target
wins where it counts, with gut-level values and character." It's no acci-

dent that Wal-Mart's union-backed critics built a grassroots campaign against the retailer in 2005 by focusing on its corporate character rather than the quality of its products. Wal-Mart fought back with employee testimonials about the company and community-building efforts such as rushing to the aid of Hurricane Katrina victims.

Hill and Goebel would not say this, of course, but Applebee's relatively soft scores on food quality could grow into a Gut Values problem for the company. The chain's own research shows that quality food is part of a good social occasion or family night out. Truly bad food cannot be covered up by nifty marketing or even an authentic sense of community, particularly now that the chain's competitors have begun to mimic Applebee's community-in-a-chain approach. "We've worked hard for this bond, this brand," Hill said. "We aren't about to blow it."

## OTHER CONNECTORS: A HEAVENLY BRAND

A few miles from Applebee's headquarters in exurban Kansas is a wildly successful megachurch run by Adam Hamilton, author of a church-marketing book entitled *Selling Swimsuits in the Arctic*. Several of the chain's executives attend the church, which might help explain why Hill considers his improve-the-world mission statement quasireligious. "There's something evangelistic about what we do."

Other companies are more overt about using religion to help make a Gut Values Connection. In-N-Out Burger, a California-based fast-food chain, has included tiny notations for Bible verses in some of its burger and drink packages. Hobby Lobby plays only Christian contemporary music in its 362 stores. Chick-fil-A sandwich shops close on Sundays so employees nationwide can attend church with their families.

The Walt Disney Company promoted its 2005 Christmas movie *The Chronicles of Narnia: The Lion, the Witch, and the Wardrobe* by previewing it for religious audiences, using the same public relations company that had promoted Mel Gibson's *The Passion of the Christ*.

Michael Novak, a theologian at the American Enterprise Institute, told *The New York Times* last year that religion is like yeast in dough: "It's in every part of life, so for it to show up everywhere is only natural—in commerce, politics, sports, labor unions and so forth."

It's even on the cups of Starbucks, which for the first time is mentioning God on its "The Way I See It" campaign. "You were made by God and for God, and until you understand that, life will never make sense," reads a quote from Rick Warren on Starbucks' cups.

Warren, featured in our next chapter on megachurches, said he recognizes the synergy between selling products and selling God, especially when he sees company CEOs working with evangelical zeal to create a sense of belonging for employees and customers. "Starbucks doesn't sell coffee; they're selling community," Warren said. "Applebee's has an environment that says 'Home.' It's about creating roots in a rootless society."

Take it from one who knows.

---

Navigating the Stormy Present
## How to Be a Great Connector

1. **Make and Maintain a Gut Values Connection.** Applebee's, Starbucks, and other successful companies give their customers and employees a sense of community and purpose.
2. **Adapt.** As sales softened and competitors narrowed Applebee's advantage, the company hustled to figure out what was happening. Applebee's and Starbucks also took advantage of societal changes, such as the rise of exurbia (Applebee's) and home offices (Starbucks).
3. **LifeTarget.** Applebee's "segmentation" study of customers was not unlike President Bush's methods of studying voters.
4. **Talk Smart.** Applebee's and other successful companies narrowcast their message through the channels heard by their targeted customers.
5. **Find Navigators.** When Applebee's sought out local leaders before opening a store, it hoped to find Navigators who could help bring their friends, family members, and associates to the restaurant. Chapters 5 and 6 will explore how businesses can profit by finding more Navigators via Internet communities.

# 3

---

# RELIGION:

## A Cause Greater than Yourself

*There is an enormous need to build . . . I call it the person. That's more than self-respect; it's also the awareness that there is something beyond you, and something beyond the moment, and something that is not only greater than you but different from you.*

—Management guru PETER DRUCKER,
on the success of megachurches

### Selling Coffee and God

VIENNA, Va.—The first thing you notice is the Starbucks coffee shop. It looks out of place, but it's a sleepy Sunday morning, so you order a small cup. "Tall?" the girls chirps. No, small. "Tall?" she repeats. You relent: Okay, a tall. "God bless you," she says, handing you a cup of coffee and change for your two dollars. "And welcome to our church."

You've just stepped inside McLean Bible Church, one of the fastest-growing congregations in the country. It is located sixteen miles from the White House, in an exurban community just west of the busy mall traffic at Tysons Corner. The church averages nine thousand worshipers every week, nearly as many people who live in this city.

You park in a two-tier, 2,500-space parking garage, exchanging friendly waves with the off-duty Fairfax County police officer who helps move traffic from Route 7 to the immaculately kept fifty-two-acre complex. You spot a familiar face. Is that Kenneth Starr? Could be; the former Whitewater prosecutor attends the church, along with members of Congress and the Bush administration.

The 283,000-square-foot church building is three stories high, mostly brick, and sunk into a hill. From the outside, it looks like a community center, and in a way it is: Pastor Lon Solomon's church is a hub of social services and social activity. Once inside, it's clear this is no ordinary church. You're more likely to spot a plasma TV screen than a crucifix. The preacher doesn't ask for money. There is none of the mysterious orthodoxy that flummoxes newcomers at, say, traditional Roman Catholic churches: kneel, stand, sit; kneel, stand, sit.

"Welcome," says a church worker named Elizabeth. You assume that's her name because it says so on the paper label over her breast pocket. "This is for couples in their twenties and thirties who've been married several years." She sets her Starbucks cup down to usher you inside a room between the church's massive glass entryway and the café, past a sign that reads, "Small Group Connections." There are about two dozen couples sitting in folding chairs, gathered around a man who is talking about tuition and pensions.

"We have dozens of these small groups, all with different interests, to make you feel more connected," Elizabeth says. "It makes this big place seem small."

It does seem like a friendly place. The man knows everybody's names, and nobody else is wearing a tag. He gives one woman a hug when she worries out loud about being able to save enough money to put her son through college. A yellow flier posted in the "Newcomers' Room" says that there are more than five hundred small groups that meet around the city each week. The church's snazzy Web site explains, "Our hope is that your small group will become your closest friends and people you will turn to in a time of need." Another first-time visitor, a thirty-something man with two children in tow, silently soaks in the tour before whispering to nobody in particular, "What kind of church *is* this?"

## WHAT KIND OF CHURCH *IS* THIS?

It is a megachurch, defined by experts as a Protestant house of worship with an average weekly attendance of 2,000 or more. Part of a fast-growing $7.2 billion industry, megachurches bring community to places that lack it—suburban and exurban America, where land is cheap and there is a continuous influx of middle-class families. These social hubs are led by charismatic pastors with the skills set of corporate marketers. Rick Warren and other megachurch preachers are not just selling the Word of God; they're selling a connection. "It's all sales," writes megachurch pastor Adam Hamilton in *Selling Swimsuits in the Arctic: Seven Simple Keys to Growing Churches.* "I've come to see that every sermon I preach is, in a way, a sales presentation."

The megachurch movement is the third side of our triangle—the source of our final, *and perhaps best,* example of how to appeal to anxious Americans in this era of change. Standing foursquare at the busy intersection of politics, business, and religion, Warren and his fellow megachurch pastors shed light on how to find voters and customers in a dynamic marketplace.

Like Bush, Clinton, and Hill, successful megachurch leaders adapt to demographic and social change; they target potential worshipers based on their lifestyles; and they use multiple communication channels to deliver messages that are relevant to people's lives. More than most political and business leaders, megachurch pastors specialize in the mysterious art of word-of-mouth marketing and the use of Navigators. But these are mere tactics. The key to any great church leader is his or her ability to speak to people's hearts, not their heads. They use those lifestyle-driven tactics to build and maintain Gut Value Connections based on two virtues: community and purpose.

## Community

Megachurches provide a social sanctuary for the growing number of disconnected Americans, especially exurbanites who've uprooted from familiar-but-changing neighborhoods to settle farther away from cities. The key is the church's "small groups," or clubs, that divide massive congregations into cozy clusters of people with similar interests. A successful megachurch is not an impersonal congregation of 10,000 people; it is 1,000 congregations of 10 like-minded friends, knit together by common beliefs, values, and lifestyles.

"They long for a place, a heritage, and commitments, however fleeting," said Scott L. Thumma, a megachurch researcher at the Hartford Seminary's Hartford Institute for Religion Research. "Megachurches offer these persons a history, a narrative tradition, and programs to which they can commit." Fresh out of the seminary twenty-five years ago, Rick Warren sent a letter to prospective worshipers that did not mention God or the Bible but instead made a simple Gut Values appeal: "Meet new friends and get to know your neighbors!"

## Purpose

Megachurches offer people a meaning in life beyond hard-charging careers and harried schedules. Megachurches exist to fulfill Jesus' "Great Commission," his call to recruit people into Christianity through evangelism. Some seek to answer their calling through external projects, such as adopting a poor inner-city neighborhood or sponsoring overseas charities. Whatever the mission, Warren's theory is that a purpose-driven church offers people a cause greater than themselves.

There is a lesson here for candidates and corporations trying to connect with anxious Americans. "I am absolutely convinced that megachurches have blossomed, at least in part, because they have responded creatively to the new needs and interests of people in a new cultural reality," Thumma said. "There is much to learn from megachurches—and it isn't all about being big."

It's about connecting with people through the Gut Values of community and purpose. "We all want purpose and people in our lives," said Warren, one of the most influential church leaders in the world. "Anybody who can deliver those things will succeed."

## WHO ARE THESE PEOPLE?

Megachurch worshipers tend to be under sixty years old and are often under thirty-five. Most earn between $20,000 and $75,000 a year. They are generally married with young children, and a large number of them have joined the church in the last five years, according to "Megachurches Today 2005," a study conducted by Thumma and others for the Hartford Institute and the Leadership Network. Most megachurches are located in new exurbs (45 percent) or older suburbs (29 percent). This is the land of Circuit City, Home Depot, Wal-Mart, and other big-box stores, where people appreciate institutions with large parking lots and huge inventories of amenities.

The congregations are largely misunderstood and badly stereotyped by political and business strategists who, because of their prejudices, ignore or insult a major part of America. Let's start by busting a few myths.

*They're not all white.* Megachurches tend to be more ethnically and racially diverse than traditional churches. "Megachurches Today 2005" found that nearly 20 percent of the church congregations were minorities. More than one third of megachurches had a 20 percent or more minority presence. One of the nation's largest churches, Joel Osteen's Lakewood Church in Houston, reported its congregation to be 40 percent white, 30 percent African American, and 30 percent Hispanic.

*They're not all poorly educated.* Several studies show that about 40 percent of people who attend megachurches hold one or more college degrees, a number as high as if not higher than that of traditional churches.

*They're not all gun-toting, gay-bashing Republican Party pawns.* While most megachurch pastors consider their congregations to be politically conservative, megachurches rarely are politically active. Just 16 percent of megachurch pastors said they had partnered with other churches in political activities in the past five years, and three fourths said they had never done so, according to the 2005 study.

The source of megachurches' political influence has less to do with the pastors' sermons than it does with their network of small groups, which offer what one expert called "an indirect mechanism for coalition building." The Bush team was far less interested in what pastors said about politics from the pulpit than they were about what worshipers discussed with friends, family, and neighbors in the weekday small-group meetings.

Democrats should be plugging into the megachurch's social networks. According to the 2004 election exit polls, people most likely to attend megachurches (suburban and exurban residents who said they went to church at least once a week and were non-Catholic Christians) broke down this way:

- 60 percent were women.
- 16 percent were black and 7 percent Hispanic.

- 29 percent called themselves Democrats.
- 20 percent called themselves independents.
- 53 percent didn't have kids at home.
- 28 percent said they were liberal.
- Two thirds earned less than $75,000.
- Half had at least some college education.
- Two thirds did not own guns.
- Just 27 percent believed abortion should be illegal in all cases.
- 39 percent believed gays should have the right to get married or be in civil unions.

That's not exactly a GOP profile. Though there are no reliable political surveys of megachurch worshipers, these data suggest that Democratic leaders should stop stereotyping and start targeting.

"We've all heard the rumors. You know, they're snake handlers who talk in tongues, rednecks who don't read *New Yorker* magazine or who don't read at all, and down-the-line Republican conservatives," said Bob Buford, the founder of Leadership Network, which helps fast-growth churches grow faster. "It's stupid and beyond bogus. And it's against the self-interest of political and business leaders to think of them that way."

Regardless of their political persuasion, megachurch worshipers practice a theology that is solidly conservative. Most churches call themselves evangelical, which typically refers to Christians who believe the Bible is the literal word of God. "But they are not all crazy, rampant Holy Roller types," Thumma said. "Less than four percent would even think of themselves as a fundamentalist. You can't be a fundamentalist megachurch because the fundamentalists' idea is to keep people out and the megachurch leader's goal is to bring people in." Thumma said he suspects that the congregations are a bit more moderate than their pastors, because church crowds tend to be relatively diverse.

Megachurches' ties to denominations are tenuous at best. In the 2005 survey, nearly 40 percent of megachurches said they were nondenominational. The reason for this is embedded in the marketing approach of megachurches: most appeal to people who have never gone to church or who stopped going because the mainline churches in which they were raised no longer seem relevant to their lives.

## THE BOTTOM LINE

Megachurch leaders are as serious about business as they are about religion. They're savvy CEOs and lifestyle-based marketers pushing a high-concept product: eternal life. According to Thumma, "These are not just churches, they are also corporations."

Bill Hybels's Willow Creek Community Church in suburban Chicago established a separate training association run by a Harvard MBA. John Jackson, the senior pastor of Carson Valley Christian Center in Minden, Nevada, calls himself a "PastorPreneur." Warren's Saddleback Church in Orange County, California, has dozens of weekday affinity groups for everyone from motorcycle enthusiasts to weight watchers. Sundays are business. "Jesus taught in the temple and the marketplace," Warren said.

Hamilton, the Kansas pastor who warns against selling swimsuits in the Arctic, applies a corporate model to his ministry. "Most of the first-time visitors to your church will come as 'consumers.' If they are considering becoming involved in a local church, they will 'shop' for a church the way they shop for a doctor, a grocery store, or a restaurant," he wrote in *Leading Beyond Walls*, a how-to manual on growing a megachurch. "For many unchurched and churched people alike, the primary 'product' they will be evaluating is the worship service."

Megachurches are successful corporations. Their numbers have doubled from about 600 in 2000 to more than 1,200 today, according to the "Megachurches Today 2005" study. In 2005, the average megachurch

### Megachurches by the Numbers

- 74 percent suburban or exurban
- 20 percent minority congregations
- 3,585 average weekly attendance
- $6 million average yearly church income
- $5.6 million average yearly church expenditure
- Typical yearly worshiper income between $20,000 and $75,000
- 1,200-plus in United States, up from 600 in 2000

had $6 million in income, with an average expenditure of $5.6 million, the study showed. Average weekly attendance grew nearly 60 percent in just five years, from 2,279 people to 3,585.

A dozen of the nation's largest churches, including McLean Bible Church, catered to a total of 156,000 worshipers each Sunday in 2005, according to figures the church leaders shared with one another at joint planning sessions sponsored by the Leadership Network. Those twelve churches were on course to grow by another 22 percent by 2007.

Some megachurches are so successful that they're opening franchises, becoming veritable McChurches. At least half of all megachurches use multiple venues for worship as well as satellite locations to increase seating capacity. Of those that don't have satellite campuses, nearly 30 percent plan to build one.

If megachurches are the flashy new sports car of religion, traditional churches are the Edsel. The Catholic Church is struggling with a long-term decline in U.S. attendance, exacerbated by sex abuse scandals. Large Protestant denominations, which dominated the twentieth century, including the United Methodist Church and the Episcopal Church, have lost more than 1 million members in the past ten years.

This speaks to the central point of this book: people and institutions that embrace change tend to succeed—from Presidents Bush and Clinton to Applebee's, Starbucks, and Apple Computer. Those who ignore the whims of their customers or scoff at the public's shifting lifestyles and values lose ground to their competition.

## ADAPTING: FOLLOWING GOD AND THE POLLS

### "I Have No Fear Here"

VIENNA, Va.—You're grabbing another cup of coffee in the McLean Bible Church's buffet-style restaurant when you realize why people turn to a place like this: it's packed with kids and their parents, and they're hanging out together.

One boy, about ten, jumps up from his seat at one table and gives his father a jelly-stained kiss. A girl at the next table asks her mother, "Is this Hanging with Mom Week?" The mother replies, "Next week, honey." Two teenage boys bolt from the pizza line and head out of the restaurant, following the thunderous first beats of a gospel/rock song in a nearby community room.

Aida Mesfin calls this her refuge from a cold, hectic world. The thirty-three-year-old married mother of two is finishing lunch with her daughter, Mariam, three, when she's asked why she comes to McLean Bible Church.

"I have no fear here," says Mesfin, who lives thirty minutes away in Alexandria. "Alexandria used to be safe, but it's not so anymore. You worry about your kids if they're outside. You worry about your husband if he's not home. And worst of all, you feel isolated. People don't trust each other anymore. They're closed up in their houses. Not here, not in an environment like this where there are people like you supporting you."

She is interrupted briefly by her sister, who is trailed by Mesfin's two-year-old, Elshadai, and the sister's own two children. "Time to play, kids," the sister says. She's taking one child to an art class and the others to day care so the grown-ups can attend Bible study.

Mesfin, who moved to the area from Ethiopia fourteen years ago, says she rarely interacts with her neighbors in Alexandria. "But this place," she says, holding her hands out, palms up, "is all community."

Her children go to church summer camp and enjoy "Golf with Daddy" days. She and her husband enroll in Bible study classes and frequently attend midweek special events. Church isn't just for Sunday around here. It's a 24/7 proposition—from nurseries to marriage counseling, psychological services, first aid training, concerts, and special assistance to people in hospitals.

At a nearby table, Todd Walmsley, thirty-eight, of Great Falls, Virginia, eats with his wife, Lisa, and their three children. There's a puddle of milk in the middle of the table. Walmsley says he and Lisa used to attend a Presbyterian Church but tired of the pomp and formality. They started at McLean Bible with a cup of coffee in 1996 and stayed, hooked for life by friendships made in a small group for young couples.

When one of their three children fell ill recently, a member of the church health staff visited the hospital. One night, their telephone rang at home. "It was Lon, calling to say he was praying for us," Walmsley said. "You have any idea what that meant to me and Lisa to have our pastor call?"

## Rick Warren and Swimsuits in the Arctic

Rick Warren likes to say that God called him from Texas to Lake Forest, California, to start a suburban church for baby boomers twenty-five years ago. Whether you believe that or not, we appreciate the fact that census data and polling helped seal his pact with the Lord.

Warren knew that he wanted to convert nonchurchgoers into church regulars, so he began his search in three states with the highest percentages of "unchurched" people: Washington, Oregon, and California. He quickly narrowed his focus to Seattle, San Francisco, San Diego, and Orange County. "These four metropolitan areas were all growing in the last 1970s, and that caught my attention," he wrote in *The Purpose-Driven Church*, a best-selling book on creating megachurches.

In the book, which has become the marketing Bible for fledgling pastors, Warren quotes Scripture to justify his use of secular strategies. "Proverbs 13:16 says, 'Every prudent man acts out of knowledge.' To me, that meant I should find out all I could about an area before I committed to invest the rest of my life there." One afternoon, he discovered that Saddleback Valley in Orange County, California, was the fastest-growing area in the fastest-growing county in the United States. "This fact grabbed me by the throat and made my heart start racing." New people meant new churches, and Warren thought he knew churches.

Still in seminary school, he flew to California in October 1979 and spent ten days consulting realtors, chamber of commerce types, bankers, county planning officials, residents, and local pastors. (Remember Applebee's local heroes program? These are the same people who are called on by a manager when a new restaurant opens in town.) Warren graduated two months later and drove with his wife and baby to Orange County, their hand-me-down furniture packed in a U-Haul truck. He stopped at the first real estate office he spotted in Saddleback Valley. "My name is Rick Warren. I'm here to start a church," he told a realtor, Don Dale. "I need a place to live, but I don't have any money." Dale found the family a condo to rent, got them their first month's rent for free, and became the first member of Saddleback Church.

Warren spent his first twelve weeks in the area knocking on doors, then summarized his findings in an "evangelism strategy" written in the words of disgruntled "unchurched" residents he had surveyed:

- Church is boring, especially the sermons. The messages don't relate to my life.
- Church members are unfriendly to visitors. If I go to church, I want to feel welcomed and not embarrassed.
- The church is more interested in my money than in me.
- We worry about the quality of the church's child care.

Years later, he said, "I don't know if I'd call it a marketing study. I just wanted to get to know folks I intended to preach to." As we unravel his business strategies throughout this chapter, you'll see that Warren knew more about selling God than he lets on.

One thing that sets Warren apart from the scandal-ridden evangelists of the 1980s and '90s is that he does not broadcast his sermons on TV. His influence stems from the network of pastors—thousands of them—who have read *The Purpose-Driven Church* or bought his programmatic material. The book has been translated into twenty-five languages and used as a training manual for 350,000 church leaders worldwide. It tells pastors how to pitch their product to a fast-changing public. *Forbes* magazine publisher Rich Karlgaard called it "the best book on entrepreneurship, business, and investment."

But the sales of that book have been dwarfed by the success of a follow-up. *The Purpose-Driven Life* has sold more than 25 million copies, making it the best-selling hardback in U.S. history. It opens with an in-your-face greeting to baby boomers: "It's not about you. The purpose of your life is far greater than your own personal fulfillment, your peace of mind or even your happiness. It's far greater than your family, your career, or even your wildest dreams and ambitions. If you want to know why you were placed on this earth, you must begin with God. You were born by his purpose and for his purpose." The book touched a chord with a baby-boom generation moving uncertainly into middle age after a heady, all-about-me start.

"One of the reasons for the success of my book . . . is that people are hungry for meaning in their lives," Warren said during a visit to Harvard University in 2005. "There is a renewed interest in spirituality. That doesn't necessarily mean there's a renewed sense of interest in religion. But after forty years of what I would call the generation of me-ism, there is an epidemic of loneliness. We have lost our ability to create communities."

He cited polls indicating that 96 percent of Americans say they believe in God. More than 120 million attend church every Sunday, which Warren likes to say is more people on any weekend than are in attendance at all sporting events in America during an entire year.

Thus, this gifted salesman with the instincts of a politician had surveyed the social landscape and sensed a shifting in the winds: self-indulgent baby boomers were looking for meaning from their nail-biting, ladder-climbing lives. He found the fastest-growing area in the nation's fastest-growing county, figured out what the people craved, and found a way to give it to them—in church, and in the name of God. As you'll read in the next section, Warren and other megachurch leaders discovered new ways to deliver a 2,000-year-old message.

Indeed, adapting is the key to success in the religious business. Nearly 60 percent of megachurches reported that one or more services had changed in the last five years, according to the 2005 study. Only 5 percent reported no changes. Almost every megachurch holds multiple worship services to make the times convenient to busy worshipers. Playing to different tastes, nearly half conduct at least one service that is different from their main program (Saddleback, for example, has had a tropical-themed service).

The services are culturally relevant and current. Most megachurches use electric guitar or brass and drums in their services, along with cutting-edge visual projection equipment. The "Faith Communities Today Study 2000" found that the megachurches with the highest rate of growth were the ones who conducted contemporary services.

In 1990, when he was starting a United Methodist Church in Leawood, Kansas, Adam Hamilton did some research and discovered that most of the new churches in the fast-growing area were conservative theologically, patterned after Bill Hybels's wildly successful Willow Creek Community Church. "We felt there was room for a church that was moderate theologically and offered worship that was more traditional and slightly liturgical," he wrote. "We offered the right product for this particular market, and a product no one was offering in quite this same way."

Hamilton, whose church is located near Applebee's national headquarters, warns that many old-line church leaders, like his fictional Arctic swimsuit salesman named Bob, cling to a product that doesn't fit the customers' needs. "We pastors and church leaders could learn a thing or two from Bob. Often, we insist on selling swimsuits in the Arctic, when what the people really need is something entirely different. Our swimsuits are our 'sacred cows'—those programs, ministries, or ways of doing church that we're comfortable with, but that may not speak to or reach 21st century people. Our task, if we are to develop churches and ministries that are growing and life transforming, is to understand the needs of the people with whom we seek to minister," he wrote.

The same could be said for political and business leaders who need to connect with voters and consumers: Understand their wants and give them their needs. Don't try to sell them swimsuits in the Arctic—those policies or products you're comfortable with but that may not interest or motivate them.

## TARGETING: DEMOGRAPHICS, PSYCHOGRAPHICS, AND CONSULTANTS

### "The Greatest Deal Ever Offered!"

VIENNA, Va.—The cafeteria empties out—and Walmsley, Mesfin, and scores of others fill the stairs leading to a sprawling corridor. It's as cavernous as a train station, with carpeting, and is built to handle the foot traffic created by thousands of people funneled each Sunday between the church's bookstore, on one side, and its information desks, on the other. You don't stop to ask any questions; the flow of the crowd is slowly but relentlessly pushing you into the larger of two worship centers.

Solomon has already begun his sermon. This is no ordinary evan-

gelical preacher. To start with, he's Jewish. The rest comes out in his
sermon: Born and raised in a Jewish home in Portsmouth, Virginia,
he attended the University of North Carolina at Chapel Hill, where he
was a chemistry major. While in college, Solomon drank, gambled,
and later sold and used drugs. He contemplated suicide but in the
spring of 1971 was convinced by a street evangelist to accept Jesus as
his savior.

Now, thirty-four years later, he's standing behind a clear glass
podium with a thirteen-piece band behind him. His stage is
equipped with the same lighting system as the one used at the Kennedy Center and features ninety-two loudspeakers. The 2,400-seat
auditorium is two thirds full for one of four services held at McLean
Bible this weekend.

He gives thanks to the housekeeper who helped raise him and
"prayed me into the kingdom of God." You get the feeling that he
tells this story frequently, perhaps as a way to assure worshipers that
no matter how serious their troubles, he's seen worse. Though this is
an upper-middle-class, upwardly mobile congregation, many people
here are saddled by debt because of mortgages and other costs of
suburban striving. Some are lonely. Others work too hard and spend
too little time with their families. Many have their own psychological
demons. Not unlike most Americans, they are buffeted by the winds
of change in society. Solomon promises them consistency, a connection, a cause greater than themselves, and, ultimately, eternal life.
Today's sermon message is typically upbeat and guilt-free: Once you
find Christ, you'll never lose your spot in heaven—no matter how
badly you screw up.

"When Jesus says that as followers of Christ we will never perish,
we can take that to the bank!" Solomon says. "You need to grasp this.
This is the greatest deal ever offered to man! Take it!"

## Saddleback Sam and Samantha

His polling complete, Warren felt he knew his audience and their
needs. "Hello, neighbor!" read his first letter to his Lake Forest, California, community. "Let's face it. Many people aren't active in church
these days. Why? The sermons are boring and don't relate to daily living. Many churches seem more interested in your wallet than you.

Members are unfriendly to visitors. You wonder about the quality of nursery care for your children." He promised friendships, contemporary music, dedicated nursery workers, and "positive, practical messages." The letters were mailed to 15,000 people ten days before Easter.

As his church grew, so did the sophistication of Warren's targeting. Much like Presidents Bush and Clinton and companies like Applebee's, Warren urged churches to segment people based on their lifestyles. He said they should be grouped and targeted according to:

- Where they live
- Their religious and spiritual backgrounds
- Their age, income, education, occupation, and other demographic data
- Their "psychographics," which he called "just a fancy way of referring to people's values, interests, hurts and fears. Long before businesses became enamored with psychographics, Christian missionaries were identifying the differences between cultures." Warren was describing LifeTargeting.

"For your church to be most effective in evangelism, you must decide on a target," he wrote in *The Purpose-Driven Church*. "Discover what types of people live in your area, decide which of those groups your church is best equipped to reach, and then discover which styles of evangelism best match your target."

Warren's targets at Saddleback were baby-boomer, unchurched, white-collar couples. He even had a name for them—"Saddleback Sam and Samantha"—personalizing his target just as President Clinton did with the so-called Soccer Moms and President Bush did with Terrorism Moderates. Warren can describe Saddleback Sam down to the tiniest details: a wife, two kids, massive debt, a health and fitness nut who prefers casual attire over formal. That last finding is why Warren never wears a suit when he preaches. "I follow Paul's strategy given in 1 Corinthians 9:20: 'To the Jews I became like a Jew, to win the Jews.' "

By the time he wrote *The Purpose-Driven Church* in 1995, Warren had the names of 31,000 people in his database who occasionally attended Saddleback Church. They represented 10 percent of the people living in the area. These people were ripe for converting into official, tithing congregation members.

Warren also kept track of the number of regular worshipers (5,000) and the number of the nonmembers (5,000) who typically attended Sunday services. He considered it the sign of a healthy church when regular worshipers recruit such a large number of newcomers. These recruiters are the Navigators we will write about in chapter 6, and they're not exclusive to Saddleback Church. According to the "Megachurches Today 2005" study, 95 percent of megachurches claimed an emphasis on evangelism and about the same percentage encouraged members to recruit nonmembers.

By contrast, just 75 percent advertised on radio or TV. "Several research studies indicate that congregations grow by word of mouth, as participants invite friends," the 2005 study said.

In *Branded Nation,* a book that lauds the marketing tactics of megachurch leaders, James Twitchell said it's good corporate sense to target people who don't attend church. In any business, wily marketers sell to the audience that precedes use, not the one that is already using, he said.

> The first rule of Marketing 101: Target the audiences just on the entry edge of consumption. Find them before they buy, before they listen to competing brands, and you will get them for life. A little expense up front and they will consume far longer than some middle-aged wanderer who will haphazardly take or leave your brand. If you ever wonder why American advertising is targeted at adolescents, it's because it would take about $350 of marketing to get a 50-year-old male to change his beer choice, but you can get an 18-year-old to try your brand for $50.

Like business and politics, the church industry has a consultant class. Warren has sold and given away advice to thousands of pastors through his book and through Saddleback programs. Another great teaching church is Hybels's Willow Creek, where a Harvard MBA, Jim Mellado, runs an association that earned $17 million in 2004 by providing resources and training events to 12,000 member churches from ninety denominations.

FaithSpan, located in Woodlands, Texas, claims to be the leader in graphic design and strategic consulting for churches. "Our niche is helping churches go to the next level," said a company executive, Robert Rizzo. "When a fast-growing church realizes they can't do it themselves any longer, that's when they come to us. They want somebody who can create an identity that is uniform and that creates, essentially, a brand for a church." He said that there are still a surprisingly large number of churches that refuse to invest in demographic research, despite the success of those that have bowed to the science of microtargeting. "This field will only get bigger as people catch on to it," Rizzo said.

Thumma said he suspects that the most intuitive megachurch leaders, giants such as Warren and Hybels, could succeed without targeting and marketing strategies. "They might be informed by the values they see reflected in the data. But in fact, they have a vision for what God is calling them to do, and they portray that vision in a way that people find appealing, that people find sincere and that people find authentic."

It may be the same in politics and business—that visionary and lucky politicians and CEOs might be able to forge Gut Values Connections on instincts alone. But why try? And even when a leader succeeds without using LifeTargeting and other tactics (e.g., Schultz of Starbucks), maintaining the precious Gut Values Connection will be difficult without strategies that help an enterprise keep pace with change. The key is not to start thinking of the tactics as more important than Gut Values.

## The Strategic Church

"Say, I've got a question for you," said Jim Mitchell.

"Fire away," replied Steve Stroope.

"How do you draw attention to your brand while opening a new franchise?"

"Signage," Stroope answered, firm and decisive as any CEO in the room. He sounded like the character in *The Graduate* who needed just one word to declare the secret to corporate success in the 1960s: "Plastics."

Stroope continued, "Lots of signage. We're pouring tons of money into the facility to let people know who we are, and that we're in their town now."

If you didn't know better, you'd swear that Stroope was an executive at Applebee's or some other corporation putting down roots in a new community. But this wasn't a business meeting, it was a church meeting. Stroope is pastor of Lake Point Church in Rockwall, Texas. Mitchell heads The Chapel in Akron, Ohio. Each had preached to more than 9,000 people the Sunday before they met at McLean Bible Church with representatives of ten other megachurches, including Saddleback and Willow Creek. Each church leader stood at an easel that displayed schematic drawings of their plans for expansion. Their employees (each church sent at least two representatives) circulated through the small room asking questions of the other church leaders.

It looked and sounded like a trade show for God.

"Why are you putting a multisite twenty miles instead of forty miles from your main campus?" asked one church leader of an easel-guarding representative from North Point Community Church in Alpharetta, Georgia. David McDaniel patiently replied that their demographic studies show that a new church forty miles away would quickly fill to capacity without easing crowding problems at the main campus in Alpharetta. On the other hand, a satellite church just twenty miles away would draw people from both Alpharetta and the new community, which would create empty seats in both churches. Studies show that people like empty seats around them, he said, so they'll get them at North Point.

On the other side of the room, Stroope explained how he uses polls, focus groups, and "psychographics" to determine not only who lives in his church areas but how many are married, who has children, what they do for fun, "basically, how they live and what motivates them," he said.

It's the same sort of data used by the Bush campaign to find people who might vote for the president if approached with the right message.

Stroope pored over data about Mesquite, Texas, after deciding to open a satellite church in the blue-collar town. He quickly realized that potential worshipers in Mesquite couldn't be courted in the same manor as upscale Rockwall residents. "I might have a big-game cookout here, but not here," he said, pointing first to Mesquite on his easel and then to Rockwall.

LifeTargeting, a new concept in politics, has been used to help churches grow for at least a dozen years. Percept Group Inc., a California-based church consulting firm, conducted more than 100,000 surveys and layered those results with consumer data from the same firm used by Clinton's team in 1996. A company vice president, Tom Hoyt, said its system segments worshipers into fifty lifestyle segments (e.g., *Young Up & Comers*) to help churches identify potential worshipers and craft messages that appeal to them.

"Our first thought when we put this all together was it would be perfect for political campaigns. Businesses were already doing it," Hoyt said. "That was twelve years ago. Why the political people just found out about it, I have no idea."

## COMMUNICATING:
## MARKETING GOD AND EXPLAINING BANANAS

### Taking Care of Business

VIENNA, Va.—Lon Solomon's services are easy on the eyes, ears, and butts.

High-definition screens display bullet points from the sermon throughout the sanctuary, always a beat or two ahead of Solomon's delivery. When the band and four singers perform a rousing set of rock-style gospel songs, the lyrics are scrolled down from on high—no bulky songbooks needed here. In both cases, the words share screen time with MTV-style close-ups of Solomon and the band.

The theater-style seats are well padded, and there are enough of them to fit several thousand worshipers inside the sanctuary and still give most people an empty seat next to them. Megachurch polling shows that few things turn people off more than crowded pews.

While the adults hear from Solomon, three hundred teenagers stand shoulder to shoulder in one of the church's many community rooms. Under dimmed lights, they hold hands and sway as a twenty-something guitar player sings rock gospel songs. A handful of teens wander the room, collecting cash donations from their peers.

Swept up in this wave of audio and visual stimuli, you don't realize until midday that something is missing. There's hardly a religious icon in sight—no crucifix, no candles, and certainly no statues of saints. Indeed, there's no obvious link to any religious denomination. What kind of church is this? A very successful one. Solomon makes that clear with the first sentence of his pitch to church newcomers. "We have an operating budget of $16 million annually," he says in the Newcomers' Room between services.

## A Poll-Tested Message

Years ago, Solomon decided to start a ministry geared to young adults. He commissioned several polls and demographic studies to discover, among other things, that 250,000 men and women in their twenties lived in Washington, D.C., and its suburbs. "Wow," he recalls thinking when he first got a look at the data. "I didn't know that."

Now the wildly successful youth ministry, called Frontline, "is a reflection of the values of Generation X and Generation Y—small-group involvement, community mindedness, and many service projects, because that's what these generations care about," Solomon said. The services are held Sunday evenings, and the sermons are structured inversely to the ones given hours earlier.

"Normally, we say, 'Here's what the Bible says. Here's what it means and what it means for your life.' In a postmodern service, we do it the opposite way, because [young adults] value their own experience so highly. We do it like this: 'Here is a truism from your life. Here is a biblical proposition it illustrates, and here's the biblical truth behind it.'

"You end up explaining the same bananas, only you do it in a different way." Evening service. Inverted sermons. Specialized ministries. How did Solomon know that this would be the way to communicate to the younger generation? "We did a lot of focus groups," he replied.

Sounding like one of the many politicians in his flock, Solomon quickly added that he uses polling and focus groups to learn how to communicate the Lord's word, not to shape His word. "That's the danger. Do we allow that information to shape our message? It would be like a politician staking out his position on polls. To me, that's wrong."

## Scriptures, Symbols, and Slogans

Warren gives pastors plenty of advice on creating an atmosphere that resonates with people. Have people greeting visitors at the door (like Applebee's and Wal-Mart do), memorize the names of regular worshipers (as good politicians do), dress casually (Warren wears Hawaiian-print shirts), sprinkle sermons with anecdotes from the pastor's own life ("I used to do some pretty raunchy things, too," Solomon says), play upbeat, contemporary music (retail businesses do it), and keep the sermons short (the public's attention span is shrinking).

In his books and Saddleback programs, Warren urges church leaders to use scripture, symbols, slogans, and personal stories to communicate their messages. "Why? Because it will have limited value if people can't remember it," he wrote.

A good sermon makes the word of God relevant to the lives of harried baby boomers by using scripture to help cope with everyday problems: debt, marriage problems, drug dependency, snotty children, infidelity, fears of crime and terrorism. That's what Solomon was attempting to do at the McLean Bible Church when he assured his imperfect congregation that they had a spot in Heaven thanks to "the greatest deal" ever offered.

We witnessed a stunning example of connecting at Willow Creek Community Church, when a guest preacher, Mike Breaux, delivered a slickly produced sermon called "Mugged by the Mirror." Part of a four-sermon series delivered in July 2005, Breaux's talk was accompanied by music, dance, and a miniplay about a woman with poor self-esteem. "When I look at my body in the mirror, the first thing I notice are the parts I think are inadequate," intones the actress.

In the church's cafeteria, watching the performance on a huge screen with two hundred other hungry worshipers, sat Angela Davis, thirty-seven, and her daughter, Annie, eight. Turning to her daughter, Davis sobbed and said, "Man, this hits close to home." The sermon continued as Davis's sobs grew louder. Annie began rubbing her mother's arm. "It'll be okay, Mommy. It'll be okay," she said between licks of her ice cream cone.

Preaching isn't enough, Warren writes. Churches also must use slick brochures, banners, articles, newsletters, bulletins, videos, cassettes, and songs to get the word out. "We believe that if we keep saying the same thing in different ways, one of those ways will capture the attention of every member," he wrote. "Utilize as many different media as you can to keep [the message] before your people."

Another marketing tactic is the lack of denominational tags and religious symbols at Saddleback and most other megachurches. The idea is to give the so-called unchurched an experience they would never expect in a house of worship.

That's what the coffee shops, greeters, small groups, and other megachurch amenities are about—making the sanctuary accessible and appealing to irregular churchgoers. For the same reasons, many pastors announce during collections that "guests" are not required to pony up. It's the same concept that compels car dealers to put minikitchens in their waiting rooms, where customers can seek comfort from what is traditionally a stressful experience, dealing with car salesmen.

Megachurch leaders aggressively are spreading their views through the ever-expanding menu of media channels. Glossy magazines, or "Biblezines," package the New Testament for niche markets—one hip-hop version is aimed at teens. Christian music is aimed at the next generations of big spenders, too, with lyrics sung to alternative rock and "screamo" (yes, the heavenly lyrics are screamed).

Megachurch leaders are technologically savvy. The first thing a newcomer notices at Willow Creek Community Church is the bank of computers at the entrance cued to the church's home page. Hybels's church also has four video-editing suites. Most new church buildings come equipped with wireless Internet access, and many pastors make their services available on iPods. Some megachurches have music studios and record labels. Computers project the words of sermons and hymns onto huge screens, and carefully regulate the room temperature. Churches use computers to keep track of attendance, organize volunteers' interests, and customize form letters to members. For instance, at least one church used its database to generate personalized birthday cards from the senior minister. "These elaborate systems allow for a technological intimacy with otherwise unreachable spiritual CEOs and ministerial board members," Thumma said. Warren brags that Saddleback's 1992 Web site was the first for a church.

Pastor Mark Batterson, who preaches in movie theaters in and around Washington, D.C., does podcasts and produces mock movie clips to preview upcoming messages. "I'm in the research and development branch of the Kingdom of God," he said.

Hamilton summed up the preacher-marketer's duty this way: "You may have done your homework and know exactly what kind of worship, programs, or ministries would meet the needs or speak to the hearts of the people you hope to attract, but if you fail in the implementation—if you don't get the product right—your efforts will come to naught," the pastor wrote in *Selling Swimsuits in the Arctic*. "So, is your music done well? Is your service accessible? Are your sermons relevant, passionate, biblical, and helpful and do they include excellent illustrations with a touch of humor? Will a visitor find our program worth coming back for, or a waste of time?"

Some of the same questions apply in business and politics. Are you relevant and passionate, and do your products or policies speak to the hearts of the people you hope to attract?

## CONNECTING: COMMUNITY, PURPOSE, AND AUTHENTICITY

### Pigeonholed

VIENNA, Va.—This group of seven first-timers, sitting in a small room lit softly by lamps, is hanging on Solomon's every word.

He tells the newcomers that the church's mission—their mission if they choose to return—is to help the poor in Washington's inner city. If anybody in the room wants a church that focuses on foreign missions, they're in the wrong place, Solomon says. With his round face, stocky build, and stern demeanor, the pastor could pass as a brother of former Attorney General John Ashcroft. He implies that politics is off the table, too. "In this town, if you take a position on any issues, they pigeonhole you—you've lost them. 'Oh, they're right-wing Republicans.' "

Yet, he says, there are two issues that are nonnegotiable: the church's opposition to gay rights and abortion. He explains that gun rights, school vouchers, and other current events won't be mentioned in his sermons, but it's not hard to guess where he stands. "We've found that if people find Christ," Solomon says, "those issues take care of themselves."

He turns the session over to an employee, spins on his heel, and heads out the door to the next service.

## "Longing for Belonging"

The ancestors of today's megachurches were the evangelical leaders of the nineteenth and early twentieth centuries—Congregationalist, Methodist, Presbyterian, and Baptist pastors who expanded their churches to provide social services. The Roman Catholic Church formed tightly knit parishes that offered education, health care, and scores of other community services. In some parts of the country, people identified their neighborhoods by their parishes: "I'm from St. Jude's, what about you?" It was an era of immense transition and social upheaval, with an explosion of new technologies and the economy shifting from an agrarian system to the industrial age. There was intense anxiety as people struggled to fit into the new economy and sought new ways to connect with each other. Traditional community-building activities were suddenly passé.

Some church leaders rushed to fill the void, creating organizations such as the YMCA and the Chautauqua Association. Both of those organizations eased the way for Protestant ministers to "make their peace with leisure," according to the historian R. Laurence Moore. The Chautauqua Association, founded in 1873, combined religious and social activities into two-week Sunday school programs featuring sermons, devotional meetings, fireworks, bonfires, humorous lectures, and music.

Multipurpose churches sprang up across the country at the turn of the last century, according to *From Meetinghouse to Megachurch,* a 2003 book by Anne C. Loveland and Otis B. Wheeler. In Denver, the Trinity Methodist Episcopal church had several parlors, a kitchen, and a music room on its lower level. In 1926, a gym and locker rooms were added. At the turn of the century, the Bethany Presbyterian Church had a swimming pool in the basement, shuffle board courts, billiard and pool tables, and rooms for games and reading.

Josh Lankford, the supervising architect of the A.M.E. church, observed at the time that social and recreational facilities were "particularly fitted for our church in the larger towns and cities, for there are many who come from other places, who either join or come under care of the churches, who know few people in the place, except those who they meet at the church, many have no homes or family in that city, and they use the church and its compartments for both their spiritual *and social temple* [emphasis added]."

Russell H. Conwell, who pastored the Baptist Temple in Philadelphia from 1882 to 1925, could have been speaking for this century's megachurch leaders when he said, "God, in His providence is moving His church onward and moving it upward at the same time, adjusting it to new situations, fitting it to new conditions and to advancing civilizations, requiring us to use *the new instrumentalities* [emphasis added]."

Flash forward one century, and the circumstances are eerily similar. People are being jolted by change as the industrial era gives way to globalization and a technology-driven economy. Community organizations that served twentieth-century Americans now seem antiquated or are dying: labor unions and scores of men's clubs such as Moose Lodges, Optimist Clubs, Rotary Clubs, and other civic organizations. As they did a century ago, successful churches are the ones filling the need for belonging and purpose in a new century. Warren and other megachurch leaders are using modern technologies and marketing techniques—"new instrumentalities," as Conwell might call them—to get the word out: *Meet new friends and get to know your neighbors.*

"It's a natural result of years of narcissism," Warren told us. "We have glorified the individual over the community, which has created a generation of very lonely people. Years ago, there wasn't the mobility that there is today; you might stay in one town for life and have generation after generation involved in everybody's lives. Now, with mobility, everybody is spread all over. We have fractured families. And we as a society have more competition for our time. It's very possible for me to come home at night, click the clicker in my car, and drive right into my garage and be home without having said hello or good-bye to a neighbor. We have this longing for belonging."

## Small Groups and Shrinking Unions

The cornerstone of Warren's approach is a small-group program, designed to turn a church with a membership of 40,000 into a cozy community. Joining a small group is the first, essential step of joining virtually any megachurch, and Warren has one for every conceivable need or talent: couples' groups, singles' groups, a group for women with breast cancer, one for mountain bikers, and even one called "Geeks for God Ministry" for Cisco-certified networking professionals.

"People are not looking for a friendly church as much as they are looking for friends," Warren wrote in *The Purpose-Driven Church*. "The average church member knows 67 people in the congregation, whether the church has 200 or 2,000 attending. A member does not have to know everyone in the church in order to feel like it's their church, but he or she does have to know *some people*."

Warren told us that the emergence of small groups and other church services is a direct result of the public's growing distrust of politicians and the mainstream media. "Fundamentally, we are drowning in information and starving for meaning," he said.

Buford, the church adviser at the Leadership Network, said the evangelical church experience became "a bit well prepared, too handled" during what he calls the megachurch's Proclamation Phase of the 1980s and 1990s, the height of TV evangelism. Small groups are the first step in the big-church movement's Demonstration Phase, a response to "a growing demand for authenticity and not hype," Buford said.

One of the biggest influences on the megachurch movement was the business guru Peter Drucker, who saw organizations such as Saddleback Church as the fulfillment of his business theories. Drucker had long argued that successful managers rallied people behind a worthwhile cause. He also believed that people find meaning in life through community and that, because people spend so much time at work, employers needed to develop a sense of community in and around the job. When he realized that there was little traction for the concept in an era of downsizing and outsourcing, Drucker turned to nonprofit organizations. He found that churches play a critical role in creating community. "The community needs a community center," he said. "I'm not talking about religion now, I'm talking society. There is no other institution in the American community that could be the center."

Drucker, whose death in 2005 was mourned by Warren and other megachurch leaders he had advised, left a profound impact on Buford and his Leadership Network. "Pastoral megachurches [are] surely the most important social phenomenon in American society in the last 30 years," Drucker told *Forbes* magazine in 1998.

Because of their training and proximity, small-group leaders at megachurches are natural Navigators—average Joes whose opinions on life, politics, and the latest gadgets and products hold great sway in an age of media fragmentation. They are the type of people—often the same people—the Bush campaign recruited.

Hybels of Willow Creek discovered through polling that one fourth of worshipers were drawn to church by a role model—somebody they know whose life was fulfilled by religion. This is why the Bush team collected church lists. It was not so much the pastors' positions on abortion, gay rights, or other social issues that made megachurches a political force. Nor was it the voter's guides made available to about 20 percent of their congregations. What made megachurches a political asset was their networks of like-minded people through which the Bush campaign could talk to voters about *anything*—not just the social issues pushed by pastors and the Christian Coalition. Certainly, when their

LifeTargeting called for it, the Bush advisers would aim abortion and gay rights messages at certain people. But education, health care, and the war on terror were just as effective with others. The key for Bush was getting influential people in those networks to persuade their friends, family, and associates to vote GOP. "You're far more likely to vote if you get one call from one of these guys than six [campaign] robocalls," said Robert Putnam, the Harvard professor who wrote *Bowling Alone*, the best-selling study of the decline in civic engagement in America.

Putnam, who is working on a book about the community-building powers of megachurches, has sounded an alarm bell for Democrats. "I think there is a chance that the evangelical church movement will be to the next twenty or thirty years what the union movement was to the Democratic Party—that is, the most enduring organizational structure that there is day in and day out, because it's not just about politics. It's about another part of people's lives that they care about," said Putnam, who invited Warren to Harvard for the 2005 address.

That kind of talk scares Andy Stern, the president of the Service Employees International Union, because he knows Putnam is right. Stern, who engineered the breakup of the AFL-CIO in 2005 while promising to drag organized labor into the twenty-first century, has his team studying the community-building successes of megachurches, as well as the efforts of some businesses to tap people's desires to connect. "We all could learn from megachurches and companies like Applebee's about how to give people a sense of belonging," he said.

Sitting cross-legged on a couch in his Washington office, Stern said he believes that unions have lost their place in communities. One and two generations ago, union members hung out in union halls, drinking beer, playing cards, and even bowling. It was in this environment they picked up the values of the Democratic Party, as if by social osmosis. Now those union halls are virtually empty. "The members are more likely to go to a megachurch than a union hall, because they're getting so much more there," Stern said. "And they're learning to be Republicans."

A charismatic fifty-six-year-old former social worker, Stern said he's not looking to draw people back to union halls. Those days are gone.

But he doesn't see any reason why more labor unions don't follow the SEIU's example and offer programs that make organized labor relevant to workers' everyday lives. Applying for college loans, picking a good school, saving money, dealing with marital problems—all these issues and more can be dealt with by a union. He wants members and potential members to see SEIU serving a bigger purpose than negotiating contracts and filing grievances. "Unions are too transactional now," he said.

More Democrats ought to think like Stern. As we already showed, the evidence suggests that the Democratic Party has more allies sitting in megachurch pews than anybody in Washington realizes. There is no reason why Democrats can't secure church lists and survey congregations for potential supporters, just as Republicans do.

The small-group concept is a blueprint for organizing people, especially in the isolated precincts of exurbia. Corporations and campaigns need to start helping like-minded people find one another, give them purpose and power, and let the organization build from the bottom up, rather than top down.

Warren pointed out that political parties could certainly learn from megachurches. "You have to do three things," he said. "Find out what people need, then get them into small groups, and then give them something to do." That last point is the most important, because "you can't just tell people to vote, you have to get them involved in your cause."

Democrats seem fixated on their message, as if changing the way they frame words will help them make inroads in exurbia and its churches. Such tactics will help, but only on the margins. The key is making a Gut Values Connection. Democrats could start by becoming a part of the community—by going to the churches, shopping at the box stores, and, yes, eating at Applebee's. Get to know these people and how they live. Following their lifestyles is the path to their votes.

## Big Menus

One of the distinguishing features of a megachurch is its service menu, with many offering cradle-to-grave programs. Sunday school programs are packed, with an average weekly adult attendance of 856 and nearly as many children under eighteen, according to a 2001 study by Thumma. More than 70 percent of pastors surveyed in 2001 said teenagers were deeply involved in church activities.

Megachurches sponsor Bible studies, prayer groups, youth activities, men's and women's ministries, spiritual retreats, job fairs, vocational training, bulk food distribution, community service programs, parenting and marriage classes, sports and fitness teams, and self-help seminars such as a program in Houston for sex addicts. Success breeds success, because friends tell friends about their newfound communities. "A congregation this large creates a social vortex which draws others to it," Thumma said in a 1996 article.

Megachurches rival Disney World for fun, games, and profit. Some churches provide roller rinks, pools, gymnasiums, racquetball courts, and weight rooms. Prestonwood Baptist Church in Plano, Texas, sold 70,000 tickets, the cheapest at $20, for a lavish Christmas festival that included a 500-person choir.

Kids are bringing their parents to church, especially in places such as Edmond, Oklahoma, where Groeschel's Life Church features a "Toon Town" of 3-D buildings, a sixteen-foot-high slide, and an animatronic police chief who lays down the town rules.

United Methodist Church of the Resurrection, the Kansas church that has a few Applebee's executives in its congregation, is about to join the ranks of megachurches that build and run shopping malls. The concept serves two purposes. First, malls have parking lots, and megachurches are always in need of a place to put worshipers' cars. Secondly, sales generate money for the churches' missions.

## Beyond the Horizon

### WHAT TO LOOK FOR IN MEGACHURCHES

Given their recent history, we suspect that megachurches will continue to evolve and thrive. In coming years, expect to see:

- Partnerships with business seeking to tap huge, impressionable megachurch communities. Churches could form retailing co-ops like Sam's Clubs or sponsor credit cards, raising money for their missions.

- Exploration of new markets, including blacks, Hispanics, and other minorities in the United States as this becomes a majority minority nation, and non-Christians abroad.
- An increase in off-site churches or "planting" by mother churches, creating a virtual franchise system in U.S. religion.
- Less focus on pastors and the church campus and greater emphasis on community ministries created and controlled by worshipers with the help of the mother church.
- A pro-environment evangelical movement. "I don't think God is going to ask us how he created the earth," the Reverend Rich Cizik told *The New York Times*, "but he will ask us what we did with what he created."
- New strategies to identify Navigators in megachurch congregations, especially in the small groups.
- Pressure to abstain from political activity. Younger pastors such as Batterson find politics to be a turn-off to younger worshipers. "Sure, I'll talk about abortion and gay rights, but in a really upbeat, nonthreatening way," he said. "Nobody wants intolerance at the pulpit."

## Maintaining the Connection: Adapting

Despite this remarkable record of success, the megachurch as we know it *must adapt* if the evangelical movement is to keep pace with a fast-changing society. The status quo is not good enough for political and business leaders; why should it be for religious men and women? As you read earlier in this chapter, some megachurch leaders already are experimenting with planting "franchises" far from their mother church. Others, such as Warren, are big into offering several different styles of worship at a single site. But many leaders believe the future of megachurches lies in creating smaller, community-based ministries, a concept that makes sense to us given what we've learned about the public's growing sense of empowerment and need for belonging.

Pastor Robert Lewis of Fellowship Bible Church in Little Rock, Arkansas, thinks his big church is getting small. "I looked up one day and realized I'm like the driver in that little car in *Jurassic Park* because I feel like I'm about to be eaten up by change in the church," he said. Lewis, a member of the Leadership Network board, is one of a growing number of big-church leaders who believe the public is starting to demand a shift in focus—away from pastors and big glitzy stage shows and back to community-based churching.

"All of a sudden, we're seeing more and more people who are bored, who have superficial religion, and who blame the church. They're leaving the church and going out and doing their own thing," he said. "People want intimate, hands-on participation, do-it-for-themselves deep commitment. They don't want to sit in a megachurch for the rest of their lives and listen to all these programs and the pastor."

But the megachurches won't disappear, not if they adapt. Fellowship, Willow Creek, and many other megachurches are putting more resources into programs that support local ministries conducted out of people's homes, backyards, and neighborhood coffee shops. At Willow Creek, Mellado said, they've created a whole system of local pastors who build and support ministries that serve people who may never come to the church's massive suburban Chicago campus. Fellowship helped a worshiper who wanted to provide marriage and family counseling for medical students at the University of Arkansas at Little Rock. The program was a hit and is now part of the curriculum.

"People keep changing so we need to change, too," Mellado said. Lewis said this doesn't necessarily mean an end to the huge facilities and sprawling campuses, "but the large church is going to have to get leaner, and provide more equipment and support to people and let them do their own ministries."

Dick DeVos, the Michigan gubernatorial candidate and former Amway executive who sits on Mellado's board, said the small group he runs out of his home meets once per month. "Not that this is a replacement for the church at this point, but we do view that as a possibility." Eventually, the megachurch may evolve into a facilitator of sorts "that hooks people with needs to somebody who has a need to give," DeVos said.

It's a sign of the times, really. Americans living in this age of technology are seizing more control of their lives. If they could vote on political ads for the liberal MoveOn.org in the 2004 campaign, create their own music library on an iPod, self-select their news on the Internet, and build their own car accessory package online, why can't they custom-order their religion?

"Big churches need to be like Home Depot," Lewis said, without a trace of sarcasm. "Their marketing approach is, 'You can do it. We're here to help.' Tomorrow's church needs to be like that: You can do it. Get out in the community. Go out in your neighborhood, go follow your dreams, and we'll be a place you can come to for help. You can do it."

## Maintaining the Connection: Authenticity

We didn't set out to portray Warren, Hybels, Hamilton, Lewis, or any other megachurch leader as a saint or superstar. We're not that naive. Surely, some will fail to adapt to the tidal waves of change washing over the country. Others may fall to scandal, repeating the cycle of greed and corruption that shamed TV evangelism in the 1980s and '90s and fuels skepticism about the megachurch movement today. "This guilt by association is unfortunate," Warren said.

The purity of their product requires church ministers to be careful about avoiding scandal. People don't expect their political and business leaders to be squeaky clean, but ministers are held to a higher standard.

"Some of the same things we're seeing with George Bush now—a leader losing his credibility—can happen in the megachurch movement," Thumma said. He said the megachurch leaders least likely to lose that connection are those who avoid TV and toil in relative obscurity, building churches and networks while keeping their finances transparent. Some megachurch leaders are reveling in the limelight. For example, Joel Osteen of Lakewood Church is a ubiquitous presence on TV with his toothy smile and syrupy sermons.

"Leadership is influence, and influence is given to you by credibility," Warren said. "People are looking for a credible voice. Every day, people are checking on your credibility. It's really just humility. Humility is not denying your strengths; it's being honest about your weaknesses. I make mistakes every day."

Whether in politics, business, or religion, Warren said, "It's the guys who don't hide it, who own up to their mistakes, who don't spin stuff. They're the ones with credibility."

---

Navigating the Stormy Present
## How to Be a Great Connector

1. **Make and Maintain a Gut Values Connection**. Rick Warren and other megachurch leaders are not just connecting to people through scripture. They are offering a sense of community and a higher purpose in life.
2. **Adapt**. Rick Warren, Bill Hybels, and others recognized the enormous potential in appealing to spiritual Americans who did not attend church.
3. **LifeTarget**. Well before the practice entered the political world, fledgling church leaders had their communities analyzed based on their consumer histories and other lifestyle cues. How else do you avoid selling swimsuits in the Arctic?
4. **Talk Smart**. As Solomon put it, sometimes you need to explain bananas in a different way.
5. **Find Navigators**. Virtually every small-group leader is one.

# PART II

# Great Change

# 4

## Anxious Americans

We got too complicated
It's all way overrated
I like the old and outdated
Way of life.

—"Back When," country song by TIM MCGRAW

IN A SUN-DAPPLED CORNER of the Dubuque Family Restaurant, coffee and conversation flow faster than the nearby Mississippi River. Nobody is pleased with the direction the country has taken.

"We're struggling to keep our house," said a plumber, Glen Naab, fifty-three, his bright blue eyes clouding over. He and his pals talk and tease and argue over the same strong coffee at the same Iowa diner in the same way, day after day—all without resolving a central question: Why does the country seem on the wrong track?

"It's hard to put my finger on it, but things are a mess in this country right now," said Lewis Dowell in the spring of 2004, pulling off a John Deere hat and running his hands though his hair. Maybe it's the fact that his retirement check from John Deere is larger than the salaries of some workers who followed him into the company workforce. "That's shocking and sad," he said.

Nodding his head, Naab said his adult children were struggling more than he ever had to raise families. "Both work long hours and find it tough just to make ends meet," he said.

Steve Harris, fifty-seven, a Vietnam veteran hunched over his coffee like a bear guarding its cub, said his generation had had the option of keeping one spouse, usually the wife, at home. If the family needed extra money or one breadwinner lost a job, the other could go to work.

"Now if a family is barely surviving on two salaries, what happens when they lose one?" asked a fireplace salesman, Rick Stein, sixty-one.

"The house goes back to the bank," replied Naab, mixing sarcasm with the day's coffee. "Isn't that the American way?"

Judging by dozens of interviews we conducted for this book, one thing unites an otherwise self-polarizing public—a perception that life in this unrivaled superpower, the richest country in the world, is not quite right, that change is coming too fast and leaving too many people behind. Besides voicing concerns about job security, health care costs, the Iraq war, and terrorism, Americans speak wistfully of simpler times—when children could play safely outdoors, people's values were reflected in popular culture, and each generation seemed destined to do better than the last.

Now that you've learned about Presidents Bush and Clinton, and Hill and Warren—the Great Connectors—it's time to explore the great changes in society that are forcing these and other leaders to adapt. From the "recentering" of lifestyles and a rise in civic reengagement to the gathering power of Navigators and the formation of a Tribal Nation, a fast-changing public is altering America's way of life. This chapter focuses on that first element: people's changing attitudes and lifestyles.

This is an anxious America. With the fall of the Berlin Wall and the end of the Cold War, people became a restless audience to a confluence of events: the dot-com bubble and the ephemeral affluence of the 1990s; globalization and sudden competition for jobs and power from overseas; the industrial age giving way fitfully to the era of technology; and, finally, the September 11, 2001, terrorist strikes on Washington and New York.

This is a resilient America. People responded to the crush of change by taking matters into their own hands. They sought a better balance between work and play. They reconnected with one another and their communities. They demanded more time with their families and more control over their frenetic lives. Americans became more spiritual and less trusting of government, business, and religious institutions. This is the context for the rise of community, purpose, and authenticity as potent twenty-first-century Gut Values.

Contrary to conventional wisdom, the American way of life did not suddenly change with 9/11. It was already in a warp-speed transition when the terrorist strikes accelerated change, deepening and confirming public sentiments that had been percolating since the 1990s. The same can be said of another national tragedy, Hurricane Katrina in August 2005. The misperception afterward was that the government's fatally inept response on the Gulf Coast shattered the public's trust in the political system. In fact, Americans had been losing faith in government for four decades. *Katrina only deepened and confirmed their skepticism.*

## PRE-9/11: THE ONSET OF CHANGE

Lori Nowak noticed the change in the mid-1990s. "The economy turned around and things were going gangbusters, but something wasn't right. I felt empty inside," said the thirty-four-year-old Woonsocket, Rhode Island, homemaker between bites of lunch at her local Applebee's. "I needed something more out of life."

It hit Charlie Roy about the same time. "With the world going nuts, I realized the only thing I can rely on is myself, my family, and my friends," said the fifty-four-year-old Cumberland, Rhode Island, teacher. "All the other priorities I had as a younger man were no longer a priority."

Julian Sowa started looking at life differently after the dot-com bubble burst in March 2000. Tech stocks plunged, wiping out trillions of dollars of wealth on paper and helping to push the country into the 2001 recession. "I lost a big piece of me in the market," said the systems operator from suburban Chicago. Eating dinner one night at an Applebee's a few miles from the Willow Creek megachurch, Sowa said he had to strip life down to its basics after the go-go '90s. "I had my wife, my home, and a good life. I decided to focus on the precious things."

Weary of change and skeptical of the status quo, Americans entered the twenty-first century unsure where to turn for answers. So they turned to one another. With the help of new technologies, people seized more control over their way of life—checking in at the office while pushing the kids on a park swing or e-mailing Mom in Florida every day. They felt empowered and obliged to help others. More Americans agreed that "people have a definite responsibility to help people in their community who are less fortunate than they are" (55 percent, up 6 points from 1995 to 2001), according to a Roper analysis.

"Rather than look to forces beyond themselves—their congressman or senator, the White House, the nation's major corporations—Americans have increasingly looked to themselves for answers," wrote Ed Keller and Jon Berry in their groundbreaking *The Influentials*, based on their access to three decades of Roper surveys. "They are saying, in effect, 'I'm a resourceful person. I can figure out a lot on my own. And I can connect to others to help me solve the problems I cannot resolve with my own resources, to create the life I want.' "

Their firm first documented the mood shift in 1993, nearly a decade before 9/11. In a special report to clients, the survey firm stated that Americans were "sobering up" financially and becoming more realistic. "Americans are taking greater responsibility for their actions." Even as the economy recovered and wealth abounded, the trend toward self-reliance and control continued, and Roper's analysts gave it a name—the "Age of Autonomy." In the business world, this meant the rise of smart shoppers who rejected brands that carried a premium price and used new tools, particularly the Internet, to find brands that offered quality *and* a good price.

Voters started shopping around, too, according to Keller and Berry, "playing Democrats and Republicans off each other, much the same way they were playing brands against each other to get better value in the marketplace—individuals leveraging the one thing they have, the vote, to exercise their demand for more accountability on the national level." It was this attitude that gave rise to Ross Perot, a quirky billionaire with few political skills who nonetheless won 19 percent of the presidential vote in 1992 and 8 percent in 1996.

A few months before the 9/11 attacks, Roper analysts began telling clients that Americans were "recentering" themselves. The "about me" 1990s were giving way to an "about connections" millennium, and "working vacations" were being replaced by "longer vacations." In ways both large and small, the social fabric of America was already changing *before* 9/11:

**Family:** Spending time with families became the top leisure activity of most Americans (63 percent, up 3 points from 1997, according to Roper), and "protecting the family" rose to become the No. 1 value of Americans (cited by 53 percent of respondents in a 2000 Roper analysis). Nearly half of Americans said just before the attacks that being a good spouse or parent defined success for them (up 11 percentage points from 1985).

**Work:** One third of Americans said they would rather have a boss who understood their need for flexibility than one who would help them advance their careers, Roper reported, and a majority preferred a job offering flexible hours over one offering opportunities for advancement.

**Priorities:** Money was still important to people, but for different reasons. The mid-1990s saw a rise in the number of Americans who said money brought them pleasure. Freedom and comfort were the oft-cited benefits of money in the late 1990s. But at the turn of the century, a Roper analysis noticed a big jump in the percentage of people saying that money meant they could contribute to society (up 13 points from 1995 to 2000), leave something to their heirs (up 12 points), or otherwise help their children (up 6 points).

**Connecting/community:** More Americans agreed that "people have a definite responsibility to help people in their community who are less fortunate than they are" (55 percent, up 6 points between 1995 and a pre–terror strikes 2001 Roper analysis).

**Nesting:** More people brought home takeout food, a fast way to enjoy a family meal at home (64 percent, up 5 points from 1998, according to Roper).

**Identity:** People's chief source of identity was their home (34 percent, up 8 points from 1996) and causes to which they contributed (24 percent, up 5 points), according to Roper.

**Leisure activities:** After rising throughout the 1990s, the percentage of people often spending leisure time on work-related chores began dropping (down 6 points since 1998 to 33 percent in 2000). Spending time with families became the top leisure activity (up 3 points from 1997), along with relaxation (up 5 points) and companionship (up 4 points). A growing number of people said they would choose a longer vacation over a shorter workday, with growing numbers identifying travel with seeking comfort or the experience of new places, Roper reported.

**Stress:** Higher numbers of people said they were reducing levels of stress in their lives (36 percent, up 10 points from 1998, according to Roper).

**Values:** Two out of five Americans thought the government needed to do more to promote traditional values, according to a CBS/*New York Times* poll in July 2000. A Hart-Teeter survey conducted for *The Wall Street Journal* in 1999 found that 60 percent of American adults thought there needed to be more respect for traditional values. Both numbers had increased in the 1990s.

**Faith in institutions:** A January 2001 Harris poll found that a majority of Americans didn't trust institutions like churches, large companies, the White House, or even public schools.

**Security:** The bombing at the 1996 Olympics in Atlanta and the Y2K terror fears heightened the public's concerns about terrorist strikes well before 9/11. In a July 1996 CNN/Gallup poll, half of the respondents said another bombing was "very likely" to occur in the United States. More than one third worried that they or a member of their family would be the victim of a terrorist attack. In December 1999, 61 percent of respondents said they expected terrorism to strike on New Year's Eve.

At the turn of the twenty-first century, Americans were both harried and hopeful. They expressed optimism about the future of America, the effect of technology on society, and even the long-lamented institutions of marriage and family, according to Keller and Berry of Roper. Americans seemed to think that after years of spiraling out of control, perhaps things were spiraling *into* control. It's that sentiment that produced a spike in patriotism and public spirit after the attacks. Keller and Berry wrote in *The Influentials*:

When the 9/11 terrorist attacks on the World Trade Center and the Pentagon occurred, this resilience, resolve, and renewed sense of faith in the nation came to the surface. Rather than sinking, the spirit of Americans rose. The resilience and resolve might have come forward without the events of the preceding decade, the turning inward for solutions, "more realistic attitude," "determination to address critical issues," and "taking greater responsibility" that we saw in 1993. It probably would not have happened as readily, quickly or strongly, though. Meaningful trends (as opposed to fads) tend to unfold over a long period of time. The spirit that many saw in the nation in 2001–2002 had been building for more than a decade.

## POST-9/11: THE ACCELERATION
## OF SOCIAL CHANGE

The horror of September 11, 2001, reaffirmed for most people the necessity of continuing to adjust their lifestyles to get the most out of every precious day. Social trends that began in the 1990s were cemented into a new order. This was most evident, of course, on the issue of security.

Five months after the attacks, an NBC/*Wall Street Journal* poll found that 85 percent of the public believed the country was likely to be attacked "in the next few months." While most people *expected* terrorism to strike the United States at the turn of the new millennium, after 9/11 they *feared* it would happen. Charlie Roy began to ride around Boston's suburbs with a survival kit in his car. He had another one in his home. "We've got the water and some money and a few other things," he said in 2005. Roy was eating with his wife (she didn't want to provide her name). "We've also got the sticky stuff. What's it called? Duct tape. We're not sure what it's for, but we know one day we'll need it and we'll be ready!" he said with a nervous laugh.

Cumberland, Rhode Island, where Roy was a teacher, is a bedroom community that is home to hundreds of people who commute to Boston for work. His school held its first terrorism drill after the 9/11 attacks. That's a sad fact of life in post-9/11 America—antiterrorism planning at schools that reminds parents of the duck-and-cover drills they did during the Cold War era. The deadly siege of a school in Beslan, Russia, weeks before the 2004 U.S. presidential election gave voters, particularly parents, a harsh reminder of terrorism's indiscriminate horror.

"Flying doesn't make me nervous anymore. But what really gets me is that sense that it could be *anybody* trying to get me," said Lori Nowak. She was having lunch with her mother and her two children at Applebee's in the old mill town. "I know nothing is likely to happen way out here, but I get an icy feeling in my stomach every time I think about terrorism. And it's hard not to think about it."

After the attacks, protecting the family became even more important. In 2002, nearly six of every ten employed Americans said family was their top priority (up 14 points from 2000, according to Roper). American Demographics/NFO WorldGroup reported a year after the attacks that 74 percent of parents said they were setting aside more family time. The percentage of people eating several meals per week with their families increased after 9/11 at a slightly faster rate than before, according to Teeter polling.

Solitary activities such as watching TV declined in popularity, while spending time with kids and social activities such as going to church and sporting events gained popularity between 2000 and 2003, according to the Harris Tracking poll. American Demographics/NFO World-Group surveys showed that 20 percent of Americans reconnected with old friends after the attacks, and nearly as many reached out to lost family members. About 10 percent made a career change. Every year since the attacks, U.S. Census data has shown an increase in the number of people who say they do volunteer work.

The public's aspirations continued on the get-a-life path. In 2003, Roper noted a big jump in the percentage of people who said owning a vacation home was something they wanted (61 percent, up 10 points from 2000), along with a stay in a luxury hotel (54 percent, up 17 points), a nicely decorated home (49 percent, up 8 points), eating at a pricey restaurant (47 percent, up 11 points) and owning an expensive car (45 percent, up 10 points). The percentage of people who said their home, music, car, and clubs were an expression of themselves increased substantially from 2000, according to Roper's 2004 report.

The notion that a person's values were out of sync with those of the rest of the country was not new, but the "values gap" widened after the attacks. People felt that many of their most cherished values—including honesty, friendship, stable relationships, faith, open-mindedness, and spirituality—were not as important to the American culture overall, according to Roper surveys. This was a continuation of the trend that had begun before the attacks.

Tracy Tallent certainly felt that way. The forty-five-year-old Iowa mother said it angered her that the cable company would not let her block MTV. She didn't want her children watching racy videos. "It's not just politics. It's the whole moral thing with me. I love this country and don't want to see it disintegrate," she said.

Kenny Ziegemeier, fifty-eight, manager of the American Legion post in Saint Peters, Missouri, bemoaned the coarsening of American culture. It may sound petty, he said, but there's a bigger problem afoot when swearing in public has become commonplace and children sit in front of televisions for hours. "I've seen people change. I've seen the economy change. I've seen our nation's security change," said Ziegemeier, a white apron spread across his lanky frame. "It can't be good."

In Arkansas, Janet Lloyd, forty-five, of Conway said the job of parenting is made harder by politicians and business leaders who make bad examples of themselves with unethical or illegal behavior. "It's a hard world to be raising children in," Lloyd said.

The public's faith in government and other institutions briefly increased after 9/11 but returned to the decades-long downward trend within six months. The fatally slow response to Katrina reinforced people's skepticism of public and private institutions. Two months after the hurricane, a Pew poll found that Americans expressing increasingly negative views of a wide range of institutions, including the federal government, Congress, and corporations. Nearly six months later, an AP-Ipsos poll showed that public confidence in government disaster readiness had actually fallen 7 percentage points since September 2005, when images of death and chaos were still fresh in the nation's mind.

People tried to be optimistic, but sometimes it was hard. Lucy Werenicz, a suburban Minnesota mother who had been out of work for months, said she had high hopes for her new job—but money was still tight. She's typical of Americans who feel uneasy even when economic indicators are high and their own personal financial situations are okay. "I'm worried about losing my house. I'm tired of worrying about it," said the Coon Rapids woman. "I'm tired of worrying about my friends being out of work. I'm just tired, you know. This world makes you tired."

## A NEW CIVIC ORDER

Change is a cyclical creature. We live in a time not unlike the turn of the twentieth century, when people struggled to cope with the shift from an agrarian society to the industrial age. *(Today it's the industrial age giving way to the technological era.)*

A dynamic marketplace in the early 1900s ushered in new technologies such as autos, radios, phones, jukeboxes, and vending machines that both complicated lives and gave people more control over their lifestyles. *(Now it's computers, e-mail, the Internet, cell phones, iPods, and assorted gadgets that both vex and enhance our lives.)*

Political and corporate leaders failed the turn-of-the-century working class, giving rise to reformers such as the trust-busting Teddy Roosevelt. *(Nobody has staked this fertile ground this century, though John McCain portrays himself as a reform-minded maverick.)*

Finally, old forms of community building such as knitting bees and barn raisings became irrelevant at the dawn of the twentieth century, prompting people to create new ways to connect. Scores of fraternal and civic organizations such as Optimist Clubs, Rotary Clubs, Moose Lodges, and the ubiquitous union halls became the nation's gathering spots for decades. *(Television, urban sprawl, technology, and other societal shifts made those twentieth-century civic groups increasingly irrelevant at the start of this century, but people are now finding new ways to connect.)*

There is also a rhythm to history and the crises that mark it. William Strauss and Neil Howe argued in their 1997 book *The Fourth Turning* that American history has unfolded in approximate eighty-year cycles, each dividing into four twenty-year "Turnings." The First Turning is always an upbeat era of strengthening institutions and weakening individualism, when a new civic order replaces the old vanguards. The Second Turning is an "Awakening," a passionate era of spiritual upheaval. The Third Turning is an "Unraveling," "a downcast era of strengthening individualism and weakening institutions, when the old civic order decays and new values start to emerge."

With the end of the Cold War, the 1980s and 1990s were a period of unraveling that Strauss and Howe compared to the 1760s, the 1850s, and the 1920s. "During each of these periods, Americans had recently achieved a stunning victory over a long-standing foreign threat . . . yet that victory came to be associated with a worn-out definition of collective purpose—and, perversely, unleashed a torrent of pessimism," they wrote. Third Turnings were marked by culture wars, political partisanship, a rise in anti-immigration sentiments, and an inclination to be more protective of children.

Each of those periods was followed by a Fourth Turning—"a crisis, a decisive era of secular upheaval, when the values regime propels the replacement of the old civic order with a new one," Strauss and Howe wrote several years before the 9/11 attacks fit neatly into their theory.

Let's take a look at how 9/11 helped shake up the "old civic order" in politics, business, and religion.

## Politics

On September 9 and September 10, 2001, President Bush's pollsters called 603 voters to get a sense of his political prospects nine months into his first term. The results were not cheering. Some 55 percent had a favorable impression of Bush, down about 10 points since his inauguration. His job approval rating also was tumbling; Gallup had it at just 51 percent. It was clear that Americans had doubts about their new president.

The economy was the top issue for 19 percent of those polled by Bush's political team, followed by Social Security and "the breakdown of the American family" (another sign that a pro-family trend was underway *before* 9/11) at 17 percent each. Education was at 14 percent. No other issue made it into the double digits.

Voters thought Bush's priorities didn't jibe with their own. A plurality of voters (21 percent) believed he cared most about tax cuts, an issue that only 6 percent of voters put at the top of their list. There was no connection.

The Bush team didn't even bother to ask about foreign policy. Then came 9/11.

The country pulled together for a brief time, and President Bush's approval rating climbed above 80 percent. Many say he squandered an opportunity to unite the country behind a cause: volunteerism, a truce in partisan politics, or serious wartime sacrifices.

"Instead he just told people to go shopping and get on an airplane," said Senator John McCain, a potential presidential candidate in 2008 who generally backs the president's war-on-terror policies. "It's the basic nature of the American people. They used to belong to Rotary Clubs, Elks Clubs, and other volunteer organizations like that. Now they're looking for new forms of community—a new sense of purpose— and it's up to leaders in politics, business, and even religion to provide a sense of that."

Spurred by fear and patriotism, a majority of the public backed Bush's efforts to expand law enforcement powers with the so-called USA PATRIOT Act. Some voters and members of Congress had second thoughts by the end of 2005, when Bush's political standing was much weaker.

Hard-liners on immigration also found a stronger voice in the post-9/11 world. With the public viewing immigration reform as a national security issue, more than two thirds backed the concept of a national ID card, according to a Pew poll. In early 2006, Americans were evenly divided on President Bush's decision to order eavesdropping on suspected terrorism-related calls inside the United States without warrants.

Historians may write that President Bush ultimately failed to capitalize on the public's post-9/11 goodwill, a judgment that will hinge on the outcome of the war in Iraq and the global war on terrorism. But there is no doubt that his response to 9/11 helped him forge a vital Gut Values Connection that carried him through his reelection campaign.

A crisis can define a leader. In the spring of 1995, then-President Clinton's popularity was at the lowest point of his presidency when the Oklahoma City bombing gave him a chance to reestablish a Gut Values

Connection. He flew to the site of the crime and united the country in condemnation and mourning, much as Bush would do a few years later atop a fire truck. John Harris, in his Clinton biography entitled *The Survivor*, wrote that the speech spoke volumes about Clinton and the American presidency. "His sermon underscored how the explosion had transformed President Clinton's standing. It was the nature of the American system, where the president is both the administrator of government, like a prime minister, and in a more mystical sense the leader of the people. President Clinton, whose emotions were the same as those of citizens everywhere, was helping the nation cope. And even the part of the nation that deplored President Clinton in other contexts seemed to appreciate it," Harris wrote. A poll by NBC News and *The Wall Street Journal* found that 84 percent of Americans approved of President Clinton's handling of the attack in Oklahoma City.

Like the man who would succeed him, President Clinton rose to the occasion. He booked an appearance on *60 Minutes* shortly after the bombing (the last time he had been on the show was in 1992 to confess having caused pain in his marriage) to propose a package of new laws giving the government more power to investigate and prosecute terrorists. In May, he went to Michigan State University to denounce militias (Timothy McVeigh and his confederates had ties to the Michigan militia). "There is nothing patriotic about hating your country, or pretending that you can love your country but despise your government," he said. "How dare you suggest that we, in the freest nation on earth, live in tyranny."

Harris uncovered a strategy memo by Clinton consultant Dick Morris that discusses how to use Oklahoma City to his advantage. "A. temporary gain: boost in ratings," Morris wrote, according to Harris. "B. More permanent gain: Improvement in character/personality attributes—remedies weakness, incompetence, ineffectiveness found in recent poll. C. Permanent possible gain: sets up Extremist Issue vs. Republicans."

Seven years later, President Bush's political team produced a strategy memo for his reelection. It listed ten issues of focus, leading with "War on Terror (Con't)."

Despite the machinations of their political teams, Presidents Bush and Clinton didn't win reelection because of the terrorist strikes. They won because the national crises *gave them the opportunity and the obligation to connect with people in a meaningful way.* And, to their credit, they did so. The attacks on Oklahoma City and on 9/11 were such a jolt to the American psyche that voters were willing to suspend temporarily their skepticism and give their president the benefit of the doubt as each made his case for unity and common purpose.

The measure of a truly great politician is the ability to create and sustain that connection, whether at war or in peace.

## *Beyond the Horizon*

### HOW TO CONNECT IN THE FUTURE

#### War: *Modern Campaign Tactics Will Be Deployed in Future Wars*

Imagine how the invasion of Europe would have played out had cable TV covered D-Day, with U.S. soldiers filing blogs from the bloody beaches of Normandy. It would have been immeasurably more difficult to maintain public support had the full effect of the bloodshed—not to mention the many snafus—been made known globally in an instant. But that's what war will be like in the Information Age. In Iraq today, U.S. troops are going outside the chain of command to learn about the battlefield. E-mails from home, blogs written by fellow soldiers, and Internet connections to U.S. media outlets give troops real-time access to news from the battlefield. Al-Qaida and other Islamic extremist groups have poisoned the Muslim public's view of the United States by exploiting the Internet and other modern communication tools. The American government has failed to match the enemy's sophistication. "Our enemies have skillfully adapted to fighting wars in today's media age, but for the most part we—our country, our government—has not adapted," conceded Defense Secretary Donald H. Rumsfeld in February 2006.

In future wars, the speed and flow of information will require the Pentagon to use all the tools of a twenty-first-century campaign to assess and affect public opinion and maintain troop morale. That includes polls, LifeTargeting, use of Navigators, a major presence on the blogs, and a communication infrastructure that responds to criticism and developments 24/7 rather than just when Washington is awake. Just as politicians poll and ponder whether a race can be won before launching a political campaign, the next commander in chief will need to be intensely aware of public opinion before leading the country to battle. War was never intended to be so democratic. The Information Age will have a huge impact on the nation's willingness to fight and sustain future conflicts.

## Business

The U.S. economy experienced a huge boom in the 1990s until the tech bubble burst. Global competition and the fitful transition from the industrial age to a tech-info era cooled economic growth and caused Americans to feel more anxious about their financial security. And then came 9/11.

The attacks not only rocked the fiscal foundation of the economy, they gave Americans more reason to fret about their place in it. People were also more skeptical in general, which affected their view of the corporate world. In a 2004 Roper analysis, a large and growing majority of Americans felt that advertising was "shown in too many places" (80 percent, up 5 points from 2002). They also said that ads encouraged people to use products they don't need (79 percent, up 12 points from 2002) or are bad for them (69 percent, up 11 points from 2002) and are a nuisance that interferes with Internet use (58 percent, up 15 points). One fourth of all Americans said they couldn't depend on getting reliable products from businesses (26 percent, down 7 points from 2001).

In Roper's 2003 analysis for clients, the firm said its polls showed only 40 percent of the public agreed that "what's good for business is good for the average person," down 8 points since 1999 and the lowest since 1981. Roper called it the return of the "Y.O.Y.O."—You're On Your Own economy. Even with relatively low unemployment, a majority of Americans didn't think there were enough *good* jobs available.

Nearly seven in ten thought job security was a thing of the past. The appetite for discounts and deals increased. In growing numbers, people said they were waiting for sales before buying, comparing prices in ads, buying in bulk, and frequenting shopper promotions. There was hope for companies that had established strong brands.

Roper analysts found that trust or authenticity was the No. 1 attribute of the best brands—the best way to make a Gut Values Connection. People who are living with uncertainty want good values (home, car, and DVD sales exploded when their costs declined); they want their aspirations met (travel, a comfortable home, comfort food); and they demand authenticity (a product they trust and can count on).

A company that delivers these qualities gets, in return, intense loyalty from its customers. Yet most companies associate their brands with wealth, power, status, and other "success" values. With so few companies understanding (much less responding to) consumer's true gut-level desires, people are willing to give those that do the benefit of the doubt. This is why a company like Applebee's can avoid a public relations meltdown when a fingertip is found in one of its salads, as happened in 2005.

## Religion

Church attendance across the nation soared by as much as 25 percent in the weeks following 9/11, higher still in New York and Washington, which were directly hit by the attacks. Rick Linamen, executive pastor of the Scottsdale Bible Church in Arizona, said his average congregation of 6,000 swelled by a third on the first Sunday after 9/11. "Like everywhere else in the country, people were scared and looking for comfort anywhere they could find it." A month after the attacks, a Pew Research Center poll reported that 78 percent of Americans believed that "religion's influence is increasing in our society" compared with just 37 percent who had held that opinion six months earlier.

But the hopes for a churchgoing revival were quickly dashed. Some churches, such as Linamen's, returned to normal attendance levels within a week or two. Others maintained the higher levels a bit longer, but U.S. church attendance was back to its pre-9/11 numbers within a year—with no end in sight to the decades-long downward trend. Yet the curve continued upward on spirituality—the vague measure of the importance people place on prayer, belief in God, and the pursuit of purpose through religion. People may be losing faith in religious institutions (a year after the attacks, Gallup found just 45 percent of respondents expressing confidence in religious institutions, down from 60 percent the previous year and the lowest in decades), but that doesn't mean they're losing *faith*.

A *Newsweek* poll in 2005 showed that just 45 percent of respondents said they attend church weekly, virtually the same figure reported by Gallup nearly four decades ago. Even those numbers are surely inflated because people don't like to admit they're religious shirkers. Researchers who actually count heads in church say about one in five Americans attends weekly services. Yet the impulse to find some form of spiritual fulfillment by getting closer to God is rising. *Newsweek* found that more Americans described themselves as spiritual (79 percent) than religious (64 percent). Two thirds say they pray daily. One third of the public meditates.

"People are less religious in terms of active and fervent support of traditional church worship and much more interested in their personal spirituality and learning more about other religions and various aspects of Buddhism and the like," said Scott Thumma, the Hartford Seminary religion scholar and megachurch expert. He and other experts said they noticed an increase in spirituality in the 1990s, and the trend accelerated after 9/11. "There's a huge chunk of Americans creating their own facts and putting stuff together and going outside traditional religious institutions," Thumma said. They're seeking control of their spiritual life, just as they're charting their own course in politics and business.

A March 4, 2004, Roper analysis suggested that people are increasingly finding practical benefit in spiritual practice. Almost three in four of the public thought praying was moderately or very effective for personal health, up 8 points from 1996, the report said. Two in three Americans had tried prayer in their efforts against physical problems or illness, up 6 points from 1999. The number of people who said prayer helped improve their lives rose 9 percentage points from 1996 to 2004.

Jim Mellado, the Harvard-trained president of the Willow Creek Association, a network of 11,000 churches in thirty-five countries, said attendance at Hybels's services skyrocketed after 9/11 and returned to the normal rate of growth in six to eight weeks. Harder to measure was the increase in spirituality, he said. "9/11 was a very significant catalyst for spirituality, but . . . there were other dynamics going on in the culture as well that resulted in increased attention around spirituality," Mellado said. "I think people are searching for answers. They're not necessarily looking for them in church, which I find very sad because that's the business churches are in."

He's not sure why there's a gap, but he knows it predated 9/11. "It's not 9/11, though 9/11 added to it. It's the culture shift we've seen happening in the last ten or so years. Time was getting squeezed. The family unit was getting squeezed on all fronts, so I think people responded by seeking more meaning and purpose in life by spending more time with family instead of going to church. Maybe they coached the kids and spent less time at work. But that didn't necessarily translate into more time at church."

# 5

## The 3 Cs: Connections, Community, and Civic Engagement

*We're bowling together to be together.*

—DIEDRE, organizer of an online bowling club

WHEN HURRICANE KATRINA swamped his New Orleans neighborhood, seventeen-year-old Jamie Ferrande ripped the door off an abandoned refrigerator and used it as a life raft to ferry his four younger cousins to safety.

Jamie and the cousins found his aunt, Troy Marcelin, and spent a day together on a highway overpass before moving to a hotel roof. They waited there for days before a helicopter plucked them from their perch and took them to the New Orleans airport. That's where Jamie called an old friend in California, Mark Miller, on a borrowed cell phone.

"I trusted him," Jamie said. "I knew he was going to come through with something, but I didn't know what."

What happened next explains why the term "community" means much more than it did a generation ago, before e-mail, cell phones, instant text messaging, blogs, and other information technologies gave the people power to reach far outside their neighborhoods and satisfy their cravings to connect, to belong, or to help. Eleven years after Harvard professor Robert Putnam declared that Americans were "bowling alone," they're coming together. More than at any time in a century, Americans are fulfilling their desire for civic engagement and personal connections.

• • •

Jamie's friend Miller didn't have money to relocate the New Orleans refugees, nor did he have room to house them. "But, you know what? I will find a way," Miller said.

He did—with the help of scores of strangers from across the country united only by the Internet and a burning desire to succeed where government had failed.

Kim Curtis, the Associated Press reporter who chronicled Jamie's odyssey, reported that Miller turned to craigslist.org, one of several community-focused Web sites that posted offers of help after Katrina hit the Gulf Coast. Miller spotted an offer of housing not far from his home and sent an e-mail. Susan and Gene Knight quickly replied. They had a space for Jamie's family in the home they had just sold in Arcadia, an affluent suburb of Los Angeles, and they would take the guests with them when they moved to their ranch in Pinon Hills, near San Bernardino.

Now Jamie and his family needed transportation. They were making their way from the airport to a temporary shelter at the former Kelly Air Force Base in San Antonio when Susan called the Red Cross in San Antonio and asked about travel vouchers. No such thing, she was politely told by a Red Cross volunteer, who then hung up and took another call.

Coincidentally, the Red Cross volunteer's next caller was Elizabeth Etheridge, who had been reading craigslist.org postings about transportation needs. The volunteer told Etheridge about the plight of Jamie and his family. "I started e-mailing everybody I knew to get as many tickets as I could," Etheridge told the AP.

She spotted a craigslist ad placed by Greg Billock, a thirty-one-year-old Google employee who had piled up frequent-flier miles on Southwest Airlines. He and his wife donated four vouchers, and they persuaded friends to kick in three more to get Jamie's family to the Knights' home.

When every other institution failed them—the federal, state, and city bureaucracies as well as even the Red Cross and other private relief groups—Jamie and his family turned to one another and to their ad hoc community for help.

"There's sort of self-organizing groups that get together and make things happen," Billock told the AP, explaining how disparate strangers had managed to help Jamie and his family.

Across America, people are investing their time on their own terms to be a part of self-organizing groups that make things happen— connecting online and offline, short term and long term, for the greater good or just for kicks. They are creating what Putnam calls "social capital," the measure of civic activity and personal connections that improve the quality of life. Americans are helping their fellow citizens, expanding their social networks, and influencing decisions in business boardrooms, political campaigns, and churches.

Some people are inspired by civic-minded impulses. Others just want to hook up with like-minded people. Whatever their motivation, Americans are sparking a revival in civic involvement after more than forty years of decline. This chapter redefines the word "community" for the twenty-first century, creates new categories for civic engagement, and illustrates through the eyes of several average Americans the new ways to create social capital. As an Internet-savvy dog club organizer told us, "There's never been a lonelier time—and there's never been more ways to keep from being lonely."

These are unsettling times. The war on terror, the war in Iraq, economic insecurity, a spate of natural disasters, the loneliness and isolation of a highly mobile, hard-wired populace in an era of sprawl—these things and more create an emptiness in America. This is a nation filled with people searching for assurance from one another or the sense of purpose they get from causes greater than themselves.

John McCain, the Republican Arizona senator on target for a 2008 presidential bid, bluntly appeals to that instinct in voters. He sees it writ large in the service of young men and women in the U.S. military and on a much smaller scale at a grocery store near his home in Arizona, where he stops for coffee, a newspaper, and conversation. "It's our new town square—places like this where people gather informally and nod, say hello, and maybe exchange some small talk," McCain said. "I think we're finding ourselves more and more isolated in our social lives, and the traditional ways that brought people together have gone by the wayside. I don't think bingo parlors exist anymore, and VFWs and Elks Clubs and Moose Lodges are growing emptier every day. So we're casting about for new ways to connect and new ways to serve. Some of us find it over coffee. Others stand ready to do bigger things."

This is good news if you're a political, business, or religious leader. The public's insatiable hunger for connection offers enormous opportunities to create Gut Values Connections with voters, customers, and worshipers.

If you're a typically disconnected American, this chapter brings good news, too, because in the history of mankind there's never been so many ways to build new relationships, strengthen old ones, and create and control your sense of community. In times like these, when government, business, and social institutions rarely fail to fail, perhaps the only thing the people of Applebee's America can count on is one another.

## THE NEW MEANING OF COMMUNITY

Today's community is what you make of it, where and how you want it. *Merriam-Webster's Collegiate Dictionary* defines community as "the people with common interests living in a particular area"—practically synonymous with the word "neighborhood." But a neighborhood is just a place where people happen to live. These days, a community is the social circle they choose to inhabit.

"The Internet has knocked down the traditional barriers to participation and community," said Scott Heiferman, cofounder and CEO of Meetup (www.meetup.com). Americans are no longer limited by the neighborhoods where they own homes, the places they drive their cars, the airfare they can afford, or the long-distance calls they make—not even by the oceans and lines on a map. Everybody—and anybody—is a potential neighbor.

Advances in transportation and technology allow people to connect beyond the traditional gathering places (town squares, union halls, parish churches, and social groups such as the Rotary and Optimist

Clubs) with anyone, anywhere. On top of that, successful political, business, and religious leaders have already begun to capitalize on the public's growing desire to connect and belong.

So we have people zipping past dozens of mainline churches to visit megachurches an hour from their homes, where they worship with fellow evangelicals on Sunday and break up into social groups on weekdays. *That is a community*.

Or we have a dozen or so antiwar Democrats finding one another through an Internet site in 2003 and meeting monthly at a bar in suburban Washington, D.C., to discuss the fledgling presidential campaign of a little-known candidate named Howard Dean. *That's a community*.

Or we have 130,000 supporters of President Bush gathering in living rooms across the country on the same evening after receiving campaign e-invitations from their neighbors and friends. *That's a community*.

Or we have an Applebee's restaurant in Shreveport, Louisiana, that was so important to Lucille Ann "Luann" Atchley that her obituary said she was survived by "the employees and friends at Applebee's where she enjoyed dining regularly." *That's a community*.

Americans are reaching out to one another in so many ways. In their living rooms, on their front porches, through housing associations, card clubs, PTA meetings—all the traditional avenues for building relations, plus millions of new e-routes. We found three types of people whose actions exemplify the emerging new spirit of American community.

**Social entrepreneurs.** These are people using the Internet and other technologies to hook up with others both online and offline. Tens of millions of people are playing fantasy sports and interactive video games, making new friends, or staying in touch with old ones. Instant messaging has made a big thing out of small talk. Facebook, MySpace, and similar Web sites help people expand their social networks online. eHarmony and other Internet dating services fulfill people's short-term social needs and fuel the hope of finding a long-term "soul mate." Nearly 2 million people with more than four thousand separate interests have found one another through Meetup. There are "Meetups" for everyone: stay-at-home moms, pug lovers, Italian speakers, *Star Trek* fans, and belly dancers.

**Civic entrepreneurs.** These are people who connect with others primarily to help their communities. Thousands of them found ways to help after Katrina, driving to the Gulf Coast and donating to charities. Citizen journalists are using their Internet blogs to address issues ignored by the mainstream media, a phenomenon that affected the 2004 presidential election.

**Social capitalists.** These are the growing number of people who are doing both—hooking up *and* doing good deeds. A group of Meetup belly dancers raised money for Katrina victims. U.S. soldiers used an unofficial Web site to learn battle and training techniques from one another. Bloggers revealed a flaw in a popular bicycle lock, forcing the company to recall the locks and reexamine its relationship with the vast online biking community.

Social capitalists often step in where government, business, and other institutions either can't or won't take care of people's needs. As people lose faith in these institutions, the demand for social capitalists rises.

Skeptics will say that while technology is making it easier for people to connect online, relationships formed by social entrepreneurs are short-lived and might not ever involve person-to-person contact. But any production of social capital is a good thing for society, and furthermore, the Internet is nurturing more offline relationships than most people realize.

You could go on the Meetup Web site now and find a bowling club in New York City that flouts Putnam's theory of civic disengagement. They're no longer bowling alone. "It's meant to be ultracasual and appealing to people who are mediocre to poor bowlers and don't have friends who want to go bowling," said Deidre (she did not want her last name published), who organizes the monthly get-togethers at a Chelsea Piers bowling alley. "We make it irreverent as possible. It's not a bowling league. It's a social league."

Some may wonder why we included civic entrepreneurs and examples of people rising to help victims of Hurricane Katrina. After all, these were onetime actions that did not create a permanent community. But that does not make them any less important to our discussion about civic engagement: when government failed the Gulf Coast, they leaped into the breach. If that is not a testament to America's spirit of community, nothing is.

## A CLAMOR FOR COMMUNITY

Whether people are using new technologies or more traditional channels, a new spirit of engagement is flourishing in America. In their 2003 book *The Influentials* that inspired some of the Bush campaign strategies, Ed Keller and Jon Berry said the importance of community had been growing since the mid-1990s. The trend was most pronounced among Navigators (they called them Influentials*), grassroots opinion leaders who tend to be on the leading edge of social trends. Keller and Berry reported a 14-point increase in the percentage of Navigators who said people have a responsibility to help the less fortunate; a 10-point increase in the percentage of those who said business should consider society's interests; and an 8-point gain in the percentage of those expressing a responsibility to their neighbors and community.

Three fourths of Navigators said "the community I live in is an important part of who I am."

Americans in general are becoming more civic-minded. In the year following the September 11, 2001, terrorist strikes, the U.S. Census for the first time asked Americans whether they regularly volunteered— and 59 million said yes. Experts expected the number to decline as the post–September 11 civic spirit receded, but that has yet to happen. The number of volunteers climbed to 63 million in 2002–03; 64 million in 2003–04; and 65.4 million from September 2004 to September 2005, according to the Bureau of Labor Statistics' analyses of census data.

John Bridgeland, head of the White House Domestic Policy Council and USA Freedom Corps during George W. Bush's first term, urged the Census Bureau to add the question to its survey in 2001. He said the growing numbers reflect a new spirit in America. "People are starting to

---

* Influentials℠ and Influential Americans® are, respectively, a service mark and a registered trademark of GfK NOP.

realize what the Founding Fathers meant by 'pursuit of happiness.' It's not what they thought it was—going shopping, buying a big house, or chasing the fast-track career. It is what the Founding Fathers intended. When you come to the end of your life, how will you answer this question: 'What did I do to help my community, my country, and the world?' People are asking that question now, and they're answering the call. They're not always doing it in traditional ways, but they're doing it," said Bridgeland, who now runs Civic Enterprises, a public policy firm that helps corporations, nonprofits, foundations, and governments develop policies to strengthen communities. He noted that one of the longest-sustained applause lines of President Bush's 2002 State of the Union address was this call to service: "We want to be a nation that serves goals larger than self. We have been offered a unique opportunity, and we must not let this moment pass."

Even skeptics such as Putnam point to recent increases in voter turnout and the rise of megachurches as evidence that the nation may be entering a period of community renewal. "If the trend goes down for thirty years and then goes up for three or four years, we can't be sure whether it's just a blip or part of a long-term trend," he told us. "But it's a positive sign, no doubt."

Putnam's best-selling book was loaded with research on the raft of fraternal organizations and clubs (the Shriners, Knights of Columbus, and Elks Clubs, among others) that grew out of the last period of social upheaval—the turn of the twentieth century, when America was transitioning from an agrarian to an industrial society. Membership rolls grew until the 1950s and 1960s, when they began a steady descent. Putnam used a variety of surveys to track drops in other forms of social capital. He blamed the declines on pressures of time and money, mobility and sprawl, technology and the mass media, and generational shifts.

What went little noticed was Putnam's suggestion that this would not be a permanent condition. "It is emphatically not my view that community bonds in America have weakened steadily throughout history—or even throughout the last hundred years. On the contrary, American history carefully examined is a story of ups and downs in civic engagement, *not just downs*—a story of collapse *and* of renewal,"

Putnam wrote. ". . . Within living memory the bonds of community in America were becoming stronger, not weaker, and . . . it is within our power to reverse the decline of the last several decades."

Putnam found reason for hope in the country's next generation of leaders, particularly those who were in high school and college during the September 11, 2001, terrorist attacks. "Perhaps the younger generation today is no less engaged than their predecessors, but engaged in new ways," he said. High levels of civic-mindedness mark *Generation 9/11* as a special one. While other age groups returned to normal levels of civic engagement a few months after the attacks, Putnam said after the publication of his book, those who were in high school or college on September 11 maintained their enthusiasm for politics, religion, and volunteering. Voting rates among eighteen- to twenty-four-year-olds are increasing two to twelve times faster than other age groups. Surveys show that young adults are expressing heightened interest in government and social issues. In many ways, members of Generation 9/11 are more like their grandparents' generation than their parents' generation. The so-called Greatest Generation maintained its high levels of civic involvement throughout their lives, something that can't be said for their boomer children.

Unlike Putnam, we don't draw the line at Generation 9/11. It is our contention that Americans in general are increasingly investing in social capital, and they are *engaged in new ways* that are hard for twentieth-century social scientists to measure.

## NETVILLE: THE FUTURE OF WIRED COMMUNITIES

Critics contend that the Internet and other technologies are pulling people apart, reducing civic engagement more than building it up. They are wrong. Technologies nurture old connections and help create new ones, as we will illustrate later with stories about Meetup, instant messaging, video games, war games, and citizen journalism.

A Pew Internet & American Life Project study released in 2006 found that the Internet and e-mail expand and strengthen offline social ties. Internet users have larger social networks than nonusers, and they get more out of them, according to the study. People who e-mail their close friends and family on a regular basis also telephone those same people 25 percent more than non-e-mailers. Heavy e-mail users are 50 percent more likely than non-e-mailers to also meet their social contacts in person, the study found.

"The larger, the more far-flung, and the more diverse a person's network, the more important e-mail is," said Jeffrey Boase, a University of Toronto sociologist who coauthored the report. "You can't make phone calls or personal visits to all your friends very often, but you can 'cc' them regularly with a couple of keystrokes. That turns out to be very important."

People not only socialize online, the report said, but those who use the Internet are far more likely to seek information and advice from their friends and family than those who don't. Forty-five percent of Internet users—about 60 million Americans—say the Internet has played an important or crucial role in helping them deal with at least one major life decision in the previous two years, such as a family health crisis or finding a job. That is a 33 percent increase from a similar survey in 2002.

Keith Hampton, an assistant professor in the Annenberg School for Communication at the University of Pennsylvania, knows firsthand the power of technology to draw people together. When he was associated with the Massachusetts Institute of Technology in October 1997, Hampton moved to a Toronto exurb (he gave it the pseudonym "Netville") and began a two-year study on the impact of cutting-edge information and communication technologies installed in the community. Netville was built from the ground up with a broadband high-speed computer network supplied and operated free of charge by a consortium of private and public companies that wanted to test its impact.

At the time, Netville was growing fast and housing was booming. Commuting time from Netville to Toronto's downtown was 45 minutes at best, twice as long at rush hour. Homes ranged in size from 1,700 to 2,600 square feet, were typically built on small lots, and ranged in price from $195,000 to $255,000. The typical Netville home had three bedrooms and a study. Of the 109 homes that comprised Netville, 64 had access to the network services, which included an online jukebox, online health services, local discussion forums, entertainment and educational applications, and twenty-four-hour, seven-days-a-week technical support. The remaining homes were not connected.

"Wired Netville residents—those connected to the local computer network—recognized three times as many, talked with twice as many, and visited with 50 percent more of their neighbors compared to their non-wired counterparts," Hampton wrote.

Intense local politics flourished in Netville. "Within the first nine months that homes had been occupied, Netville residents had begun an organized campaign to pressure the developer into addressing their problems and concerns," Hampton wrote. He estimated that more than half of the households were involved in active protests against the developer, despite the fact that the housing problems were "little more than routine for a new residential development." They organized though e-mails and meetings, both online and offline.

Within the first few months, a neighborhood e-mail tree was used by residents for a wide range of community-building activities, including exchanging introductions; organizing barbecues, parties, and other informal activities; exchanging information on local services; sharing information related to the local government; and helping children locate potential friends and ask for help with homework.

"The great thing about e-mail lists is that you're not presented with visual cues that would normally affect how you form new social circles," Hampton told us this year. "Usually when we form ties, it's based on similar ages and genders. We'll be pushing a buggy and chat with somebody else pushing a buggy. The e-mail list allows a whole different array of clues to be sent out not necessarily based on gender, age, race, and ethnicity. We find those visual clues are disappearing, and people are forming bonds with a more diverse group of people, based on similar hobbies, interests. It's more about lifestyles than life cycles."

The last half of this chapter will highlight a few of the many ways people are building twenty-first-century communities.

# TWENTY-FIRST-CENTURY CIVIC ENGAGEMENT:
# THE POWER OF COMMUNITIES

## Meetup

Wendall Wu pops the volleyball high in the air and on a gentle arc to his teammate James Davies, who spikes it past the opposing players. Wu, Davies, and their fellow teammates applaud.

Standing on the sideline, Katie Paradiso, twenty-three, joins in the applause, giggling, and turns to a stranger standing next to her. "I can't tell you how glad I am that I found these people."

Paradiso found them on the Internet. Just a month earlier, she was sitting in her Forestville, New York, home in front of a computer, scanning the Internet for anything she could learn about Arlington, Virginia. Paradiso was about to start graduate school at Marymount University in the Washington, D.C., suburb and knew nobody from the area.

An avid player, she typed in the word "volleyball" on the Google site, and it directed her to Meetup, the Web site that helps people find others with similar interests. A few more keystrokes, and she found a group of volleyball enthusiasts who play near Marymount. Better still, they also get together outside the gym at local restaurants and bars. Paradiso had found herself a community of *social entrepreneurs*.

"I love volleyball, and I wanted to meet new people," she said. "The Internet allowed me to do both."

Wu, the organizer of Paradiso's new social circle, is a psychiatry resident at nearby Georgetown University. He pays a few dollars each month to Meetup for use of the site to organize his volleyball club. It tells people when and where to meet and provides message boards for them to communicate. With his wide, dark eyes and tall, muscular physique, the young doctor has no trouble finding dates or making friends. Still, he likes how Meetup cuts away at the barriers to socialization. "I find it difficult to meet people in bars and stuff because most of us probably don't have common interests. It's much easier to find friends if you know from the start you have at least one common interest, that one core thing, that binds you together."

Meetup was founded in 2002 and its mission is as simple as it is ambitious: revitalize community in America. Its cofounder Scott Heiferman was living in New York during the September 11 attacks and was inspired by the community spirit that rose seemingly out of nowhere. "It was always there, but it took the attacks for people to realize how much they really needed each other," he said. "People do have more to give."

The Meetup Web site provides social entrepreneurs the tools to give more of themselves to one another. It is a collection of local interest groups that organize online and meet regularly offline. The majority of Meetup participants are female; a plurality of them are baby boomers. Anybody can start a Meetup about anything: witches, knitters, food lovers, stay-at-home moms, books, Elvis, poodles, and thousands of other categories.

In the fall of 2004, Harvard professor Putnam gave Heiferman the National Conference on Citizenship's Jane Addams Award for civic entrepreneurship (named after the Progressive Era reformer who decried the lack of public services in the late nineteenth century). Calling Heiferman's creation an example of using online tools to build offline relationships, Putnam declared, "We know there are genuine connections, real new connections, created by this new technology."

Some Meetup clubs grow into bastions of civic entrepreneurship and grassroots organizing.

Roberta Bailey likes pugs—the jowly, wrinkly faced breed of dog she keeps as a pet. She also likes punk rock and people. Through Meetup, the Manhattan photographer found a way to combine her interests: she organized a group of Pug owners who fought to save a legendary punk venue. "I got off my butt and did something cool," she said. Bailey organized a "Million Pug March" in Washington Square Park to show support for the venerable club CBGB. It's as close to political activism as she has ever come.

Philip Lutz is a divorced father who believes that he and others got "raw deals" in custody cases. He used Meetup and other Internet tools to organize meetings of divorced men who lost custody of their children. Gathering in homes, churches, and community centers in the Philadelphia area, the men swap stories, complaints, and advice. One of Lutz's groups found a sponsor for a fathers' rights bill in the state legislature, and he worked his e-mail list to build support. "When we get together in a group, they realize they're not alone—and they can do something about their problems," Lutz said.

Cindy Seip, forty-one, organized gatherings of belly dancers in Fort Lauderdale, Florida, who ran an online auction that raised $484 for Katrina victims. Still, the group's primary purpose is to hook up and hang out. A favorite activity is taking their husbands to shows that have nothing to do with belly dancing. "We do the kind of things our parents used to do—go out on the town or get together and play cards or whatever," said this social capitalist. "The TV and computer took all of that away for a while. We could just sit at home and be away from everybody. Now, Meetups are one way that we not only meet people online, but we get together face to face."

For some people, Meetup is just a way to vent. Adam Wolbaum, twenty-three, is into the gothic subculture in his hometown of Edmonton, Alberta, Canada. A brooding, sharp-tongued parttime telemarketer, Wolbaum started a Meetup group to inspire relationships among youngsters who revel in their status as outcasts. Its 180 participants, including an active core of about 20, raised money for Katrina victims, staged water fights, and "pretty much just hung out." The group's Meetup site offers a glimpse into the goth culture, if not the yearning for connection in all of us. One posting by "Vanesti" starts out, "Well, it's that wonderfully depressive time of the year again. It's my birthday on Oct. 5th. I'm poor, depressed and oh so lonely. No relationship with a guy (which I really bloody want). Feel like I have no friends (mostly cuz I've been being a hermit)."

Wolbaum said he thinks he knows Vanesti. "She's a new girl who just started showing up. We'll start watching her back. She's one of us now. Actually, she's always been one of us. Now she's found us."

Heiferman said a perfect world would have a Meetup for everybody "because there's somebody out there for everybody." In the twentieth century, people gravitated to fraternal organizations that were designed to serve the masses. Today, technology and mobility are allowing people to put themselves into smaller, intimate categories. This is a Niche

Nation, where politicians and companies LifeTarget and megachurches sponsor small groups centered on hundreds of disparate hobbies. In a nation of niches, why shouldn't there be a Meetup (or something like it) for everybody?

## Instant Messaging

MontoyaMom: hey sweetie. Did u call?
JessieGirl: yea.
JessieGirl: I can't believe a/b ashton and demi!
MontoyaMom: me either—they are so kaballah.
JessieGirl: weird.

A community can be as small as two social enterpreneurs and as intimate and familiar as this exchange between Harvard sophomore Jessica Coggins (JessieGirl) and her mother, Regina Montoya, fifty-one (MontoyaMom). Montoya missed her daughter's telephone call but caught up with her on AOL's instant message. They "IM" each other daily, which makes Montoya a rarity among baby boomers. Nearly two thirds of people between ages eighteen and twenty-seven use instant messaging, according to the Pew Internet & American Life Project's 2004 survey. Less than a third of leading baby boomers (ages 50 to 58) such as Montoya use the technology.

JessieGirl: I went to pfoho (a Harvard dorm) last night.
MontoyaMom: cute guys rights?
JessieGirl: ooooh yes. except I didn't see my 'mr. pfoho.'
MontoyaMom: who is? isn't he the preppy guy
JessieGirl: no. well.
JessieGirl: he's a little preppy.
JessieGirl: he is TALL.
JessieGirl: and dorky in a good way
MontoyaMom: from where
JessieGirl: Montana
JessieGirl: I didn't know ppl lived there
MontoyaMom: You can't be preppy if u are from Montana.

Montoya first started using instant messaging on a regular basis when her daughter went away to college. She said it's a great way to stay in touch. Indeed, nearly one in three teens who use instant message or text messaging do so to communicate with their parents. The mother said she occasionally uses instant message to chat with her friends and colleagues. "They get surprised when I do," she said. By contrast, Jessica routinely uses instant messaging to communicate with her peers and estimates that just 20 percent of her IM chats are with her mother. Montoya is a Dallas lawyer and the CEO of a Washington-based Latino advocacy group, a job that requires her to travel often. "I always have a computer with me," the mother said. "This is how we keep in touch."

MontoyaMom: is he a repub?
JessieGirl: I think Montana and I think the Unabomber
JessieGirl: he's liberal!
MontoyaMom: and nasty hair, a beard carrying a rifle
JessieGirl: mommy!

Jessica said her friends admire her mom for instant messaging. "It's really cool to be a with-it mother," Montoya said, laughing. Mother and daughter said they rarely talk by telephone now, but they feel closer than ever because of the informal and continual IM connections. "I keep up a lot more with what's going on, and I have more of a day-to-day sense of the issues. Occasionally, it will occur where the conversation gets more complicated, and then I'll ask if I can call. Then we stop and call each other," the mother said.

JessieGirl: I like my nip/tuck!
MontoyaMom: but you need to check first [on direct TV]
JessieGirl: ok
MontoyaMom: hey just told ur dad. Call him b/c he would love to talk
MontoyaMom: he is so proud
JessieGirl: that I watch nip/tuck?

In August 2005, AOL's instant messaging system had 195 million users, up from 70 million in 2000. Other instant messaging services experience similar growth. People share more than words through instant messaging. A Pew study in 2005 found that half of IM-using teens have included a link to an interesting or funny article or Web site in an instant message. Nearly half have used IM to send photos or documents. Almost a third of teens using IM have sent music or video files via the technology. Some instant messaging programs allow people to reach out to others beyond their immediate acquaintances. A third of instant message users have posted a profile for their IM screen name that others not on their buddy list can see, according to Pew. Other instant messengers using the same IM program can conduct random searches, locate an individual, and contact them. "In addition to conducting conversations, IM users post profiles and add people to buddy lists to expand their social circles," reads the 2004 Pew Report. And there's nothing like it to help keep an existing social circle intact. Nearly a third of teens who use IM or text messaging will use those tools to communicate with their parents.

> **JessieGirl:** jay harris is having an open house
> MontoyaMom: who is jay harris
> **JessieGirl:** our house master
> MontoyaMom: what's his background?
> **JessieGirl:** jewish studies
> **JessieGirl:** he's definitely one of the top three house masters.
> MontoyaMom: cool.
> **JessieGirl:** I loooooooove you.
> MontoyaMom: and I luv u.

## Howard Dean

While President Bush tapped into church lists, gun clubs, and other existing social networks, Howard Dean's team used the Internet to create new ones.

It all started pragmatically enough when Dean was a little-known former Vermont governor on an underdog's quest for the Democratic presidential nomination. His campaign manager, Joe Trippi, found a cheap, easy way to organize supporters via the Internet: the Meetup Web site. In June 2003, witches were the No. 1 Meetup group, but Dean-for-president supporters were quietly climbing the charts because of a link at the campaign Web site. It was so easy to do: the Dean site routed supporters to Meetup.com, which put them a keystroke away from getting an invitation and directions to the next Dean Meetup at a nearby bar, coffee shop, or restaurant.

That's how Diana Read found herself sitting beneath an "Electrify Your Love" ad board at a bar in Tysons Corner, Virginia, Running a hand through her curly white hair, she turned to the man sitting next to her and asked, "Have you been here before?" Under any other circumstances, that would have been a pickup line. Not here. Not on the first Wednesday in June 2003, when there were 259 Dean-for-president Meetups taking place in 239 cities, including this bar in suburban Washington with twenty-five Democrats meeting in the back. Most of them knew each other from past meetings. It had the feel of a club, a Dean club.

"Time to break out the checkbooks!" shouted Austin Morrill, a high-energy real estate agent who seemed to be in charge of the meeting.

"How's the kids?" a housewife, Amy Rothstein, asked the woman sitting next to her. Picking a piece of popcorn off her wood sweater, Janet Hooks sighed and said, "They're driving me crazy. I don't get out enough. This is a godsend."

The next day, Dean was giving a speech in Washington. "The Meetup people have made it possible for me to no longer just be an insurgent candidate because they've given us an organization that we otherwise would have had to pay for," he said.

Standing behind him, campaign signs in hand were three people from the Meetup meeting the night before, including Rothstein. "Friends stick together," she said. "These are my friends. This is my cause in life now."

By the time Dean dropped out of the race, 640,937 people had registered as supporters through the candidate's Web site; 188,941 of those had signed up to receive notices of meetings in their areas. About 75,000 of them actually attended a meeting, according to Matthew

Hindman's *The Real Lessons of Howard Dean: Reflections of the First Digital Campaign*. It was a milestone year for community building via the Internet; Bush had an astounding 2 million people in his database by the time Dean dropped out.

"I think I tapped into a craving for community in a society where we are becoming increasingly isolated from ourselves," Dean said in 2005. Many of his 2004 supporters had considered themselves disenfranchised from the political process, but through Meetup and other efforts by the campaign they suddenly felt as though they were part of an important enterprise.

"What made Dean was our ability to tap into that hunger to belong," Trippi said. "Nobody else did that on the Democratic side."

The Internet did not create the desire to belong, nor did it give politicians the ability to prosper from that sentiment. The craving to connect has always been there. Smart politicians have always tapped into it. But the Internet and other technologies allow political campaigns to connect exponentially more people to one another.

"It's given people faith in strangers again," Trippi said. "I would never nail a sign to a telephone pole inviting people to my home and giving my address, but on the Internet you can have 175,000 people setting up Dean house meetings and showing up, bonding, and belonging. People let their guard down on the Internet for some reason and bond in ways they never would normally."

Karen Hicks organized the house parties for Dean. While the Internet helped bring people together, Hicks said what followed was traditional political organizing. Trained staff helped hosts put together invitation lists and pitch Dean to their friends and neighbors. "The most valuable people to have reaching out to other people are folks they know and trust," Hicks said. "I think people are looking for a referee nowadays. If you're somebody outside of politics, you're most likely not paying attention to the back and forth and the tit for tat. It's all kind of a blur to you and looks the same unless somebody you consider to be credible—a neighbor, a friend, or even a casual associate—makes sense of it for you."

Real community building took place over pastries and coffee. "We had story after story of people actually getting to know their neighbors through this. They lived next door to each other for ten years. Maybe they waved and said hello but they always wondered what it looked like inside the other person's house. The Dean campaign brought them together, which they'd been hoping to do for years but either didn't have the time or opportunity," Hicks said.

It's fashionable to dismiss Dean's organizing tactics because his candidacy flamed out in early 2004. But that is a mistake. The former Vermont governor failed to win the Democratic nomination *because he was a flawed candidate*, not because his grassroots efforts were flawed. He got as far as he did because of his bottom-up organizing tactics, not in spite of them. In opposing the Iraq war and denouncing Democrats who backed it, Dean projected strength, principle, and authenticity. But as 2003 ended, the former Vermont governor committed several gaffes that caused voters to wonder whether he was capable of being president. Dean no longer connected. Once a candidate loses the Values Connection, the best tactics in the world can't save him.

E. J. Dionne Jr., a columnist with *The Washington Post*, captured the essence of Dean's legacy in an article written shortly after his campaign collapsed. He said that critics who mocked the campaign for its community-building methods failed to recognize that a sense of fellowship has always been a reason people join political campaigns.

"The style of the Dean campaign was different suited to a new time and generation. But don't knock the Deaniacs for trying to create a sense of community," he said. "In providing an alternative to the soulless model in which so much campaign work is parceled out to private vendors, they were answering a real demand."

The demand has never been greater with new technologies making it even more intense, a golden opportunity for political, business, or church leaders willing to do what's necessary to give their organizations a soul.

## Fantasy Sports

Ilan Graff is a junkie. A fantasy sports junkie. A Harvard graduate who now works the New Democratic Network in Washington, D.C., Graff plays fantasy football with people associated with the interest group; he plays fantasy baseball with fellow Harvard graduates and their friends; and he is commissioner of a fantasy basketball league with current and former Harvard students.

It's a time-consuming obsession that gives Graff what many young men dream of—control of a major league sports team (even if it's only the statistics-laden jock dream-world created by Graff and his pals). That leads us to a second benefit that fantasy sports give Graff and 30 million others who participate: a sense of community.

"It's a great complement to existing friendships, an easy way to stay in touch," Graff said. "It's also a good way to widen your social circle. There are several people in the baseball league that I had never met. The league gave us something to talk about when we first came face to face."

In fantasy sports, a group of people (nine of ten are men) run mock athletic leagues. The games begin with a "draft" at which the participants take turns picking players off professional league rosters. Drafts can be live or online. Various Web sites help hook up participants, keep track of draft selections, and offer message boards that allow the participants to brag and gripe to one another—virtual "trash talk."

For the remainder of the sports season, the participants compete against one another, gaining points based on the production of the players they draft or obtain later in trades. Some leagues still keep statistics by hand, though Internet leagues let technology handle that chore. Trades can be negotiated live, over the telephone, or via the Internet.

Most fantasy sportsmen are social entrepreneurs making new connections and nurturing old ones. A University of Indiana study in 2000 found that 90 percent of participants cited maintaining friendships as the most important reason for joining a fantasy league, far outpacing other reasons, including being a fan of the sport, having fun, and competing for bragging rights.

"I can believe that," said Daniel Okrent, a legendary journalist credited with inventing Rotisserie baseball (named after the New York restaurant that Okrent and his pals frequented), the forerunner of numerous fantasy sports games. "One of my two best friends in the world was somebody I met on opening day of my first draft."

During the 1979 off-season, Okrent was on a flight from Hartford, Connecticut, to Austin, Texas, when he came up with the idea. "I don't know what prompted me that day other than I was missing baseball," he says. "I had no idea it was going to change the way people look at sports forever."

A month later, Okrent and nine or so pals met to discuss rules. They held their first draft in April 1980. "In connection with your theory that this is a community builder, I don't think any of us knew more than three or four others among us during that first draft." A quarter century later, the group was still going strong and met up at the 2005 World Series, save for one founding member who had quit the league in 1981 and another who had died.

"Who knew? It's kind of stunning. It grew very rapidly in the 1980s, because of the ten of us, eight were in the media and wrote about the teams. That spread the word. Once the Internet took off in the 1990s, that's when it really zoomed," Okrent explains. "I think it being a fantasy is part of the appeal. It allows you to be that one thing you'll never really be—the general manager of a baseball team. Then there's no question that personal interact is an element of it." Unfortunately, Okrent said, the Internet has made it possible to draft, trade, and track scores without any personal interaction, except via e-mail.

That hasn't stopped Dan Epstein, a Harvard student, from keeping tabs with friends from college as well as from his high school track team through a fantasy sports league. "Everybody wants to belong to something," he says. "This is what I belong to and what I do to stay in touch."

Professional sports leagues recognize a bottom-line benefit to this community builder and market their product to fantasy sports enthusiasts. More than 12 million people play fantasy football alone, and the average participant belongs to at least two leagues, spends nearly three hours per week managing his team, and shells out $154 per year on league fees, stat-tracking services, and specialized news and information, according to an article by John Moore on MarketingProfs.com. The Fantasy Sports Trade Association (proof that there's an interest group for everything) estimated that the leagues were a $3 billion industry in 2005.

## Video Games

Growing up in rural True, West Virginia, Kemp Peterson had a close friend who lived forty-five minutes away. They kept in touch by playing online video games, starting with StarCraft and later Halo 2. At college, he plays with his roommates as a group against different "clans" or forms alliances with people he's never met but who have earned a spot on his "friends list."

For many Internet video game players, cyberspace clans become communities that help online social entrepreneurs make connections. According to Peterson, clan groups are "like a group of friends going to play basketball together."

Peterson and his clans are far from alone. Online video gaming is a $1 billion industry. The number of broadband subscribers grew from 5 million in 2000 to 39 million in 2005 and is projected to grow to more than 60 million by 2010, according to one study. Pew Internet & American Life Project surveys show that 70 percent of college students say they play video, computer, or online games at least once in a while. One in five says that gaming helps them make new friends as well as improve existing relationships. Nearly two thirds of students surveyed agreed that gaming helped them spend time when family and friends weren't available. Roughly the same numbers said that gaming takes little or no time away from their friends and family.

"You hang out on a virtual basis," Peterson told one of our researchers, fellow Harvard student Eric Lesser. "You definitely associate them with personalities beyond their style of game playing." He found that games like StarCraft reward players who form communities or clans that work together toward a common objective. A leader always emerges. "If you have a clan, there's going to be a leader of that clan."

## Battle Lessons

It started with a book entitled *Taking the Guidon*, an attempt by Majors Nate Allen and Tony Burgess to explain how to command an army company. Once they decided to post the book on the Internet in March 2000 and, a year later, build a second site designed just for lieutenants,

Allen and Burgess had created themselves a community of social capitalists.

In this case, the common bond was not a block, a neighborhood, or some other geographic location. It was their ranks—captains and lieutenants—and they used the password-protected sites to exchange information about training, fighting, and raising families. They were helping fill in the gaps of normal military training. According to an article by Dan Baum in the January 17, 2005, issue of *The New Yorker*, there are discussion threads on everything from mortar attacks to grief counseling and dishonest sergeants. "Some of the discussions are quite raw. Captains post comments on coping with fear, on motivating soldiers to break the taboo against killing, and on counseling suicidal soldiers. They advise each other on how to kick in doors and how to handle pregnant subordinates. Most captains now have access to the Internet at even the most remote bases in Iraq, and many say they'll find at least ten or fifteen minutes every day to check the site."

The advice is precise and pragmatic. The soldiers are giving one another information and guidance that they're not getting or not getting in time from the larger institution that is the army. Baum collected snippets of conversations posted on CompanyCommand.com and PlatoonLeader in the past year:

> Never travel in a convoy of less than four vehicles. Do not let a casualty take your focus away from a combat engagement. Give your driver your 9mm, and carry their M16/M4. Tootsie Rolls are quite nice; Jolly Ranchers will get all nasty and sticky though.

## Hurricane Katrina

Jamie Ferrande and his family, the New Orleans refugees, benefited from a national sense of community after Hurricane Katrina. But so did many others. As local, state, and federal governments bungled the response to the August 2005 natural disaster, civic entrepreneurs filled the breach with a there-by-the-Grace-of-God mentality that is steeped in American culture.

"It's heart-wrenching," a substitute teacher, Liliette Pena, told the Associated Press, stifling sobs as she stood in a long line at Dodgers Stadium in Los Angeles to donate $100. "I'd like to think that if anything like that happened in Los Angeles, people back East would do the same thing."

Americans set new standards for ingenuity and generosity, filling trucks with donated clothes, water, food, and medicine, then driving through the night from hundreds of miles away. They went to the Gulf Coast because it was the right thing to do or because they vaguely felt that their good deeds would be repaid should calamity strike their families. And they gave. More than $500 million was donated in the first ten days, nearly double the amount that poured in from the nation in the same period following the September 11 terror attacks.

In Arkansas, state officials were first told to expect three hundred evacuees. Nobody came. Then the state was told to prepare four thousand meals for a fleet of buses. No buses arrived. Suddenly, without warning and in the middle of the night, more than nine thousand refugees showed up at a National Guard post. "It rained people on us," said Governor Mike Huckabee, a Republican.

While the Federal Emergency Management Agency floundered, Huckabee and his team turned a network of church-run camps (normally used by children and families in the summer months) into temporary communities for refugees. Each camp had a designated mayor and police chief. Some had clothing stores, barbershops, and "mini–M.A.S.H units" to take care of the sick. When the promised aid from FEMA got lost in a tangle of bureaucracy, the state helped refugees find jobs for themselves and schools for their children.

"These were instant communities, and you'd be amazed at how smoothly they functioned," Huckabee told us. "Not just because of what we did at the state level, but because of what the church officials, local volunteers, and average Joes did by pitching in and helping out. In the midst of this misery, which is what these people were going through, I found this sense of community uplifting."

Cyberspace played a major role in connecting and reconnecting people after Katrina struck. Tens of thousands of people shared stories of grief, searched for the missing, and found comfort in messages they posted across the Internet. On the largest Web sites, such as those run by the American Red Cross and Yahoo!, the names of more than

200,000 missing people were posted shortly after the disaster. Storm victims posted pictures of themselves taken with cell phones. Some kept Internet-based logs.

One such blogger was Kaye D. Trammell, who later wrote in a *Washington Post* op-ed piece what the Internet meant to her as she waited out the storm. "I was without power, sitting alone in my dark apartment with winds howling all around me. My blog was the only thing keeping me calm. It connected me to people out there waiting for my next post. These people were talking back to me, feeding me information from the outside world about what was happening. Even though this was my first hurricane 'alone,' it was also my first in which I was comforted from around the world."

## Citizen Journalists

Trammell's blog did more than bring her comfort. It also brought news of Katrina's devastation to the outside world. She provided intimate, first-person context to the mass media's coverage. There were hundreds of blogs filed by citizen journalists like Trammell, an assistant professor in the Manship School of Mass Communication at Louisiana State University. "These blogs no longer belong to the bloggers but to the community, as a centralized mechanism for communication and comfort in the face of natural disaster," she wrote.

In general, blogs are a virtual community—just as real and active as the traditional neighborhood. In his book *We the Media*, the newspaper columnist Dan Gillmor argues that technology is changing the media industry by creating a communications tool kit that allows anyone to become a journalist at little cost and, in theory, with global reach. "In the 20th century, making the news was almost entirely the province of journalists; the people we covered, or 'newsmakers;' and the legions of public relations and marketing people who manipulate everyone. The economics of publishing and broadcasting created large, arrogant institutions—call it Big Media, though even small-town newspapers and broadcasters exhibit some of the phenomenon's worst symptoms."

The reason citizen journalists are growing in power is because their blogs are communities of like-minded people who can affect change. Without a community of people reading and writing a blog, it would be no more influential than a community activist standing on a street corner with a thousand fliers and nobody around to take them.

Tens of thousands of people are taking advantage of their new powers to report from the front lines of American life. These social capitalists traffic in community news, gossip, and classified ads. One such site is Backfence.com, a Virginia-based site that bills itself as a forum of discussion of "the kinds of things that used to be talked about over the back fence." Community chatter used to be the parlance of local newspapers, which are declining in numbers and increasingly owned by corporate conglomerates. Once again, technology is allowing people to fill the role of a failing or changing institution.

In 2002, Senator Trent Lott heaped a bit too much praise on fellow Senator Strom Thurmond while celebrating the former segregationist's hundredth birthday. He said that the country "wouldn't have had all these problems over the years" if it had elected Thurmond president in 1948. The story was slow to build, barely noticed by the major media. Liberal bloggers, such as Joshua Marshall on Talking Points Memo, jumped on the case and several conservatives also chimed in, keeping the story alive until the mainstream media finally picked up on it. Five days after his remarks, Lott was forced to apologize. Two days after that, Bush called the comments "offensive"—and Lott was toast. He gave up his leadership post fifteen days after Thurmond's birthday. "While bloggers could not have brought down Lott on their own had Big Media not taken up the story, the Lott debacle was, by all accounts, a watershed," wrote Gillmor. The conservative John Podhoretz wrote in his *New York Post* column that Weblogs had claimed "their first scalp."

It wasn't their last.

In the 2004 presidential campaign, the political press corps repeatedly found itself a step behind—or totally out of step with— the growing community of political bloggers. In the spring, a group of Republican-funded Vietnam War veterans who patrolled the Mekong Delta in Swift boats similar to the ones piloted by Navy Lieutenant John Kerry challenged the Democratic presidential nominee's account of his medal-winning service. The initial news conference of the Swift Vets and POWs for Truth was largely ignored, because mainstream media news organizations didn't give the charges any credence.

A few months later, the group bought $40,000 worth of advertising time to air their ads in three states. It was a puny buy, and once again Big Media turned a deaf ear, doing relatively little to either confirm or deny the group's allegations. News organizations such as the Associated Press, *The New York Times*, *The Washington Post*, and the television networks were still playing their outdated role as news "gatekeepers," the ultimate and infallible arbiters of what Americans need to know.

It didn't fly. Thousands of mostly anonymous people, empowered by what Gillmor calls their twenty-first century tool kits, kept the controversy alive on the Internet until Kerry finally denied the charges. His decision to go public made it a mainstream story. The Swift Boat group eventually raised nearly $7 million, much of it from grassroots supporters.

That's not the only example of citizen journalists driving the news in the 2004 campaign. The blog community (it even has a name: Blogosphere) was the first to challenge the authenticity of documents used by the CBS News anchor Dan Rather to question Bush's National Guard service. Experts and hobbyists on typewriter fonts came out of the virtual woodwork, trading information and opinions as they built a case that the documents had been forged. They sent thousands of e-mails to reporters, who quickly found their own experts to confirm the data whipping through cyberspace. The network's report was discredited. An internal report led to the firing of three news executives, and Rather left the anchor chair in March 2005, his long career ending under a cloud.

In the future, political operatives and mainstream reporters covering them will be required to monitor blogs to keep pace with citizen journalists and rumormongers on the Internet. Smart political campaigns will take things a step further and assign dozens of staff or volunteers to *respond* to Internet chatter, injecting the campaign's message to the Blogosphere. These electronic communities cannot be ignored by candidates any more than a traditional neighborhood can be slighted.

There's a lesson here for corporate America. Just as the Dan Rather fiasco was breaking, Donna Tocci learned the power of the Blogosphere—in this case, brought on not by forged memos or a loose-lipped senator but by a Bic pen. On September 12, 2004, someone with the Web name "unaesthetic" posted in a group discussion site for bicycle enthusiasts an intriguing bit of news: the U-shaped Kryptonite bike lock could be picked with a Bic ballpoint pen. It was the beginning of two sleepless weeks for Tocci, the company's sole public relations executive.

According to her version of events, the company realized the next day (September 12 was a Sunday, and the twenty-five-person Kryptonite staff was off) that it had a potential problem because people reading the Internet forum had began to call with their concerns. Company officials began trying to re-create the lock picking on its products, and issued a statement on Tuesday promising some answers in forty-eight hours. Another release went out later in the week suggesting that the company would replace locks and promising further details by Wednesday of the next week.

That wasn't quick enough, not for the community of bike enthusiasts who were closely following the company's actions, exchanging information and rumor over a virtual back fence. Two days after the first posting, a number of blogs, including the consumer electronics site Engadget, posted a video demonstrating how to pick a Kryptonite lock. Every day, new bloggers joined the fray and hundreds of thousands of people were reading about the faulty locks. Eventually, Big Media caught up. On September 16, the AP reporter Theo Emery filed this story:

> BOSTON (AP)—You don't have to be the Man of Steel to open a Kryptonite bike lock.
>
> Faster than a speeding bullet, word is spreading across the Internet, through cyclist hangouts and into bike shops that all it takes to open a circular-key lock, like the one on the famous U-shaped Kryptonite-brand lock, is a ballpoint pen.

On September 22, Kryptonite announced it would exchange locks for any customer who didn't feel comfortable with their old ones. Nearly 100,000 locks were shipped free of charge to customers who returned locks that were as much as fifteen years old.

Tocci said the company played everything by the book. Kryptonite confirmed the problem with the locks, responded to complaints individually, issued several press releases, geared up for new manufacturing demands, and announced a voluntary exchange program—all within ten days. "That's remarkably fast in the old world," she said. "But a bit too slow in the new."

In hindsight, Tocci said she would have posted on the company Web site sooner that Kryptonite was investigating the claims. She also would have already built relationships with the most influential bloggers who regularly write about the close-knit biking community, just as she had done for mainstream journalists. A company blog might have helped, she said. Tocci now works with a Web consultant to learn how to detect and respond to blog-fueled crises. We'd suggest that companies keep a band of Internet-savvy volunteers or staff on standby in case a public relations crisis erupts and the firm's message needs to be catapulted into the Blogosphere, where word-of-mouth communication rules.

Tocci said she learned two lessons from the experience. First, authenticity and accountability are potent business values. "Think of a product you've had in your house for fifteen years. We're going to openly admit that it doesn't work. We're going to replace it. We're going to pay all your shipping costs and send you a new one. Most companies don't do that. We did, and we survived a major problem because we made ourselves as transparent and accountable as possible."

But her biggest takeaway is that tech-driven citizen journalists do not even pretend to be detached observers like their counterparts in Big Media. They are active members of a *community*, personally invested in how their *virtual neighborhood* is affected by a corporation or its products.

"That's why it's so easy for falsehoods to spread," she said. "When people tell you something with authority on a blog, you tend to believe them because they're part of your community."

## LESSONS FOR LEADERS:
## CONNECTING THROUGH COMMUNITY

Communities are the key to connecting.

Successful political campaigns tap into existing social networks (President Bush) or create new ones (Dean) to spread their message peer to peer. Traditional political advertising has lost influence because the media has become fragmented and voters more cynical. The best way to talk to voters is the oldest and most authentic one: word-of-mouth communication via a social network.

The other advantage of a network-based political organization is that it fosters the sense that every volunteer or paid staff member is a key contributor to a grand cause. The desire to be a part of something bigger than one's self lingers in most Americans, especially in a time of war, which is why McCain's idea of rallying voters behind some national purpose is still an effective way to forge a Gut Values Connection.

Dean barely tapped the potential for organizing political communities on the Internet. Joe Green, a Harvard senior who helped us research this book, is the founder of a social networking Web site called essembly.com that allows community members to debate issues, exchange biographical information, organize political activity, identify people who share their beliefs, and sort themselves into ideologically similar groups. The nonpartisan site is designed so that campaigns or political groups can identify supporters and get them to recruit like-minded friends to the cause.

In corporate America, the bike lock fiasco shows what happens when a business ignores its community of customers on the Internet. Blogs offer enormous potential for businesses to find Navigators on those sites.

Whether online or offline, a community gives companies a word-of-mouth communications channel that is more credible than their TV ads—a point we'll explore more deeply in the next chapter. Successful companies like Applebee's create a sense of community in their workforce and with their customers that builds loyalty.

A typical megachurch is a collection of tiny communities—

hundreds of small groups stitched together by a marketing-minded pastor who realizes that Americans, particularly in exurbia, crave a sense of belonging.

Chris Kofinis, a Democratic consultant who specializes in grassroots organizing via the Internet, said that politics, business, and religion will never be the same now that people have the tools to find and motivate like-minded souls. "At a time when we are craving community and meaning in our lives, people are using these technologies to find others with the same complaints and organize them," he said. "They don't have to just sit in a coffee shop and gripe about politics or some product. They can change politics. They can change a business. They're in control, even if many of them don't even realize it yet."

## *Beyond the Horizon*

### TEN TIPS FOR THE FUTURE

Ten steps for political, business, and religious leaders who want to take advantage of the public's yearning for community:

1. Clearly define your purpose or cause. It's what galvanizes your community.
2. Give your staff the clear sense that they're vital to achieving a common purpose.
3. Build your organization from the bottom up, not the top down. Technology makes grassroots organizing easier than ever.
4. Give your customers/voters/worshipers a say in how the product/campaign/church is marketed. Recognize that the consumer has more control than ever.
5. Tap into existing networks when possible. Create networks where none exist.
6. Be true to your purpose. Authenticity, accountability, and trust are the keys to building a bond or brand.
7. Join the online community of bloggers to catch the first whiff of a crisis and to make sure your message is heard in the cyberspace community.

8. Whenever possible, make your enterprise a Third Place, a community outside home and work for people in search of connection.

9. Donate time and money to community causes. Customers are inclined to support civic-minded companies such as Home Depot, according to Bridgeland, the former head of USA Freedom Corps. At the urging of the Bush White House, more than a thousand companies started Business Strengthening America. They urge their employees to get involved in their communities and are making it easier for them to do so by granting paid leave and organizing service projects.

10. Identifiy the community's leaders (Navigators) and get them on your side. Better still, use the Internet and other tools to create products that draw Navigators together in online communities. They can help you spot trends as well as influence consumers and voters. Businesses and political campaigns will pay top dollar to advertise on a Web site or in other media that attract these twenty-first-century opinion leaders.

# 6

# Navigators

*Information is not knowledge.*

—Albert Einstein

*A wealth of information creates a poverty of attention.*

—Herbert Simon

I N CHAPTER 3, we quoted Rick Warren as saying that Americans are "drowning in information and starving for meaning." Mixed metaphors aside, the megachurch maven put his finger on a critically important change in American society—a revolution, really—that has had an enormous impact on politics, business, and religion.

Let's start with the flood of information. In the 1950s, Americans had a choice of two or three TV networks and no way to change channels without getting off their butts. Five decades later, and it's salad days for couch potatoes; they can aim a remote control between their feet and whip through six hundred channels.

Two decades ago, Americans got their information doled out in small nuggets on somebody else's timetable. The networks required viewers to be in front of the TV at 6:30 P.M. to catch the news. Newspapers published once a day. The library was the only recourse for people who wanted more information than editors and anchors dispensed. Today, a 24/7 news cycle revolves around our lives—with cable TV, satellite radio, e-mails, telephone text messages, Internet news sites, and search engines that allow us to customize the information we get. There are more magazine titles (18,821 in 2004, up 47 percent since 1984), more over-the-air radio stations (13,535, up 44 percent since

1984), more TV stations (1,366, up 68 percent since 1984), and more cable networks (390, up from 28 networks in 1985).

In 1986, keeping in touch meant mailing a letter to a friend or making a long-distance telephone call. Today, instant messages, e-mails, cell phones, and Internet video conferences allow us to seek advice from friends and family on a whim.

When President Clinton took office, the average U.S. household received about 25 TV channels. In 2005, it had four times as many channels. In 1993, there were 130 Internet sites, and now there are tens of millions—a bottomless pit of news, entertainment, products, and virtual companionship. The number of blogs on the Internet went from practically nothing when George W. Bush took office in 2001 to as many as 30 million in 2005.

Pundits predicted that this glut of accessible information would make people more independent—that they would find the information on their own. *Who needs other people telling you what to watch, listen to, or read when you have six hundred TV channels, millions of blogs, WiFi, and an iPod?* Here again, conventional wisdom is wrong. Americans are actually more dependent on people they know and trust to guide them through the treacherous tides of change—people we call Navigators.

Americans are bewildered by the mass of messages thrust at them, and their faith in traditional sources of information has diminished. That's why political, corporate, and religious leaders need to learn more about word-of-mouth marketing and the role Navigators play influencing public opinion.

More than ever, people are seeking a gut check from friends, family, and acquaintances before making major decisions on everything from jobs, finances, and family crises to voting, buying, and where to go to church. Though they don't necessarily help people find the higher meaning that Warren had in mind, Navigators do lead people to a better understanding of these confusing, chaotic times.

A Navigator is anybody who influences an opinion in peer-to-peer conversation. It happens all the time. Recommend a movie to a friend, and you're a Navigator. Urge your brother to vote—Navigator. Drag a pal to church, help a neighbor choose a computer, or gossip about a candidate for PTA president—Navigator, Navigator, Navigator. Studies show that 14 percent to 29 percent of casual conversations have something to do with a product or a service, which means there's a lot of word-of-mouth marketing going on in everyday life.

But some people are much better at it than others. In *The Influentials*, Keller and Berry make a strong case for their theory that one of every ten persons tells the other nine how to vote, where to eat, and what to buy. You know who the master Navigators are in your community. They're the stay-at-home moms whom other mothers turn to for scuttlebutt on the new neighbor, advice on their taxes, or restaurant referrals. They're the firemen who fix the neighbors' cars, give stock tips, and always know the best electronic gadget to buy.

The evidence is mounting that a good word from a trusted friend or coworker is more likely to help a person feel connected to a campaign, product, or church than TV advertisements or celebrity endorsements.

"At a time when the number of media is exploding and marketing is becoming more pervasive throughout life, the channel with the greatest influence in America is neither the traditional media of television, radio, or print advertising nor the new medium of the World Wide Web but the 'human' channel of individual, person-to-person, word-of-mouth communication," Keller and Berry wrote in *The Influentials*. "The challenge, then, for society's institutions—business and government and the people who run them—is to adjust to this new reality in which word of mouth rules and learn the word-of-mouth rules."

More than eight in ten people tell Roper pollsters that their personal network is a primary source of ideas and information about restaurants to try. Seven in ten say that friends, family, and other people are their best sources on new meals, vacation sites, and prescription drugs to buy. Six in ten turn to other people for tips on hotels, health products, movie selections, and which brands are best.

Since 1977, the Roper firm has reported steady increases in the percentages of people who turn first to family, friends, and associates for what movies to see, car to buy, places to visit, health issues, investment tips, and home improvements. "Americans generally are twice as likely to cite word of mouth as the best source of ideas and information in these and other areas as they are to cite advertising," write Keller and Berry.

A Pew Internet & American Life Project study released in 2006 found that 81 percent of Americans had asked a close friend or family member for advice on a major decision such as a health care crisis, personal finances, changing jobs, buying a personal computer, voting in an election, or finding a new place to live. Nearly half of Americans sought help from somebody outside their closest circle of friends and family. In a sign that the new technologies may increase the reliance on Navigators, the study found that Internet users were significantly more likely to seek advice from their social circle than nonusers.

In Barrington, Illinois, a suburb of Chicago, a nondescript guy like Julian Sowa is a Navigator. He's a Little League coach, a church elder, and a regular at Applebee's, none of which would lead you to think he's someone important in his community. But he is. A computer specialist, Sowa is the guy neighbors seek out when they're in the market for a computer. "Before I plunk down $1,200, I'm calling Julian," says Bonnie Kohn, a neighbor. "Sure, I'll look at the ads in the paper and all that, but I don't consider it a good deal until Julian signs off." Multiply that $1,200 purchase times the number of people who pick Sowa's brain in any given year, and you have a force that the local Best Buy should be reckoning with.

In Pittsburgh, Pennsylvania, a stay-at-home mother, Mary Shull, is a Navigator. While volunteering in 2004 for MoveOn.org, a liberal activist group, she collected the e-mail addresses of 1,500 friends and political contacts. When former Republican Joe Hoeffel decided he might run for lieutenant governor of Pennsylvania in 2005, he put Shull on his call list alongside well-known politicians and power brokers. "Ten years ago, somebody like Mary would be as interested as she is in politics, but her circle of influence would not have extended beyond her home or block or even voting precinct," said Hoeffel, a Democrat who gave up his House seat in 2004 for an unsuccessful Senate bid. "Now she's got 1,500 other self-motivated and influential people at her fingertips and carries as much clout as half the people I've been calling."

In Spokane, Washington, Shannon Sullivan's nine-year-old son wanted to know why Mayor James E. West had used a city computer to solicit gay men over the Internet and why nobody was doing anything about it.

"He's the mayor," Sullivan replied.

"Mom, you better do something."

So she did. A single mother with a high school education and no political experience, Sullivan launched a recall campaign that used an Internet site to organize rallies and media events. It turned out that there were thousands of other people in Spokane, who wondered why nobody was doing anything about West. "I was mad at people for not doing anything. I was mad at the system, and I was mad at James West," she said after the successful campaign. "I'm not so mad anymore."

Successful leaders are not slaves to traditional mass media. Cable TV has had more viewers than the broadcast networks since 2001, increasing its share by 28 percentage points in just two decades. In the 1960s, an advertiser could reach 80 percent of U.S. women with an evening spot aired simultaneously on three national TV networks. Today, an ad would have to run on a hundred TV channels to reach the same audience. An episode of *I Love Lucy* drew 70 percent of the available audience in the 1950s. *Desperate Housewives* wins its time slot with less than a third of Lucy's ratings. The Internet's potential for advertising and communicating has just been tapped. Consider the implications when Chicago, Philadelphia, San Francisco, and several other municipalities implement plans to go wireless, making the Internet accessible and affordable to almost anybody, anywhere inside city limits.

"Twenty-five years ago there . . . was a lot more capability to influence people through traditional media. People didn't have dozens of TV channels to watch. They didn't have satellite radio. They didn't have Google and Internet ad blockers," said Dave Balter, president of Boston-based BzzAgent, a firm that specializes in word-of-mouth marketing as a media form. "Consumers are certainly in control. We need to take our case directly to them."

Major advertisers such as Procter & Gamble and American Express are shifting billions of dollars in advertising from old media to niche media and word of mouth. Broadcast TV ads "are less meaningful today because network TV isn't watched by as many consumers as it used to be," said American Express CMO John Hayes. "The couch potato has been replaced by the Web surfer."

Procter & Gamble owns Tremor, a word-of-mouth marketing company focused almost entirely on the teen market. Tremor puts Crest, Tide, Pampers, and other P&G products into the hands of young Navigators, who are urged to talk the items up to friends and family.

Pabst Blue Ribbon beer made a comeback as a "retro beer" after word-of-mouth marketing made it a symbol of authenticity and coolness. It is common practice in the clothing industry to seek out popular youngsters and give these Navigators free apparel in the hope that they'll talk about it with their friends.

Small-group leaders at megachurches are natural Navigators. Applebee's tries to create word-of-mouth buzz by contacting community leaders as part of its "local heroes" program. Starbucks gives away products to grassroots Navigators. The Bush campaign produced the most successful word-of-mouth marketing program of 2004 when its marshaled 7 million volunteers into a massive "buzz" machine.

But political, business, and church leaders need to be careful with buzz marketing. Word-of-mouth communication is effective when it is authentic, a rare burst of honesty in a plastic marketplace. "The reason that word of mouth is so powerful is that it is an honest conversation," said Balter of BzzAgent. "You can't find it with a hundred other messages waiting to be deleted from your inbox."

Trust is a key word here. People are increasingly skeptical of what they hear from official sources such as the media, government, corporations, and other institutions. The Pew Research Center in 2004 found that credibility ratings for the major broadcast and television news outlets had dropped significantly since 1996. The credibility of newspapers has also declined. When CBS anchor Walter Cronkite declared from his anchor chair that the Vietnam War could not be won, Lyndon Johnson shut off his TV and groused, "If I lost Cronkite, I've lost middle America." No news anchor holds that sway today due to a loss of both audience share and credibility.

Some media figures, such as Rush Limbaugh and celebrities such as Oprah Winfrey, have huge powers of persuasion. But their influence is limited to intensely loyal slices of an American public that are becoming more polarized, politically and socially, by the day.

As for politics, faith-in-government ratings dropped steadily after the Vietnam War and remain low after a brief post-9/11 surge. A 2005 Roper analysis found that 69 percent of people believe that "individual Americans" are solving the nation's problems (up 17 points from 1995). No other entity rates higher as a problem solver—not community groups (68 percent), governors (61 percent), the president (55 percent), or Congress (57 percent).

In a way, the clock is turning back to the pre-TV era. Consider what life was like in the first years of the twentieth century, when a flood of immigrants poured into the nation's largest cities, mostly alone or with a few family members, poor, undereducated, and speaking a foreign tongue. Almost from the moment they stepped off the boat, these new Americans relied upon somebody else for employment, security, and a sense of community. A century ago, ward bosses, precinct captains, priests, and even Mafia dons were Navigators. They helped dictate how people voted and spent their money and where they worshiped. "The ward boss said, 'You know me, you trust me, so trust this candidate. This candidate will be good for *us*.' The *us* here being those who shared what marketers now call a lifestyle," said former Democratic Party chairman Joe Andrew, who calls the bond between voter and ward boss "transitive trust."

As people gained access to more information, largely through the growth of radio in the 1950s and television in the 1960s, they no longer needed the guidance of ward bosses and other local Navigators. A candidate could go directly to the people through TV. In the post–World War II era, TV anchors had outsized influence, political endorsements were critical, and successful businessmen such as former Chrysler chairman Lee Iacocca were opinion-swaying celebrities.

But now the information flow has become a flood, a torrent of messages coming at a confused, cynical public from all angles. People are turning to one another once again. As they did a century ago, today's opinion leaders work on the grassroots level rather than from the high perches of media, politics, or business.

The twenty-first-century opinion leaders are average Americans who know lots of other average Americans, trusted souls with large social networks. These Navigators are influencing public opinion one casual conversation at a time. Often without realizing their own powers, these *Navigators* help others decide how to vote, what to buy, and how to live.

## BUSH LEAGUES

In the spring of 2004, the Bush campaign was in trouble. Senator John Kerry had just wrapped up the Democratic nomination and was riding high in the polls. The Abu Ghraib prison scandal was cutting into Bush's popularity, and the death toll was mounting in Iraq.

None of that mattered to Ed Keller and Jon Berry, two marketing gurus from New York who were paying a visit to the Bush's campaign team in Arlington, Virginia. Bush strategist Dowd was a fan of their book *The Influentials*, which included a list of twelve ways to identify these new opinion leaders. After hearing the Bush campaign's plans to adapt their book to politics, the authors walked out of the Bush headquarters to their rental car, shaking their heads in amazement. "It's over," Berry told his partner. "Bush will win."

Recalling that day, Berry later said, "They not only got the concept but were so far ahead in implementing that it would be impossible—barring unforeseen events—for (the Democrats) to catch up by Election Day."

From their e-mail list of more than 7 million people who volunteered as supporters, Bush's team built a separate database of 2 million self-identified Navigators. These were people who said they were willing to write letters to the editor, talk to others about politics, forward e-mails, or attend a public meeting.

Once a week or so, the campaign talked to these Navigators via e-mail and other means. The Internet made it possible to create a constant two-way flow of information between volunteers and the campaign. Navigators would write letters to the editor—advocating Bush's position, responding to Kerry's attacks, and helping set expectations. Talking points made sure they knew the campaign's message when they wrote letters, talked to friends, or attended public meetings. The campaign often gave them a first look at TV ads. That's a great way to create buzz; Navigators love to brag about hearing things first. They would get instruction on how to talk up Bush ads and talk down Kerry's.

In the crucial final days of the election, the Bush Navigators helped get voters to the polls. This is where Bush had a huge advantage over Kerry. While Democrats relied on a paid and often out-of-state staff, Bush's get-out-the-vote team consisted of volunteers who promoted the president inside their personal networks. Neighbors talked to neighbors. Teachers talked to teachers. Evangelicals talked to fellow worshipers. Bowlers talked to fellow bowlers. And so on.

LifeTargeting allowed Bush advisers to match a Navigator up with another voter who had similar political attitudes and lifestyles. A Michigan Navigator tagged as a Terrorism Moderate would call other Terrorism Moderates in his Macomb County neighborhood. The Bush team realized that the best media for influencing people are the oldest: everyday conversations.

By contrast, Democrats invested more money in the old ways of voter persuasion, sending legions of paid canvassers and union members into key states to knock on strangers' doors. It was impersonal and institutional. But people don't trust institutions anymore; they trust other people—particularly people they know or who come from the same walk of life.

The scary thing for Democrats is that Republicans are trying to perfect the system. Inspired by the Keller-Berry book and other research on public opinion, the Bush team analyzed its volunteer lists and determined that Navigators can easily be identified based on how they answer a handful of questions about their civic activity.

Under the Republican National Committee plan, the next GOP presidential campaign will begin asking those questions of every person it canvasses in door-to-door field work. Republicans will be able to identify millions of Navigators through this process. The RNC is also trying to find a way to identify Navigators through consumer preferences, voting patterns, and geography. In other words, they hope to draw on their LifeTargeting tactics to find Navigators. So far, that effort has met with limited success, but Republicans are still far ahead of Democrats in the art and science of word-of-mouth marketing.

## Beyond the Horizon
### SOLVING THE RIDDLE
### New Strategies

There should be a rush in corporate America to build on LifeTargeting and figure out how to determine what lifestyle habits suggest that a person is a Navigator. That would allow a business to compile a national database of the most important potential consumers. The other key is to figure out how to talk to Navigators. What communication channels do they use? Where do they get their information? What are the best media for persuading the persuaders? There will be a different answer for every Navigator. Whoever solves the riddle will swamp backward-looking competitors.

## PLAYING HARD TO GET

La Esquina's owners seemed to break every public relations rule when they opened their Manhattan restaurant without a listed telephone number or a clearly marked entrance.

They didn't advertise their July 2005 opening. They didn't invite media. They hired a publicist, Jennifer Baum, but told her not to do anything unless their risky marketing plan failed. If nothing else, the location would certainly seem to have doomed the restaurant to failure. The street-level doorway to the subterranean eatery is hidden inside a Mexican taqueria with a sign that says "Corner Deli" (La Esquina means "the corner"). For any customer who manages to find the secret portal, there are two unwelcome signs: "Employees Only" and "No Admittance."

Yet the restaurant quickly became one of the hottest spots in town, a forbidden fruit passed between friends and acquaintances in excited conversation and through culinary blogs. The owners' approach was simple: They tapped their personal networks to create a buzz of exclusivity about their restaurant. They invited the likes of Carlo von

Zeitschel, a gallery owner and great-grandson of Kaiser Wilhelm; Elise Overland, a fashion designer to rock stars; and Hope Atherton, described by *The New York Times* as a "nymphlike artist who lives down the block." There were bad-boy artist Tom Sachs, whose studio is located nearby; Terry Richardson, the British fashion photographer; and Paul Rowland, another neighbor, who owns a modeling agency that once represented Kate Moss.

"They were all Tastemakers, people who other people go to for information," Baum said, trotting out her term for a Navigator. Her bosses, La Esquina's owners, are Navigators in their own rights—keepers of wide and varied social circles. Derek Sanders is an architect married to a journalist at *Vogue* magazine; James Gersten is a longtime restaurateur; Serge Becker is known for his affiliation with some of New York's most successful nightspots; and Cordell Lochin is a former club promoter. "He's the young, early twenties I-stay-up-until-4:30 A.M. guy," Baum said. "He's got that whole thing down."

Gersten said the key to the owners' marketing strategy was starting a person-to-person chain reaction by inviting their first guests by telephone rather than e-mail, fax, or formal invitation.

"With the barrage of information out there, a simple telephone call makes a difference. Also, if you know somebody and they ask you to come, it's more valuable than if you read about it in a magazine or even if it gets a good review in a paper," he said.

The marketing strategy was designed to fit the restaurant's speakeasy flair. "We're evoking a little 1920s-style nostalgia," he said. "It makes sense to use vintage 1920s communications, person to person."

Still, Baum seemed mystified by her client's success. "It's what we didn't do that got everybody's attention. We did not do a full-fledged press kit. We did not do a big, expensive press party. Normally, when we open restaurants we have four-color pamphlets; I just opened one Monday, and we went all out. We did not do that with La Esquina."

Instead, the owners let news of their quirkly restaurant spread by word of mouth. When the tables started filling up, which took about a week, they made sure each new customer got what he or she had come for. It wasn't the food (which eventually received a so-so review in *The New York Times*); it was the shared sense of exclusivity.

"It's hard to find. It's hard to get a reservation. Once you get there, it's even harder; there are gatekeepers at every level. Nobody is allowed to take pictures downstairs without being on the list," Baum said. "You feel like you're a part of a big secret with a small, select group of people."

Baum, a veteran of New York's public relations scene, is slowly getting used to this "new" old form of marketing. For the first time, she sent an employee to the Word of Mouth Marketing Association convention in the summer of 2005. The fledging group's founding members include Balter of BzzAgent and Keller and Berry, the authors of *The Influentials*.

"I think we are turning to people we trust for information nowadays," Baum said. "That's why blogs are so popular. I see the way people respond when Mary Smith says something good about a restaurant, and they just run. They have to go. They trust Mary Smith more than all the four-color brochures I could produce."

Still, the tone in Baum's voice belied a trace of skepticism. You could tell she was itching to call the city's food critics, paper the subway system with ads, and maybe even hire a college student to stand outside the restaurant in a taco costume. She found her client's whisper campaign baffling.

"It was a little frustrating for me, I have to say. But it's what they wanted me to do," she said. "They were right, and it worked. They didn't know it would work for sure. They always had me in their back pocket. Even to this day, we have press kits ready to give out, just in case."

As long as La Esquina's owners keep giving people want they want—*a community* of pretentious obscurity (better food would help, but it's not what they're selling)—Baum can keep the press kits in storage.

## HEY, BUDDY!

We can read your mind.

Actually, we can't. But we know who can. Robin Burgener, a Canadian computer programmer, created an artificial intelligence algorithm in 1988 that interacts with people and learns from them. He put the formula on the Internet (20Q.net) in 1996 for all to try. As people played it, the formula accumulated their knowledge and grew the artificial intelligence database to more than 15,000 objects. Over time, 20Q.net grew savvy enough to almost always guess what object a person had in mind—from aglet to zebra—after posing twenty or fewer questions.

It was an Internet sensation. The link was e-mailed from person to person thousands of times, around the globe; people shared it with friends, coworkers, and family. Without a penny of promotion, 20Q spread like a virus to become a word-of-mouth success. "Hey, buddy! Can you believe what this guessed?"

Patti Saitow had to have it. The vice president of global marketing services for Radica USA, Saitow learned of Burgener's invention from a Radica engineer who was looking for Internet games for the company's inventory. She set about finding him, first with an e-mail. He didn't answer it for weeks. She sent another, then others. Finally, after she had all but given up on the Canadian, Saitow's telephone rang, and it was the soft-spoken Burgener.

"What are you trying to get in touch with me about?" he asked.

"20Q," she replied.

Burgener told Saitow that the algorithm could be converted into a cheap toy but only if the number of database objects were cut from 15,000 to 2,000. The good news was that people think of those 2,000 objects 98 percent of the time.

Now that Saitow had 20Q, she needed to promote it.

Despite its multimillion-dollar marketing budget, Radica did not set aside much money for marketing 20Q because the big spending is reserved for kid's toys. What to do? One of her bosses pointed Saitow to a May 2004 article in *Fast Company* magazine about a two-year-old Boston company called BzzAgent, owned by word-of-mouth maven Balter. It explained how the company works:

Once a client signs on, the BzzAgent searches its database for "agents" matching the demographic and psychographic profile of target customers of the product or service. Those agents, all volunteers, are offered a chance to sign up for a "Bzz Agent" campaign. They receive a sample product and a training manual for buzz-creating strategies. The idea is to make them conscious of the power of their opinion and how to communicate it effectively with others. Examples might include talking with a coworker, responding to a blog posting, chatting with a salesperson at a retail outlet—or just having an everyday conversation with someone they know. Agents are expected to file a report describing the nature of the buzz and its effectiveness. BzzAgent coaches respond with encouragement and feedback on additional techniques.

Balter had started the company with an initial assignment for 300 agents—mostly friends and friends of family—to generate buzz for a Penguin Group book. His band of agents (Balter calls them a community) now exceeds 130,000 as of January 2006. They've buzzed products as diverse as Estée Lauder facial masks, Lee jeans, and Rock Bottom Restaurants, according to the *Fast Company* article. Saitow put down the article and picked up the telephone to call Balter. "I figured, 'What do I have to lose?'" she said.

For the fraction of the cost of a TV or newspaper advertising campaign, Radica hired BzzAgent to put 3,000 agents on the case. Nine in ten of them were sixteen to twenty-four years old. The rest were thirty-five years or older. There were four times as many women as men, and three fourths had previously played single-game handhelds similar to 20Q. Only 16 percent had previous knowledge of the game. The agents, who signed up online and communicated with BzzAgent via the Internet, each received a 20Q and a slick nine-page "BzzGuide."

Palm-sized and shaped like the number "20" at top and the curl of the "Q" on the bottom, the guide excitedly told agents, "We've come across one of the coolest handheld electronic games out there. And we're thrilled to share it with you." The idea is to make the agents feel like they're part of a community, knitted together by the fun folks at BzzAgent headquarters, which is called the "Central Hive."

The guide said that 20Q had been passed from desk to desk at the Central Hive and "we couldn't believe it guessed the following things." It listed three dozen objects (from carburetor to turtle) and the Central Hive workers who were stumped by 20Q ("Toof" had carburetor and "Fletch" had turtle). Finally, the guide offered tips for spreading "the buzz" about 20Q—such as sharing it with somebody when standing in line, traveling, taking a break at work, or "watching a lame TV show" with a pal.

Balter said the idea behind any BzzAgent campaign is to maximize the agents' genuine enthusiasm. It works only when the product is worth talking about. In an age of spin and skepticism, word-of-mouth marketing traffics in a rare commodity: authenticity. The agents "are not scripted, paid or obligated to talk about the product after joining a campaign," according to a BzzAgent report given to Radica.

"Our job is to augment word-of-mouth communications that would be going on anyway, teaching people to better communicate their excitement or interest in a product," Balter said.

In the twelve-week campaign for Radica, 3,000 agents talked to 64,000 people about 20Q. Two thirds of the agents reported talking to people who planned to buy the game. Two thirds bought additional games for themselves. Nine in ten said they planned to continue "bzzing" about 20Q after the campaign ended.

Just as important, Radica learned from Balter's agents that playing 20Q was often a group activity, a lesson that helped the company reshape future marketing campaigns.

Demand for 20Q outstripped supply during the 2004 holiday season and sales were 600 percent above projections. Saitow would not disclose the cost of the BzzAgent campaign but says it would have cost six times more in traditional advertising to earn the same sales totals.

"They made a true believer in word-of-mouth marketing out of me," said the twenty-year marketing veteran. "It was the most successful marketing campaign I've ever been involved in." Society is changing in ways that makes word-of-mouth marketing more valuable, she said.

"I think consumers are becoming jaded and not buying the typical spiel they hear in the advertising world," Saitow said. "They are coming to rely more on people and associations they feel are on the leading edge because they know what advertising is—it's bought and paid for by the people who want you to buy their product."

Balter said that when he began the company he underestimated the willingness of people to be volunteer BzzAgents. The people who sign up seem to like the idea of gaining more control in the marketplace. Thus, the notion of helping to sell a product or, better yet, suggesting changes to one during a two-way relationship with a company is enticing. Most agents are also the type of people—Navigators—who like to be the first to discover something new and share it with their friends, family, and acquaintances.

## NEXT UP FOR NAVIGATORS

The Bush campaign borrowed the idea of LifeTargeting from corporate America. Now it's time for business to mimic the Bush campaign and work harder to recruit Navigators. If the Bush team and fellow Republicans can identify modern-day opinion leaders by asking four questions, think what Starbucks or another major company could do with its e-mail list. What if a company like Applebee's merged its analysis of potential customers with Bush's strategies to find average men and women whose opinions influence their friends, family, coworkers, and neighbors?

Berry and Keller of *The Influentials* envision a day when there will be a constant two-way stream of information between companies and opinion leaders, with influential consumers playing a role in refining products and marketing strategies. Their firm routinely surveys Influentials because these opinion leaders are social visionaries, living on the cutting edge of political, business, and social trends. The Influentials were the first people to buy digital cameras and cell phones, the first to start buying products in bulk, and the first to put post-9/11 fear of flying behind them.

"In times of change," Berry and Keller wrote, "people naturally seek a guide, someone who's been out ahead of them, who's already identified the issues, addressed them in his or her own life, and can offer good, reliable, informed insights, advice, and information about what's going on now and what's to come, someone they trust.

"Americans instinctively know this. We believe this is one reason, in this time when messages are coming fast and furious at people from seemingly all directions, Americans are placing increasing stock in the simplest form of communication, word-of-mouth advice and information from people they know and trust."

The Boston-based Balter said his company was approached in 2004 by a presidential candidate (he would not say which one) about run-

ning a word-of-mouth project for the campaign. Balter turned down
the job. "We don't do this for religious or political groups for a very specific reason. BzzAgent needs to be a bipartisan platform," he says. "We
decided long ago we needed to be careful." But Balter said there is nothing stopping political and religious organizations from tapping the
power of word of mouth.

In the religious world, megachurch consultants such as the Harvard-
trained Jim Mellado of the Willow Creek Association in Barrington,
Illinois, are already running word-of-mouth marketing campaigns
through their churches' networks of small groups to recruit nonchurchgoers. Leaders of those groups are taught how to spread their church's
mission throughout the quasi-communities. There are training sessions, Internet communications, and four-color brochures, not unlike
how BzzAgent tees up its volunteers to talk up a product. By definition,
an evangelical is someone who spreads the word of God. In practice,
most evangelizing is done person-to-person among communities of
people who live near one another and share similar lifestyles. Some surveys suggest that as many as 80 percent of Christians say they came to
Christ or the church through a friend or family member, as opposed to a
formal recruiter such as a pastor or an event such as a crusade.

Asked to describe his mission at Willow Creek, Mellado grabbed a
pen and notebook and drew what looked to be a large hill. It was a
graph of the pattern by which ideas and innovations are adopted by
megachurch leaders. On the left were the early adapters. The trend
spreaders were next, and the mainstream population was the big bulge
in the middle. Finally, the laggards were represented by the right-hand
slope. This is not new stuff; officials with BzzAgent and Tremor refer to
the same graph when they talk about their clients' targets. It's from the
1962 book *Diffusion of Innovation* by Everett Rogers. Here again is an
example of *business and church leaders literally working from the same play-
books*.

In the political world, Democrats have some catching up to do. "We
can't let Republicans beat us on person-to-person politics," said the direct mail expert Hal Malchow, who has tried to introduce Navigators
and LifeTargeting to his party. Traditional political advertising is growing less effective as voters change. "They're smart. They know when I

send them a piece of mail I have a very specific agenda—to get them to vote for a candidate—and I will say what I can get away with to support that agenda. They know it. But when a friend or even vaguely familiar neighbor comes up and says, 'Hey, so-and-so, is a really good person, a good candidate, and I'm really excited by him,' they have no agenda. They're your friend. They have no reason to say it if it's not true."

A combination of ego and foolishness has kept politics out of buzz marketing, he said. "One of the problems in politics, particularly political communications and all the consultants and all these campaigns, is everybody operates off of a lot of bullshit," Malchow said. "If you win a campaign, everybody calls you a champion and assumes you did everything right. If you lost it, you could have run the best campaign in the world, but everybody calls you a fool and ignores what you did. There's no real measurement of what worked and didn't work in the campaign, but that's about to change."

Like everything else.

# 7

# Americans on the Move

*Whether in the city or the inner-ring suburb or the outer-ring exurb or beyond, we are witnessing different effusions of the same impulse to move out and up.*

—David Brooks, *On Paradise Drive*

Inside Livingston County's sprawling new courthouse is a basement computer where the GIS Management Department keeps aerial photographs of this bedroom community sixty miles northwest of Detroit. For a small fee, the secretary types in the address—3949 E. Grand River Avenue—and prints out a 1985 picture of Howell, Michigan, the county seat. From a thousand feet in the air, the region is a patchwork quilt of farms, woods, ponds, two-lane roads, and the occasional farmhouse. She punches another key, and the 1990 picture looks the same—farm after farm, a few trees and ponds. The first hint of change comes with the 1995 photo, when a small shopping complex seems to have sprouted from one of the fields, a horseshoe-shaped invasion of consumerism near the farm at 3949 E. Grand River.

In the next few years, all hell breaks loose. The 2002 aerial shot is a busy picture of big-box stores, small businesses, chain restaurants, and parking lots stretched along a widened Grand River Avenue. Two new subdivisions look like jagged gray scars—each house linked in equal measures by ribbons of asphalt to twisting roads that snake around a pond. Urban sprawl has struck. The cookie-cutter sameness of exurbia has claimed another rural landscape.

At the center of the picture—3949 E. Grand River Avenue in modern-day Howell, Michigan—stands an Applebee's, once again at the leading edge of exurban life. This is where we found Pat Monette, a retired sheet metal worker digging into a Honey Grilled Chicken and talking about the place he has called home for ten years. "I moved out here for a better way of life," said the burly, bald sixty-nine-year-old customer, his back to the bumper-to-bumper traffic on Grand River near I-96. "It was a lifestyle decision—nothing more, nothing less."

With the cities of Detroit, Flint, Lansing, and Ann Arbor in range of commuters, the rolling, rural landscape of Livingston County is rapidly filling with families in search of bigger homes, more acreage, better schools, safer streets, and shelter from the problems of city life. "They move out here for a variety of reasons," said Livingston County Administrator Robert Block, "including racial reasons." Lifestyle choices brought them out here and their lifestyle needs determine how they vote, what they buy, and where they go to church.

The people of Livingston County are part of a great American migration that is touching all corners of the country—urban, suburban, exurban, and rural. This chapter explores how tribal life affects the making of Gut Values Connections in politics, business, and religion—not just in Michigan but in an entire nation of lifestyle pioneers.

## LOOKING FOR A BETTER LIFE

America is on the move. Nearly one in five people changes address each year and, having done so, are likely to move again. More than two in five Americans expect to move in the next five years. White middle-class suburbanites are moving away from coastal cities to what the demographer William H. Frey called the New Sun Belt. The white voting-age population in Nevada, Arizona, Colorado, Utah, and Idaho increased by more than 22 percent in the 1990s alone. African Americans are moving to suburbs in the South that have large black populations. More than 17 million—almost half of all blacks—live in the eleven states that were in the Confederacy, up a million from 2000, according to Census estimates. Hispanics are spreading far beyond the immigrant "gateways" of California, Florida, New York, Illinois, and Texas and now make up at least 5 percent of the population in twenty-eight states, up from sixteen in 1990, Frey said.

Jim Taylor of *Advertising Age's American Demographics* wrote in 2004 that the nation was entering a "third great wave of migration" spurred by the public's changing lifestyle wants. "People from the South who left to work the auto plants are retiring and heading home to the land of their fathers. Joining them are corporate transplants, the urban poor and those who are looking for an uncomplicated life as a reward for years of hard work. The motivation for migration is a warmer climate and a simpler life," Taylor said, predicting up to 50 million émigrés to the South in the next two decades.

Traditionally, people moved because they had no choice; their jobs or career advancement depended on it. Today, people change addresses simply to improve their lives. Technology, mobility, and relative affluence are allowing many Americans to build careers that revolve around their lives rather than fitting their lives around their work.

Two examples of lifestyle motivators: Skyrocketing housing prices are blamed for recent population dips in Boston and San Francisco. Warm weather and affordable living costs have fueled the rapid growth of midsize cities in Florida, Arizona, Nevada, and California, according to a 2005 census report. Those figures showed no let up in migration trends toward the South and the West, which were home to all ten of the fastest-growing cities with at least 100,000 people. Topping the list was the Phoenix suburb of Gilbert, Arizona, which grew by more than 46,000, or 42 percent, in just four years.

This is why LifeTargeting makes so much sense. When one of the biggest decisions people make—where to buy a house and raise a family—is based on their lifestyle, it stands to reason that those life choices are the best predictor of how they'll vote, what they'll buy, where they'll eat out, and how they'll express their spirituality.


## THE MIGRATION CIRCLE

Most families move to Livingston County, Michigan, from places such as Dearborn, Southfield, or Ferndale—older, inner-ring Detroit suburbs that attracted the first generation of suburbanites in the 1950s, '60s, and '70s. Those suburban pioneers left Detroit decades ago for the same reasons their children and grandchildren are now pushing farther from the city into exurbs like Howell—in search of a better way of life.

Today, the older suburbs are magnets for middle-class minorities who in generations past would have settled in Detroit. Like the white families before them, these new suburbanites believe life outside the city is best for their families. Southfield shifted from more than 70 percent white in the 1990 Census to nearly 55 percent black a decade later. Dearborn, once a white bastion run by a notoriously segregationist mayor, is now home to the nation's largest Arab-American community. Nationally, nearly one fifth of the U.S. population lives in what Brookings Institution calls "first suburbs"—caught between fast-growing exurbs and slow-growing or declining inner cities. They are often shortchanged by federal housing and transportation policies that favor central cities and outer exurbs. "Politically, they are less than the sum of their parts," said Bruce Katz, director of the Metropolitan Policy Program at the Brookings Institution.

Then there is Detroit. The once-booming auto giant has seen its population cut in half since the 1950s, when it peaked at nearly 2 million. The Motor City now has fewer residents than it did in the 1920s. The depopulation is due in part to the region's reliance on the auto industry and industrialization in general. But another factor is "white flight." It began in the 1950s, when Detroit lost 23 percent of its white population, and accelerated after the 1967 riots and school busing of the 1970s. Nine of every ten Detroit residents are black. Though Detroit is an extreme case, most major U.S. cities have experienced population losses, especially of married couples and families (Chicago, New York, and Philadelphia each lost more than 350,000 residents between 1970 and 2000). Most people who could move did so, leaving urban cores stocked with populations that couldn't afford to leave. Despite some success in attracting high-income singles and empty nesters, the nation's cities have yet to experience a major resurgence. A few years ago, Chicago was seen as the great hope for city life when the 2000 census found that the Windy City had gained population in the 1990s, the first time that had happened in five decades. But then the city's population declined 1.2 percent between 2000 and 2004.

Experts blame a weak economy and post-9/11 safety concerns for driving people out of cities, but say there is still hope. "Traditional urban America isn't going to die," according to Joel Kotkin, an author and authority on global, economic, political, and social trends. "Instead, city living, as urban analyst Bill Fulton has put it, will likely become primarily a 'niche lifestyle,' preferred mostly by young, the childless, and the rich."

## TRIBAL NATION

Why are families throughout the country abandoning one suburb for another farther from the city? Why are minorities leaving cities for the suburbs? Why are young singles and empty nesters filtering back into Detroit and other big cities? The simple answer is, because they can. It's human nature for people to want to be near and around others like them, people who have similar interests, educations, incomes, hobbies, habits, family status, and stages of life. Like modern-day clans, we're choosing sides and moving together, creating a self-polarizing Tribal Nation.

One exurb might be inhabited by the White, Upwardly Mobile Family tribe as well as the Hockey-Loving Retail Workers clan. A few miles away reside the Blue-Collar Factory Town tribe. An old-line suburb is home to Black Middle-Class Strivers, living in uneasy peace with the Second-Generation Immigrant Entrepreneurs. The Gentrifiers, a tiny urban clan, and the Too Poor to Leave tribe both roam the city. In a tribal nation, the boundaries of states, cities, and precincts are less important to political, business, and religious marketers than are lifestyle niches. This is what calls the "red state/blue state" cliché into question.

In politics, it's impossible to ignore the concept of Republican reds and Democratic blues because each state controls a specific number of electoral votes and a candidate needs 270 to become president. But LifeTargeting will revolutionize the way strategists look at the electoral map and the tribes of voters moving around it. Democratic neighborhoods long written off by GOP campaigns contain hordes of hidden Republican voters who can now be identified and targeted. Nationally, more than 80 percent of GOP voters live outside heavily Republican precincts. Democratic strategists have long ignored potential voters living in GOP neighborhoods. In New Hampshire, for example, a Democratic LifeTargeting project identified 169,215 likely Kerry voters in 2004, and 155,836 of them live outside traditionally Democratic precincts. This is what happens when people move to communities based on shared lifestyles rather than political ideologies.

## EXURBAN TRIBES

Livingston County Supervisor Robert Block poured two cups of coffee and plopped his heavy frame into a conference room chair. His sleek low-slung new office space—built into a hill next to the nineteenth-century courthouse—hummed with activity, all of which he ignored to talk about life on the exurban frontier. "Livingston County is just like Florida," he said with a laugh. "It's hard to find a native."

About 160,000 people call Livingston County home, nearly a 170 percent increase in thirty years. County officials project that the population will climb to 187,000 in four years and hit 220,000 in 2020. Ninety-eight percent of county residents are white. The median age is thirty-six, the median income is nearly $70,000. A third of the population is less than eighteen, giving it the largest school-age population in southeast Michigan.

This exit-ramp community is a carbon copy of exurbs across the country, including Gwinnett County outside Atlanta; Scott County outside Minneapolis–St. Paul; Pinal County outside Phoenix; Loudon County, Virginia, outside Washington, D.C.; and Douglas County outside Denver. Sixty of the nation's hundred fastest-growing counties are located in the South, twenty in the West, eighteen in the Midwest, and two in the Northeast. Five of the top ten fast-growing counties (from 2000 to 2003) are located in Georgia.

Generally populated by the same kinds of people (white middle- to upper-class families) who attract the same businesses (Home Depot, Lowe's, Wal-Mart, Best Buy, other big-box stores, and smaller chains that feed off them), the nation's exurbs are the vital heart of America in terms of population, commerce, job growth, and even politics.

A housewife in Howell has more in common with a stay-at-home mother in exurban Lake Forest, California, than she has with a woman her age and income level who lives just thirty miles away in Ann Arbor, Michigan. The two exurban women are tribal cousins with similar lifestyles, while an unmarried, liberal career-minded professor at the University of Michigan might as well be from a different planet. "Detroit is a million miles away from me," said Debbie Kromer, forty-nine, of Hamburg in Livingston County, "but Orange County [California] looks and feels like home to me."

According to census data, Kromer and other women in Livingston County are far more likely to be married and raising children than women in nearby Washtenaw County (Ann Arbor), and the medium household income is almost $20,000 higher in Livingston County than in Washtenaw County. A better match for Kromer would be the exurban precincts of Williamson County outside Austin, Texas, where the percentages of married families and income levels are on a par with those of Livingston County.

Politically, Kromer also has more in common with an exurban woman in Texas than the average female voter a few miles away in Ann Arbor. According to exit polls, suburban women were far more likely to vote for Bush and favor his economic and terrorism policies than were urban women. Fifteen percent of suburban women wanted abortion to be illegal in all cases, compared to just 4 percent of urban women.

The suburbanization of America began with the rise of the automobile culture, and it accelerated in the 1960s and '70s. Since 1950, more than 90 percent of metropolitan population growth in American has taken place in the suburbs or exurbs. In the 1990s alone, suburbs and exurbs of the nation's hundred largest cities grew twice as fast as the cities themselves: 9.1 percent versus 18 percent. Today, five of every ten Americans live in suburbs and exurbs, up from three in ten in 1960. A study released by the American Farmland Trust in October 2002 reported that the United States was losing two acres of mostly prime farmland to exurban development every minute.

Beyond the automobile, scores of technological advances helped spur sprawl—from the ready availability of air-conditioning in the 1960s (making southern cities and suburbs inhabitable) to the ubiquity of cellular telephones in the 1990s (making long commutes bearable and telecommuting possible).

While families dominate, the exurbs are starting to attract people who had been migrating to cities. These include young singles starting

their first job, elderly widows and widowers, empty nesters, and divorced mothers with children. Some exurbs are becoming more racially
and ethnically diverse. In Washington, D.C., nearly half of new ar-
rivals, particularly from Asia, settled outside the beltway in the 1990s,
Katz of Brookings said. Among the nation's 102 largest metropolitan
areas, minorities comprised 27.3 percent of the suburban population in
2000, up from 19.3 percent in 1990, according to Frey.

Jobs and businesses follow the people. One third of all jobs are located beyond a ten-mile radius of central business districts. This has
created a relatively new phenomenon in America: two-way traffic jams.
There was a time not too long ago when traffic went one way: from the
suburbs to the city in the morning and the reverse at night. Now rush
hour goes both ways simultaneously because people and their jobs are
spread all over. "The suburbs now dominate employment growth and
are no longer just bedroom communities for workers commuting to traditional downtowns," said Katz. More than 40 percent of office space in
the top dozen markets is found in suburbs and exurbs, compared to the
1980s, when only a quarter of all the office space was suburban, according to the demographer Robert Lang.

In the next quarter century, the nation is expected to increase its housing, office, and business stock by 50 percent, and the great majority of that
new building will take place in exurbs. "The suburbs are where the action is going to be in the future," Kotkin wrote. "The great challenge of
the 21st century—not to mention the main economic opportunity—lies
in transforming suburban sprawl into something more efficient, interesting and human." But the rapid sprawl comes with complications that few
people notice until they're ensconced—including hellish commutes,
overcrowded schools, disappearing open space, inadequate public works,
and social disconnectedness.

## Beyond the Horizon
### SPREADING SPRAWL

People will continue following their lifestyle needs, and that migration will almost certainly take them to places that are not yet settled. Despite the intense urban sprawl occurring since World War II, the United States remains a nation of wide-open spaces. From 1945 to 1997, the amount of urban land (defined as places with at least 2,500 people) quadrupled to 65.5 million acres; still, that was less than 2 percent of the total 2.26 billion acres. Contrary to conventional wisdom, the acreage of cropland and forests has actually increased slightly since 1945. Robert Samuelson, a *Washington Post* columnist who dug up those numbers from *Historical Statistics of the United States* wrote that reforestation has offset much woodland lost to subdivisions.

## CONNECTIONS AND COMMUNITY

Block, the county administrator, knows firsthand about the epidemic of isolation. "My sense is, we're not building communities," he said. "We're just building subdivisions." His pet peeve is the proliferation of subdivisions built along busy highways without residential roads connecting them together. "They're creating little islands of housing" in a sea of sprawl, Block said. "There's no connection to community spirit. No connection to current or future residents."

Block, who served as Southfield's city manager in the mid-1980s before joining the exodus to newly minted suburbs, said he has never felt quite at home in Livingston County. He's not sure bigger is better, certainly not when sprawl occurs quicker than he can plan for it. "I have a house here," he said, "but it doesn't feel like home."

That would be no surprise to Robert Putnam, the Harvard professor whose book *Bowling Alone* fingered urban sprawl as one reason for the decline in civic engagement that began in the 1950s. Early hopes for a generation of "hyperactive joiners" in suburbia proved fleeting.

"As suburbanization continued . . . suburbs themselves fragmented into a sociological mosaic—collectively heterogeneous but individually homogeneous, as people fleeing the city sorted themselves into more and more finely distinguished 'lifestyle enclaves,' segregated by race, class, education, life stage and so on," Putnam wrote. "So-called white flight was only the most visible form of this movement toward metropolitan differentiation. At century's end some suburbs were upper-middle-class, but many others were middle-middle, lower-middle, or even working-class. Some suburbs were white, but others were black, Hispanic, or Asian. Some were child focused, but others were composed predominantly of swinging singles or affluent empty nesters or retirees."

The trend toward gated communities and the "numbing homogeneity" of far-flung suburbs has created a "formalized and impersonal" atmosphere throughout suburban and exurban life. "Rather than at the grocery store or five-and-dime on Main Street, where faces were familiar, today's suburbanites shop in large, impersonal malls," Putnam wrote.

When people pick up and leave their familiar city or suburb, they leave something important behind: a community—that sense of belonging that comes with having lived in a place for a long time, especially when the roots extend a generation or more. It takes times to build new social networks, and the first few years in exurbia can be an exercise in isolation. But, as we explained in chapter 5, technologies are helping people overcome society's barriers to community, even in exurbia.

This is more than an abstract concept to us. One of this book's coauthors, Fournier, grew up on the same block on the east side of Detroit where his parents were raised and just a few miles north of where his father's family had lived for generations. Dowd is a native westsider whose family moved to Southfield when he was young. After another generation of migration, Fournier and Dowd both have brothers living in Detroit's northern exurbs. (Fournier has a brother in Macomb County, and Dowd has two brothers in Livingston County.)

For all three brothers, the first order of business in exurbia was getting to know their neighbors—to restore that lost sense of community.

Two of them built bars in their sprawling homes, which quickly became magnets for friends and family. The interesting thing is that the exurban I-94 corridor in Macomb County is filled with the children and grandchildren of native eastsiders like the Fourniers. The exurban path along I-96 is a bastion for former westsiders like the Dowds. People move in tribes, eastsiders and westsiders. It's as if entire communities had pulled themselves out by their roots and moved twenty miles north, looking for a new and better lifestyle while clinging to remnants of the old.

Howell resident Kromer doesn't need Putnam's book to tell her about the lack of community in Livingston County. "My next-door neighbor is not friendly, and the rest of them I don't even know," she said. "They drive past my house, open their garages from inside their car, and disappear until their car comes popping back out in the morning." She moved to Howell from Redford, an established, inner-ring suburb just outside Detroit. "We had block parties, lawn sales, and people who had known each other for generations."

While the closest megachurches are in heavily populated Oakland County, several Livingston County pastors are trying to grow their churches. One of them is the Reverend Jerry Aston, who offered a family gym night, pizza dinners, and other small-group activities at Arbour Meadow Community Church, which met at a local high school. His marketing plan seemed ripped from the pages of Warren's *The Purpose-Driven Church*. "At last!!! A church designed for those who've given up on traditional church services!" the church Web site said. "Let's face it. Many people aren't active in church these days."

The site promised to "meet your needs in the 21st century" by creating a place where people can "meet new friends and get to know your neighbors. Enjoy good music with a contemporary flavor." If he follows the megachurch business model, Aston will buy land in Livingston County while it is relatively cheap, draw worshipers from suburbs closer to Detroit, and expand his congregation as Livingston County attracts more disconnected young families.

# HOMES

Of all the lifestyle reasons people move to exurbia, a big home with plenty of acreage and amenities is one of the biggest draws. The average cost of a Livingston County home increased by 250 percent from 1980 to 2000, from $63,100 to $220,097, but is still cheaper per square foot than houses in old-line suburbs.

But there's something else that people are looking for in a home beyond size and sizzle. They want an antidote to the numbing sameness and isolation of exurbia—that *lost sense of community* we talked about. They want their homes to be gathering spaces for family, friends, and neighbors—and the housing industry has quickly adapted.

Take a look around your own home. If it's a newer, exurban house, the kitchen is part of a large "great room" where family and friends gather to eat, watch TV, use the computer, play games, or just hang out. If yours is an older home, chances are you have had a wall of the kitchen torn out to create a large living space. Great rooms grew in popularity in the mid-1990s, according to major manufacturers, and orders exploded after the September 11 terror attacks. "All of a sudden, people wanted great rooms," said Gordon V. Hartman, one of the biggest home builders in Texas. "They didn't want to be holed up in their kitchen; they wanted to be able to visit with their friends or kids or whatever while working on dinner." Hartman said that the demand for great rooms in Texas doubled in the late 1990s, consistent with national statistics.

"People are getting busier and busier, so they want to go back to the way things used to be—or at least how they remember them," Hartman said. "The style changed to create more interaction because of how hard it is now, with all that's going on, to have time with family and friends. The little time you have is quality time, so we want to try to maximize every minute we have in the house."

The same mix of nostalgia and practicality brought a major change just outside the average exurban home—the porch revival. In their pre–World War II heyday, wide, sweeping porches were a gathering place for family and friends, a retreat from the heat, and a source of entertainment for those who'd sit for hours watching cars and neighbors pass by. Starting in the late 1950s, television and air-conditioning lured people inside. For a half century, homes were built with privacy as the top priority, particularly in the suburbs and exurbs. Porches or decks were built on the back of homes, if at all, and were hidden by high hedges and fences.

But now people are yearning for the bygone community, and, once again, the industry must adapt. They're building front porches again. People are coming out of their houses and backyards to visit with one another. Those who don't yet have porches are throwing open the garage door, rolling out the barbecue, and waving at neighbors from their driveway. In some parts of the country, town homes are suddenly in demand among middle-class families seeking to simplify their lives.

"Families are so busy taking children to soccer, karate lessons, hockey practice, or dance classes—and with Dad often working two jobs *and* being involved in the family—they don't have time to mow the grass, keep up the yard," said Steve Boone of Boone Builders, one of the largest home construction firms in Minnesota. "They like the house but not quite everything that goes with it."

Entire communities are being designed to meet the growing demand for self-contained subdivisions that look and feel like old-fashioned towns, with shops, restaurants, and houses all in the same complex. While most suburban subdivisions have no sidewalks, these neotraditional neighborhoods have wide walkways with trees to shade pedestrians. A typical subdivision has a long front yard to accommodate automobiles, but neotraditional developments have shallow yards to make it easier for neighbors to converse between the sidewalks and front porches.

"All of a sudden, people wanted to have more interaction in terms of walking to things. They wanted to be closer to shopping centers, closer to places for their children to play, closer to each other," said Hartman, who sold his construction firm after making a fortune on great rooms and porches. "When I look back just ten years ago, that wasn't important."

Smart companies keep apace of the public's fast-shifting lifestyles. K.B. Homes, one of the nation's largest home builders, invests tens of thousands of dollars in consumer surveys to predict what people want and how much they're willing to pay for it. "Then we go out and build it," said Marshall Gray, The division president in Tampa. "At K.B., they depend much less on me or my opinions and look strictly at what the numbers say the buyer is looking for."

## SCHOOLS AND OTHER INFRASTRUCTURE

Schools are a source of both pride and frustration in exurbs such as Livingston County. "People move out here in large part for the schools," said County Manager Block. "Then they quickly start complaining about them." The problem is generally not the schools' quality—test scores and graduation rates are higher in Livingston County than most other exurbs. The problem is overcrowding.

Enrollment has increased no less than 25 percent in each of Livingston County's five largest school districts since 1990, and one district is grappling with a 45 percent leap. The same parents who moved into the county to take advantage of its school system now complain that their children have been forced to transfer several times because the fast-growing district is constantly adjusting its boundaries.

Mike and Melissa Brewster moved from the Detroit suburb of Novi a few years ago and love their new neighborhood. Their house is twice the size of what they could afford in Novi, and they have nurtured a tight-knit group of friends. "The only problem is the schools. Growth is happening out here so quick that they can't keep up with the construction," Mike Brewster said. One of his children had to change schools three times by the third grade.

Block said it's almost impossible to provide the services demanded by new subdivisions—water, roads, sewage, and emergency response—let alone the amenities of a well-planned community. When people see their services suffering (one reason why they left the city or old-line suburbs), their commutes lengthening (fuel lost to traffic jams in 2003 could fill up every car in the country for six days of driving), and their schools overcrowding, a natural reaction is buyer's remorse. For some new exurbanites, the first taste of civic activity is joining an antisprawl campaign.

"It seems like they're overexpanding, overbuilding, overeverything right now," said Mike Salah, whose fiancée, Cindy Moran, lives in

Howell. "Cindy's trying to sell her house, but she can't because there's such a glut on the market right now."

## POLITICS

Moran fidgeted with her food while telling an all-too-typical story of middle-class squeeze. Married and divorced shortly after high school, the thirty-eight-year-old woman has four children, ages fifteen months to eighteen years, and was between jobs when we met her at the Applebee's in Howell. She was diagnosed with muscular dystrophy in the early 1990s, "and the last five years have been downhill," she said. Moran is one of 45 million Americans without health insurance. "Can't afford it, which sucks," she said, whispering so that her five-year-old daughter, Olivia, couldn't hear. Andrea, fifteen months old, threw a piece of chicken on the floor. Moran, a thin, pretty blonde, picked it up without a pause in her monologue. "I'm not really connected at all with politics, or it's not connected with me. I struggle with that all the time," said Moran. "Democrats are the party I should be with, because I lack much income, but I don't believe in the morals of that party."

She was critical of GOP health care policies, opposed the war in Iraq, and questioned the priorities of Bush's party. "They don't care about me," she said, "because I don't make that much money." And who did she favor in 2004? "I'd have to say Bush," she said with an apologetic grin, her cheeks reddening. "At least he seemed steady and would keep us safe. It might not make sense, but, you know, it just felt right voting for him."

The politics of Livingston County reflects widespread problems for Democrats on the national level. In the 2004 presidential election, Bush trounced Kerry by a two-to-one margin in Livingston County en route to winning 96 of the nation's 100 fastest-growing counties. Bush won 474 out of the 573 "micropolitan areas," small towns and suburban regions that the Census Department considered too urban to be rural and too rural to be urban.

As Livingston County's population grew, so did the GOP's margins of victory. Bush defeated Kerry by about 25,000 votes in Livingston County, increasing by nearly 10,000 votes his margin of victory in

2000. In 1996, the Republican nominee, Bob Dole, won the county by just 8,000 votes.

Kerry, who never even tried to mount a campaign on the suburban fringes, suggested after the 2004 election that the lapse had been costly. "We need to get out in these places and get to know these people," he said. Democrats need to get to know people like Brewster, the Livingston County man worried about his daughter's school, who said, "Everybody I know and trust out here seems to be a Republican. It's not the issues so much as it is the ethic, know what I mean?" They need to know and respect people like Mary Gillard, who lives in a booming new suburb outside Tampa. "I haven't always been a Republican," she said. "But it seems like everybody here is one, so, what the heck, join the club."

Notice how Brewster and Gillard voted Republican not because of any policy but because it's what their neighbors do. It's almost as if voting GOP made them part of a club. *It's a way to connect,* through politics, in a society lacking social ties. Exurban voters are not motivated by partisan labels. They're driven by the same lifestyle issues that brought them to exurbia in the first place: bigger homes, better schools, safer streets, like-minded neighbors, and a better quality of life for their families. That makes exurban voters capable of swinging in huge blocs to whatever party makes a Gut Values Connection keyed to their lifestyles.

It happened in 2005, when the Democratic gubernatorial candidate, Tim Kaine, defeated the Republican Jerry Kilgore in four exurban counties won by President Bush just twelve months earlier. Furthermore, Kaine fought Kilgore to a tie in the state's seven fast-growing counties, the same ones that President Bush had won by 13 percent. The Democrat won in exurbia because he talked about his faith and his policies in ways that showed voters he understood and cared about their life's concerns—that he *shared their values*—and would try to make things better. Kaine promised better schools and roads and vowed to help communities that sought to curb sprawl. Polls had shown that many voters wanted to retain their communities' quiet, bucolic atmospheres, one of the things that had drawn them to exurbia in the first place. They wanted better schools, another exurban drawing card. And they needed better roads to reduce their commutes, which stole time from their families.

Kaine's first ad aired on a Christian radio station. The first TV ad he ran in the fall of 2005 highlighted his experience with Catholic missionaries. In the final days of the campaign, Kilgore played into Kaine's hands when the Republican ran an ad that said the Democrat's opposition to the death penalty meant he would not have executed Adolf Hitler. Kaine, a Roman Catholic, pledged to enforce the death penalty despite his personal opposition, using the ad to shine a spotlight on his religious beliefs. "My faith teaches life is sacred," he said. That ad underscored not only Kaine's faith but convinced many voters that he would be a strong, principled leader. As Bush did on Iraq, he turned an against-the-mainstream policy into a Gut Values attribute.

Kaine also benefited from Kilgore's tired 1980s-style message. The Republican focused on Kaine's record and policies—calling them liberal—rather than his values. Kilgore should have learned from Bush's campaigns, which used the policies and records of both Gore and Kerry to label them flip-flopping opportunists with no core beliefs. Not coincidentally, those labels were the exact opposite of the image Bush wanted to project for himself—as decisive and principled. Throughout this fast-changing country, and especially in exurbia, when there is a choice between a candidate who runs on issues and one who runs on Gut Values, the values candidate will almost always win.

An April 2005 analysis by the firm of Stan Greenberg, one of the primary architects of Clinton's successful 1992 campaign, found evidence that Republicans don't have a lock on exurbia. Conducting polls and focus groups in Minnesota, Greenberg and his team concluded that the issues voters cared about most in 2004—education and health care—tend to favor Democrats, and exurbanites were willing to pay for improvements in both areas. The pollsters found that six in ten exurban voters supported higher taxes to improve schools. The findings were significant because Minnesota is historically a Democratic state that has become intensely competitive, due in large part to the GOP's success in exurbia.

Residents of the state's sprawling new suburbs were more liberal than rural conservatives on cultural issues, such as guns and gay marriage, concluded Greenberg's firm, which conducted focus groups in Scott, Hennepin, and Anoka counties. Exurbanites in Minnesota wanted their government to be more accountable; 59 percent believe it to be wasteful and inefficient. Exurban voters also were more upset than others about foreign immigration, with one in five saying it was the most discouraging thing about their state.

The wrong lesson to draw from this is that a laundry list of education and health care policies guarantees success. If that was the answer Democrats would have won the Minnesota exurbs in 2004 (Bush won exurban precincts of Scott, Hennepin, and Anoka counties). The key is to show voters you understand the challenges of life in the "stormy present"—and that you have the tenacity, authenticity, and raw abilities to help them, their families, their communities, and their country. Education and health care are good conduits for communicating those values, but it's not the issues that count; it's the Gut Values Connection.

## BUSINESS

In the twentieth-century industrial-based economy, a company would open a factory and the town's population would swell as people followed the business for jobs. In the twenty-first century, information-technology economy, highly mobile and relatively affluent Americans will move to communities that fit their lifestyles *and companies will follow the people*. This is a revolutionary shift that has transformed the employer-corporation relationship.

In exurbia, where people moved for affordable housing and now struggle to pay their mortgages and taxes, shoppers place a premium on price and values. Big-box stores such as Best Buy and Target thrive in this environment, because they can stock huge inventories of low-priced goods. Family hardware stores, decades-old pharmacies, and mom-and-pop general stores can't compete. In small towns everywhere, their shuttered doors line half-empty downtown streets.

Big-box stores give people something else that today's consumer craves: selection. American's fast-changing communities are filling with people from all walks of life and different parts of the country, with varied tastes and needs. Bigger stores can stock a variety of goods that meet everybody's needs. Home Depot is a success because it can service the all-thumbs father struggling to fix a leaking faucet, his Mr. Fix-it neighbor, and the community's largest contractor.

The change is felt not just in exurbia. Newly empowered consumers everywhere demand convenience, which explains the trend toward longer store hours. Ubiquitous 24/7 shopping malls can't be far away. Fast food isn't fast enough for people, so the restaurant business is adapting; customers can prepare huge meals in corporate kitchens, take them home, and freeze them.

Successful businesses find a way to integrate themselves into people's changing lifestyles. Wal-Mart allows people to park their motor homes overnight in its lots, a policy that improves its after-hours security and give the chain a handy core of customers each morning. It has also made Wal-Mart part of the burgeoning community of retirees who travel the country in motor homes.

Cabela's, the superstore for outdoorsmen, has made itself a destination point for families. The stores, which can exceed 175,000 square feet, offer education and entertainment attractions such as museum-quality animal displays with colorful dioramas, huge aquariums stocked with native fish, and outdoor landscapes with mountains and rivers. They are often built in rural or exurban areas, drawing a small city of chain hotels and restaurants to cater to vacationing families. Cabela's core customers are white, working-class males, many of them former Democrats who filled the Bush team's LifeTargeting sheets in 2004.

## Beyond the Horizon
### THE NEXT HOT SPOT
#### College Towns

Places such as Ann Arbor, Michigan, Tempe, Arizona, Durham, North Carolina, and Austin, Texas, will become the new "factory towns." The growing number of people who place a value on technology, information, and education will see college towns as communities filled with like-minded people. Smart businesses will follow the people, creating a business boom in the nation's college towns.

# RELIGION

Customers have the upper hand in the religion business, too. Churches that are changing to meet the needs of Americans are thriving. Those caught in the past are struggling. People are willing to drive as much as an hour, zipping past their old church, to get a better deal on Sunday, often at an exurban megachurch.

The Roman Catholic Church is an example of a religious institution that has lost its Gut Values Connection. It is a hierarchical organization in an era of bottom-up management. Catholic priests teach scripture as they did a century ago, while megachurch leaders make the Bible relevant to people's everyday lives. The Catholic Church was once synonymous with community, but now it can't keep up with a megachurch for providing community services and has no small-group structure to build connections. Finally, covering up sexual abuse by priests destroyed the credibility of an organization whose Gut Values Connection was based on integrity. The shame of all this is that the Catholic Church does not need to change its ideology one iota. Many megachurches are just as conservative as the Vatican. The problems have much less to do with the Vatican's ideology than with the perception that the church has lost touch with its parishioners.

Successful megachurches thrive in an era of mobility because the small-group concept gives people a sense of belonging. The large menu of amenities makes the church campuses veritable community centers. And the sermons are designed to help people put their harried lives into a broader, more meaningful context.

As the suburbs change, so will the face of religion. Each day brings a new mosque or majority-minority church to places such as Arlington, Virginia, and Dearborn, Michigan.

# 8

# Generation 9/11

*The young Americans of this time constituted a generation birthmarked
for greatness.*

—Tom Brokaw, *The Greatest Generation*

*They say genes skip generations. Maybe that's why grandparents find
their grandchildren so likeable.*

—Author Joan McIntosh

GEORGE HEIER WASN'T BUYING IT. "Sounds to me like
you're writing a how-to book on foolin' the public," said the
World War II veteran we met in chapter 2. Heier was sitting
at his regular table at Applebee's beneath the picture of his late wife of
fifty-eight years, four months, and four days. "Hate to tell you, mister,
but those folks don't need no help."

Heier was right; political, business, and religious leaders don't need
our help fooling the public. But they do need to be reminded that
the road to success in politics, products, and pews is to build authentic
relationships with the people they serve. Leaders need to connect. It
was not our intention to deify Presidents Bush and Clinton, and Hill
and Warren; they are imperfect men in imperfect businesses. But we do
think they are good examples of what happens when even flawed leaders stay true to their principles and make Gut Values Connections.
Their stories remind us, too, of how fragile those connections can be.

The Great Connectors start by adapting. President Clinton realized
he needed to re-aim his presidency at skeptical swing voters, and eight
years later, President Bush discovered that the shifting political land-

scape required him to find passive and inactive Republicans. Hill's team at Applebee's and megachurch leaders like Warren followed people to exurbia and gave them the single most important thing they left behind in their old neighborhoods—a sense of community.

Presidents Bush and Clinton, and Hill and Warren, understood the choices people make about their lifestyles shape their attitudes about politics, shopping, and religion; it's not the other way around, as too many egocentric strategists seem to believe. The Great Connectors use new technologies and information to build lifestyle profiles that helped them find and persuade the public. LifeTargeting is now a prerequisite for success in politics, business, and religion

Presidents Bush and Clinton, and Hill and Warren, used niche advertising and word-of-mouth marketing to talk to a public that is both distracted and distrusting. Americans today get their information in tsunamis from both traditional and nontraditional sources: cable TV, satellite radio, the Internet, e-mails, iPods, and so on. The public has little faith in the media and other traditional opinion leaders, so they're turning to people they trust. These Navigators are everyday people who may not stand out from the crowd. But they like to hear about the hottest new thing first; they try it out and recommend it to people in their large social networks. President Bush's team revolutionized the science of finding and using Navigators to validate his message. Megachurches are not far behind. Their small-group leaders build relationships with people based on the hobby or cause that brought them together—"Motorcyclists for God" or "Golfers for God"—and over time become subtle influencers of opinion. Word-of-mouth marketing and Navigator-like programs are starting to catch on in corporate America, but business leaders are not as methodical about the strategy as was the Bush team.

These tactics are all means to an end—a Gut Values Connection— that could be achieved without polls, targeting, and slick marketing. Presidents Bush and Clinton are blessed with an intuitive sense of what the public wants and needs, which made it surprising when they lost their Gut Values Connection—particularly in 1994 for Clinton and 2005 for Bush. Applebee's culture of community began with its first restaurant, not its first consumer survey. Of all Great Connectors, Warren and his fellow megachurch leaders seem to lean the least on tactics to build and maintain Gut Values Connections. But they may need to rely on these strategies more to maintain their successes as people change.

Voters saw President Bush as a strong and principled leader in 2004, even when they disagreed with him on the Iraq war. To some, his willingness to buck majority opinion further enhanced the connection. ("Even when we don't agree, you know what I believe and where I stand.") President Clinton's empathy carried him through the Monica Lewinsky scandal. Applebee's homespun atmosphere drew customers who might have liked the competitors' food a bit better. The relevance of the megachurch message has helped people overcome their skepticism with organized religion.

Two Gut Values have emerged as the most important from today forward: *authenticity* and *community*. People are starved for belonging and will pay special heed to leaders who unite them and rally them to a great or common cause. They are tired of phoniness and failure in politics, business, and religion, and, with their emerging power, can find or create alternatives to the institutions that fail them.

In nearly three years of interviews, we found Americans to be an uneasy people: many are struggling to make ends meet in a global economy; most worry about the general direction of the country; they fear that more terrorist strikes could undermine their quality of life; and they are uncertain whether their children's generation will fair better than their own. At the same time, Americans strike us as hopeful and resilient. Perhaps they sense in the winds of change an enormous potential for empowerment. The times have given people unprecedented control over information, entertainment, politics, religion, consumer goods, and their lifestyles. They talk to more people than ever. They can connect with one another and seek help from one another. People can move to like-minded communities and create e-communities, literally out of thin air, to feed their hunger for connections and purpose. Americans are as demanding as ever; they love their country, and think it deserves the very best leaders. "We need a new generation of chiefs with some guts and heart," Heier said. "I hope the next bunch gets it right."

It's important that the next generation of Great Connectors gets it right because they face stiff challenges. The problems that exist today—from globalization and terrorism to a rising federal deficit, a dependence on foreign oil, and looming entitlement crises at home—will not go away on their own. They will likely worsen and be joined by other crises we cannot fathom.

Political, business, and church leaders can prepare themselves for the unpredictable future. They can do what we did: Look just beyond the horizon to the generation on the rise. We call it Generation 9/11, the leading edge of which consists of young Americans who were in high school and college when terrorists struck New York and Washington five years ago.

We spent a lot of time studying eighteen- to twenty-four-year-olds and the rhythms of past generations on the theory that Generation 9/11 may be our best guide to the future. In fact, they are our future. What we discovered is that young Americans are a product of the trends we discussed in this book: the "recentering" of their baby-boom parents; the rise in civic engagement and the hunger for connection; increased mobility and migration; the influence of new technologies; and that intriguing mixture of optimism and skepticism we heard in our interviews at Applebee's. Here's what we found:

- Generation 9/11 is the most ethnically diverse generation in U.S. history.
- Young women outshine young men as in no other generation, and they are changing the nation's gender dynamics.
- An enormous "opportunity gap" divides those with boundless potential and others with virtually no shot at social mobility.
- They grew up with technology and continue to crave innovations that make life easier and more enjoyable and, by connecting them to other people, more meaningful.
- They have little use for old institutions and are quick to create new ones.
- They are more spiritual but less inclined to go to church.
- Balancing life and work has been a priority from their first days on the job.

In *Millennials Rising: The Next Generation*, authors Neil Howe and William Strauss (who also wrote *The Fourth Turning*) say that every fourth generation tends to be a "hero generation" and that Americans born between 1982 and 2002 are primed to be the next great one. Following the pattern of past generations who came of age amid crises, the members of Generation 9/11 are destined to correct the excesses of their baby-boom parents and fill the role of their Greatest Generation grandparents. They are drawn to issues of "community, politics, and deeds whereas the Boomers focused on issues of self, culture, and morals," Howe and Strauss wrote. Generation 9/11 will quickly rise, as did their grandparents, to power and influence, bringing with them a civic ethic that escaped their parents' generation. "Above all, there is a capacity for greatness that lies within this generation in a way that has not been seen since the (Greatest Generation) were children," according to the authors, experts in generational cycles.

Generation 9/11 is not a carbon copy of its grandparents. Its members grew up amid the Internet boom, thus witnessing an immediacy of financial success that the Greatest Generation did not experience until later in life. Unlike their parents and grandparents, Generation 9/11 harbors few illusions about finding security and longevity with a single company, thus are less likely to be loyal to their employers and will expect less loyalty from them. Generation 9/11 is intensely civic-minded, but it's not interested in structured, hierarchical community organizations such as the Kiwanis or Rotary clubs that catered to their grandparents. They'd rather build social networks with online tools such as MySpace.com, where 27 million young adults post artwork, intimate snapshots, and blogs filled with blunt and often racy commentary on their lives.

Generation 9/11 is as politically active as past generations, but its members define political action much differently. "Whereas their parents used protests, marches, concerts and sit-ins as a means of making their voice heard, and their grandparents joined unions or a political party, today's generation are utilizing technology, marketing and networking to further their political agenda," said a Harvard University Institute of Politics study in 2005. Twenty-two percent of college students said they had worn a wristband to show support for a political issue or cause. More than a third said they had signed an online petition; less than a third said they had written an e-mail advocating a position, and 18 percent had contributed to a political blog. Ninety percent of college students say that elective office is an honorable calling. Generation 9/11 cares enough to vote. About 47 percent of Americans aged eighteen to twenty-four cast ballots in 2004, up from 36 percent in 2000, according to the Census Bureau. No other age group increased its turnout by more than 5 percentage points.

Young voters favored Kerry over President Bush by 13 percentage points in 2004, an ominous sign for Republicans. Rarely does a presidential candidate win an election while losing young voters by such a large percentage. Exit polls suggest that Generation 9/11 voters tended to be slightly more liberal, a bit less evangelical, and more inclined to support abortion and gay rights than the general public.

What does Generation 9/11 suggest to us about the future?

## America Will Be a Majority Minority Nation

More than a third of young adults call themselves non-Caucasian, compared to just 12 percent in 1972, according to the Harvard study. But it's not just the number of minorities that makes Generation 9/11 a multicultural force to be reckoned with; it's the minorities' growing influence and position among the elite. Young minorities are graduating from high school and college at higher rates than at any time in history. Asian-American students are outperforming every category, including whites, while Hispanics and blacks are narrowing the education gap, especially in the lower grades. The nation's most prestigious universities are aggressively recruiting minorities from the growing ranks of valedictorians, salutatorians, and academic stars with Hispanic and Asian surnames (30 percent of Harvard's graduates are minorities). One expert called Generation 9/11 "the most globally aware and racially diverse generation in history." Technology allows them to form communities that bypass cultural and class boundaries. Generation 9/11's strong sense of familial and communal obligations is partly due to the large number of second-generation Hispanic and Asian Americans staying true to their parents' values—much as second-generation European immigrants colored twentieth-century society.

**Impact:** Experts predict that minorities will make up a majority of the

U.S. population by 2050. Texas, California, New Mexico, and Hawaii already have majority minority populations and five other states— Maryland, Mississippi, Georgia, New York, and Arizona—are not far behind, with about 40 percent minorities, according to the Census Bureau. Political, business, and religious leaders will need to be aggressive about finding niche communications that reach diverse audiences. Intolerance at the workplace or in politics will not be accepted.

## Women Will Rock

The women of Generation 9/11 are getting better grades, running a majority of student governments, and graduating from college in larger numbers than their male counterparts. In 2005, colleges were on course to give at least 200,000 more bachelor degrees to women than men, according to the National Center for Education Statistics. Women earned 50 percent more associate's and master's degrees than men. That's a stunning turnaround from the 1960s, when two thirds of college students were men. A growing number of women are playing sports in high school and college, the start of a lifetime of teamwork and competition. These girl-powered trends help explain why sexual abstinence is up and teenage pregnancy is down; the women of Generation 9/11 have big plans for the future and don't want to be bogged down by having children too early.

Impact: Family dynamics are shifting. Finding husbands with a similar or better education will be much harder for Generation 9/11 women than it was for their mothers and grandmothers. Men will have to get used to the idea of marrying up. Politics will be less of a boys' club. There will be more female politicians and a high demand for candidates with nontraditional résumés. The best and the brightest will be women, so businesses will be forced to create a more friendly and flexible workplace for pregnant women and mothers. Religious organizations, especially the Roman Catholic Church, will face intense pressure to give more power to women.

## The Opportunities Gap Will Widen

For members of Generation 9/11 with the right education and background, the opportunities will far exceed anything their parents or grandparents could have fathomed. But these may be the worst of all times for those without advantages. Rising college costs, declining rates of real income, the breakdown of two-parent families, and the erosion of welfare and other "safety net" programs are combining to create an Opportunities Gap between the haves and have-nots. Nearly half of people ages eighteen to twenty-four have no college experience, according to the Center for Information and Research on Civic Learning and Engagement, and Harvard reports that one of every four twenty-one-year-olds was raised by a single parent.

**Impact:** The Opportunities Gap will be one of the defining issues of Generation 9/11. The socially conscious high-opportunity Generation 9/11 members will make closing the gap a major political issue. Remember, it was the Greatest Generation that inspired the GI Bill and the growth of organized labor in the 1950s, two reasons for the rise of the middle class. Businesses will realize that people on the privileged side of the Opportunities Gap will pay top dollar to improve their quality of life, whether for the latest gadget, a vacation cruise, or a loaded minivan for the family. Folks on the wrong side of the Opportunities Gap will be forced to jump from brand to brand in search of value. Churches and other nonprofits will find a great cause in helping those trying to bridge the Opportunities Gap.

### Technology Will Transform Communications

Generation 9/11 doesn't get its information from the same places as its parents and grandparents. The Harvard IOP study showed that 42 percent of college students get their news from *The Daily Show* with Jon Stewart, three of every four cited cable TV, and one third read blogs for information. A vast majority prefer cell phones to traditional telephone service. Generation 9/11 is by far the fastest to adapt to new technologies, from iPods to Internet videos. The typical twenty-one-year-old in 2004 was exposed to 3,000 marketing messages per day, a total of 23 million since birth.

**Impact:** Political business and religious leaders will spend significantly less money on mass media and find ways to broadcast their messages through niche media. They will talk to Generation 9/11 one on one and *through each person's lifestyle:* a text message on the phone he's carrying; an Internet ad on the computer he's working on; a video on TVs in his gym; or a personalized video message on his iPod.

## Americans Will Redefine the Role of Religion in Their Lives

A sense of religious duty permeates Generation 9/11 and is the reason many cite for their civic engagement. A majority of fifteen- to twenty-five-year-olds have donated to church or community organizations, reported the Center for Information and Research on Civic Learning and Engagement. High schools are more likely than ever to have religious clubs. At the same time, young people express their faith in highly personal and nontraditional ways. According to Democratic pollster Greenberg, only 41 percent of eighteen- to twenty-five-year-olds said in 2005 that they were Protestant or Christian, and nearly a quarter said they had no religious preference. Still, 72 percent said they believed in God, 73 believed in Heaven, and 64 percent believed in Hell. A plurality of young adults described themselves as "religious" (44 percent), but a majority said they were "spiritual but not religious" (35 percent) or "neither" (18 percent). The generation's diversity applies to religion; America, which has basically been a Christian nation, is becoming the most religiously diverse country on earth.

**Impact:** Churches, including the most successful megachurches, will be forced to adapt to the freewheeling worshipers of the future. As we explained in chapter 3, worshipers will not be as linked to a big church facility as their parents but will demand support from their church leaders as they express their spirituality through community service and other self-directed routes. More businesses will join the ones we praised in chapter 2 for using religion to make a Gut Values Connection. Politicians must use their faith as a way to show voters they share their values, without sounding like advocates for any particular religious institution.

## Americans Will Seek Work–Life Balance

High numbers of young adults say they are depressed and feel pressured to succeed. Many feel overscheduled from an early age—the ubiquitous refrigerator calendars filled with scrawled reminders of sports activities, academic clubs, and various other appointments. They enter adulthood craving a slower pace, and they feel empowered to take control.

**Impact:** Employers hoping to attract the top talent will be forced to offer flexible schedules, more vacation time, and midlife breaks for career ladder climbing. Politicians and preachers will connect with people by speaking to the work–life balance and offering solutions.

## Money Won't Buy Status

Generation 9/11 is less concerned about what money *says about them* than they are in what money can *provide for them* and their families: a good home, safe neighborhood, quality schools, and entertainment.

**Impact:** Americans will be brand-conscious, but they won't buy a monogrammed shirt or the hot new electronic gadget to make a statement about their economic status. They'll buy a brand because it makes them part of a community (e.g., Apple's "technological lifestyle"), or because it makes a statement about their values (e.g., Nike's "Just do it").

## Failing Institutions Will Be Abandoned

Generation 9/11 grew up with a sense of entitlement—not for wealth or material goods to the extent of their baby-boomer parents, but for control. This is what happens when you grow up amid a technological revolution. Generation 9/11 has unusually high expectations of control over how they live, shop, worship, and function in the political system. They are also one of the most informed generations in American history; thus they are doubters and questioners—highly skeptical, though their political and community activism suggests that they are not cynics.

**Impact:** If a consumer product is no good, they won't hesitate to try a different brand. The same applies to a politician or political party (two thirds of young adults want a viable third-party option, according to a 2000 *Newsweek* poll). They'll be even more likely than baby boomers to shop for churches (and it was their parents' generation that fueled megachurches). They won't stand for spin from political, business, or church leaders. Just give them the facts and hope you've earned the benefit of the doubt with a Gut Values Connection.

That's a sentiment that cuts across the generations, from the Harvard students and Generation 9/11ers who helped us research this book to George Heier, the D-Day veteran who eats at Applebee's at least once a week and calls himself a Democrat-turned-Republican-turned-disgruntled-voter. "You want to know how they can get my vote in Washington?" Heier said in his whisky-sandpaper voice. He paused for a beat or two as we leaned over our coffee, not wanting to miss the sage advice that had brought us to this suburban corner of "Applebee's America" and to this table between the bar and the bathroom—beneath the picture of Mr. and Mrs. George Heier.

"They could run the joint like they run this here place," Heier said. "My place."

# Acknowledgments

THIS BOOK WOULD NOT HAVE BEEN POSSIBLE without research assistance from an incredible team of Harvard students, especially Paloma Zepeda, Jordan Pietzsch, Kelly Ward, Steve Grove, and Julie Babayan. The research crew also included Mark Beatty, Kristin Blagg, Rebecca Brocato, Mary Catherine Brouder, Matt Busch, Millie Canter, Irin Carmon, Eric Fish, Joe Green, Dina Guzovsky, Shaan Hathiramani, Daniel J. Hemel, Ai Nhi Hoang, Rachael Johnson, Adam Katz, Eric Lesser, Robert Lord, Rory Malone, Reed Malin, Anat Maytal, Jack McCambridge, Alexandra Messiter, Josh Patashnik, Elise Stefanik, Joe Tartakoff, Aidan Tait, Ariane Tschumi, Faryl Ury, and Andrea Woloski. The book got its start at Harvard's Institute of Politics with the help of Eric Andersen, Sydney Asbury, Phil Sharp, Bill White, and Fournier's "fellow fellows": Mary Beth Cahill, Brad and Julie Carson, Vicki and Bob Huddleston, Tom Newcomb, Roger Simon, and Maggie Williams.

We are also indebted to the many friends and associates who gave us their time and opinions, including Jenny Backus, Dan Balz, Bob Buford, Laura Crawford, Don Fierce, Tucker Eskew, Joe Gaylord, Bob Kowalski, Blair Levin, Mike McCurry, Walt Mossberg, Robert Putnam, Pam Rumpz, and Mike Shannon. A special note of thanks to Gary Golden, who edited and re-edited this manuscript, a selfless gesture that Kowalski would say is tantamount to the blind leading the blind.

This book would not have been possible without Sandy Johnson and the rest of the Associated Press family, including Kathleen Carroll, Donna Cassata, Dave Espo, David Goodfriend, Terry Hunt, Will Lester, and Tom Raum.

We are grateful to Alice Mayhew and Roger Labrie at Simon & Schuster.

Finally, thank you to Laurie Ellison for the tour of her pleasant corner of "Applebee's America."

# Appendix 1

# What's Your Tribe?

Political commentators insist that the nation is a collection of "red states" (Republican) and "blue states" (Democrat). The reality is that America is a collection of tribes—communities of people who run in similar lifestyle circles irrespective of state, county, and precinct lines. Because your political impulses are strongly influenced by those around you, the best way to judge whether you belong to the Red Tribe (Republican), Blue Tribe (Democrat), or the Tipping Tribe (swing voter) is to understand your lifestyle choices, not by issues or the state you live in.

To find out what political Tribe you belong to, take the following quiz:

1. You're at the counter of your local convenience store and have an extra dollar in change. You:

   A. Save it for a rainy day.
   B. Buy a lottery ticket 'cause you're feeling lucky.

2. At a picnic with friends, you open a cooler full of soft drinks and reach for the:

   A. Dr Pepper
   B. Sprite or Pepsi

3. You've won the jackpot on a game show and have a choice between two kinds of vehicles. You select the:

   A. Audi
   B. Saab

4. A free subscription to one of the following two magazines is offered to you. Which one do you choose?

   A. *US News & World Report*
   B. *TV Guide*

5. You're headed out to buy some groceries. You are most likely to visit:

   A. A superstore like Wal-Mart or large supermarket such as Kroger
   B. Whole Foods or similar organic grocer

6. You're at a cocktail party, and the only choices are gin, bourbon, scotch, and vodka. Which liquor do you choose?

   A. Bourbon or scotch
   B. Gin or vodka

7. If we opened your refrigerator, it is more likely that we would find which brand of bottled water:

   A. Ozarka or the local brand
   B. Evian or Dannon

8. You're at happy hour, and there is a special on domestic beer. Which do you choose:

   A. Coors
   B. Bud

9. Which special event would you be more inclined to attend:

   A. Monster truck show
   B. Pro wrestling match

10. If we checked your Internet history, it would more likely show that you had visited:

   A. An auction site, such as eBay
   B. A dating site, such as Match.com

11. Nothing is on network TV you are interested in, so you click through cable; do you:

   A. Stop on the Discovery Channel
   B. Tune in to Court TV

12. Between the following sporting events, which would you more likely watch:

   A. X Games or college football
   B. U.S. Open tennis or Major League soccer

---

Now tally up your answers. For every A, you receive 1 point; for every B you get 0.

Scoring system

8–12   Red, enough said.
5–7    A true Tipper
0–4    Blue, that's you.

# Appendix 2

# Changes in Technology and American Lifestyle

1937   The five-and-dime S. S. Kresge Co. takes its first step toward eventually becoming Kmart when it opens a store in America's first suburban shopping center, the Country Club Plaza in Kansas City, Missouri.

1946   The first mass-produced television set, the ten-inch screen RCA 630-TS, is available to consumers at a cost of $375 ($2,566 in 2000 dollars).

1948   Mahanoy City, Pennsylvania, becomes the first community to have community antenna television, or cable TV, which solved the problem of bad reception for television viewers in this mountain-surrounded town.

1953   Half of U.S. households own a television set.

1955   The first microwave oven is available to consumers at a cost of $1,300.

The first radio facsimile transmission is sent across the United States.

1956   America's first fully enclosed, climate-controlled shopping mall opens in Edina, Minnesota.

For the first time, consumers can buy a television with a remote control, the Zenith Space Command, at an additional cost of approximately 30 percent the cost of the TV.

1962   The first Wal-Mart big-box discount store is open for business in
       Rogers, Arkansas.

       Target opens in Roseville, Minnesota.

       Kmart opens outside Detroit, Michigan.

       Congress passes the Communications Satellite Act of 1962,
       creating the private satellite industry.

1966   Xerox introduces a fax machine that could be attached to any
       phone line. It weighs forty-six pounds and takes six minutes to
       transmit a page.

1967   Raytheon acquires Amana and markets the first moderately
       priced ($500) countertop microwave.

1969   Leonard Kleinrock's UCLA host computer becomes the first
       computer that is attached to the early version of the Internet.

1972   The first in-home video game system, the Magnavox Odyssey, is
       available to consumers.

1973   Martin Cooper of Motorola, Inc., places the first phone call
       from a cell phone.

       There are 30,000 fax machines in the United States.

1975   Sony markets the first VCR.

       HBO establishes the first operational satellite broadcast system
       to send programming to its cable affiliates.

1976   The microwave oven is in 60 percent (about 52 million) of
       American households.

1977   Apple Computer markets the Apple II, the first mass-produced,
       commercially successful personal computer.

1979    Sony introduces the Walkman.

VisiCale, the first commercially affordable electronic spread-sheet program for the Apple II, goes on the market.

1980    CNN goes on the air.

The U.S. Census reports that a majority of American homes have air-conditioning.

1981    MTV goes on the air.

IBM introduces the IBM PC, which runs on the BASIC operating system developed by Microsoft.

1983    Compaq releases the Compaq Portable, one of the first "luggable" personal computers, which costs $3,590.

There are 300,000 fax machines in the United States.

1984    Apple introduces the Macintosh, the first computer designed for use by the general public, which enables users to point and click through the operating system rather than type code.

The federal government breaks up AT&T, leading to more competition in long distance and eventually wireless (in which AT&T had predicted there would be only 1 million subscribers by 2000) and the Internet.

The Cable Communications Policy Act of 1984 is passed, providing the cable industry new freedoms to expand programming and legalizing the private reception of unscrambled satellite television programming.

Sharp introduces the first moderately priced fax machine and sells 80,000 machines in the United States in the first year.

1985   Microsoft introduces Windows 1.0.

For the first time, more television sets are sold in the United States with remote controls than without.

Nintendo markets its first video game consol, the Nintendo Entertainment System.

1989   The Prodigy e-mail platform is introduced.

The first version of the word processing program Word for Windows operating system is issued.

Fax machines number 4 million.

1990   Microsoft releases Windows 3.0, the first widely successful version of the Windows graphical user interface.

1991   Tim Berners-Lee combines hypertext with the Internet, and the graphical interface of the World Wide Web becomes accessible to a mass population, enabling users to read content with the click of a mouse and publish from their PC.

1992   American Mobile Radio Company, predecessor of XM Satellite Radio, is founded.

1993   Apple introduces Quick Take, the first commercially successful digital camera, enabling consumers to transmit photos over the Internet.

Netscape introduces its Web browser, Netscape Communicator, which allows users to access Web pages easily.

The FCC begins auction of spectrum to create five new wireless carriers in every market. The year ends with 24 million subscribers who use cell phones an average of 119 minutes per month and pay an average price of $0.47 per minute.

Number of cable television programming channels reaches 106.

1995    The Internet bookseller Amazon.com goes online.

eBay goes online and launches its person-to-person auctions.

Craigslist, a San Francisco community Web site listing events and classified advertisements, goes online.

The venture capitalist John Doerr joins forces with several cable companies to form @Home, a company designed to bring broadband to American homes.

Two percent of the public goes online at least three days a week to get news.

1996    America Online introduces an unlimited-use pricing plan of $19.99 per month.

PalmPilot, the first successful handheld computer, is introduced in the marketplace.

The first social networking Web site, SixDegrees.com, goes online.

1997    AT&T Wireless introduces the "One Rate," the first wireless plan to replace per minute pricing with a monthly charge for a large number of minutes, accelerating the price war. The year ends with 55 million subscribers who use phones an average of 117 minutes per month with an average price of $0.37 per minute.

FCC awards two licenses for satellite radio operators.

1998    America Online acquires ICQ and makes instant messaging ubiquitous among American teens.

1999    More than half of the Internet users in the United States have used a credit card to make a purchase online.

Amazon.com serves its 10 millionth customer, and AOL's Instant Messenger's 40 million registered users send 430 million messages a day.

TiVo, a maker of digital video recorders (DVR), launches its IPO.

Research in Motion markets the BlackBerry wireless e-mail device.

Cable has 1.4 million broadband subscribers, while phone companies have about 330,000.

2000 Sharp releases the first camera phone.

The year ends with 109 million cell phone subscribers, who use phones an average of 255 minutes per month and pay an average price of $0.18 per minute.

The majority of American households have an Internet connection. The percentage of American households that have Internet connections went up 44 percent in January 2000 to 59 percent by December 2000.

2001 The first time there are more wireless subscribers than active wire phone lines in the United States.

The first time cable television has more viewers than network television.

Apple introduces the iPod.

Cable has over 7 million subscribers, while telecom companies have about 5 million.

Satellite radio begins offering service.

2002 The community group NYCWireless makes free wireless, high-speed Internet accessible in Bryant Park.

Friendster.com goes online and inspires the creation of other social networking Web sites such as MySpace.com.

Within one year the number of Americans who had TiVo or another brand of digital video recorder went up from 900,000 to

1.9 million at the end of 2002. eBay acquires PayPal, the leading online payment network, and announces in its third quarter 2002 financial results that its online net revenue from U.S. consumers has increased 52 percent during the last year.

2003    One hundred twenty million Americans shop online.

2004    The year ends with 182 million subscribers who use cell phones an average of 584 minutes per month and pay an average price of $0.09 per minute.

Cable has over 21 million subscribers, while telecom companies have over 15 million.

Number of cable television channels reaches 390.

2005    Eight in ten Americans have access to the Internet from any location.

MySpace.com has 34 million unique users by the end of the year, a 443 percent increase in 12 months, making it the eighth most-visited site on the web.

Friendster.com has 20 million subscribers, the same number that the largest American Internet service provider, AOL, has.

The number of broadband subscribers surpasses the number of narrowband subscribers.

Twenty-seven percent of the public reads blogs.

2006    Seventy-two percent of Americans have gone online within the last three months from work or from home.

Apple sells its one billionth digital song on the iTunes Web site.

The CTIA wireless association lists the number of cell phone users in the United States at 203 million (34 million in 1996).

# Notes

## A Note on Sources

Interviews with average Americans were conducted in 2004 and 2005 by Fournier, some in his role as chief political writer for the Associated Press. A few quotes and scenes appeared first in Associated Press stories about the 2004 elections. Most of the interviews were conducted in Applebee's restaurants, but many took place in diners, parks, parking lots, bars, and other venues across the country.

Lloyd Hill and his team granted several interviews, beginning with a January 2005 visit by all three authors to Applebee's headquarters in Overland Park, Kansas. A few months later, Hill spoke to Fournier's study group at Harvard's Institute of Politics and sat for an interview. Hill and other company officials also granted several telephone interviews to Fournier through February 2006. Rick Warren appeared at Harvard's IOP in the spring of 2005 and granted a brief interview with Fournier. Warren also spoke with Steve Grove, a graduate student who was one of the book's researchers. Grove provided us his notes of the interview. In January 2006, Warren spoke with Fournier by telephone for the book. Presidents Bush and Clinton declined interview requests.

Nobody was granted the right to edit, delete, preapprove, or veto any material for this book. Each source understood that he or she had no control over how the information they provided would ultimately be used.

### Introduction: Stormy Present

*Bush versus Kerry:* Pre-election surveys and exit polls.

*Warren's church attendance:* Figures provided to Leadership Network, Dallas, Texas, in November 2005.

*Trends and attitude of public:* GfK NOP annual presentations to clients, 2001–2006; Roper Reports Worldwide, a product of GfK NOP; and interviews with Jon Berry, vice president of NOP World and coauthor with Ed Keller of *The Influentials* (New York: Free Press, 2003).

*Cindy Moran remarks:* Interview, March 2005, at Howell, Michigan, Applebee's.

*Presidential election results in the hundred fastest-growing counties:* Michael Shannon of ViaNovo for Dowd.

*Lincoln quote:* Annual message to Congress, December 1, 1862.


## 1: Politics: Values Trump the Economy

Much of this chapter is based on the recollections and records of the coauthors, along with confidential conversations with political leaders and strategists.

*Clinton approval rating:* CNN/USA *Today* Gallup Poll of January 17–19, 2000.

*Bush approval rating:* Gallup Poll had it as low as 46 percent (May 7–9, 2004), and it was at 48 percent just before Election Day (October 29–31, 2004).

*Bush's social networks:* Interviews with Ken Mehlman, Terry Nelson, and Karl Rove, all May 2005, in Washington, D.C.

*Dean's strategies:* Interviews with Dean, September 2005, in Washington, D.C.; campaign manager Joe Trippi by telephone in January 2006; and political strategists Karen Hicks by telephone in January 2006.

*People better informed and educated:* Interviews with Jon Berry in May 2005 and February 2006.

*Debbie Palos and Lynn Jensen remarks:* Interview at Applebee's in Howell, Michigan, shortly after the 2004 election; Palos's telephone interview in January 2006.

*Clinton 1995 news conference:* John F. Harris, *The Survivor: Bill Clinton in the White House* (New York: Random House, 2005).

*Clinton's early strategies:* Interviews with Harold Ickes in May 2005 and Mark Penn in May 2005, both in Washington, D.C.

*Clinton's polling and targeting strategies:* Primary source was interviews with Penn in May and August 2005.

*Don Baer's remarks on Clinton:* Interview, January 2005, in Washington, D.C.

*Paul Begala remarks on Clinton:* Telephone interview in January 2006.

*Galston and Kamarck on polarization: The Politics of Polarization* (Third Way Report, October 2005).

*Clinton quotes as governor:* The Associated Press archives.

*Clinton speeches as president:* The Associated Press archives.

*Bush targeting methods:* Primary sources included interviews with Alex Gage, May 2005, in Alexandria, Virginia; interviews with Rove and Mehlman in Washington. Also see Thomas B. Edsall and James V. Grimaldi, "On Nov. 2, GOP Got More Bang for Its Billion, Analysis Shows," *The Washington Post,* December 30, 2004; Tom Hamburger and Peter Wallsten, "Parties Are Tracking Your Habits," *Los Angeles Times,* July 24, 2005; Jon Gertner, "The Very, Very Personal Is the Political," *The New York Times Magazine,* February 15, 2004; Matt Bai, "The Multilevel Marketing of the President," *The Washington Post Magazine,* April 25, 2004; Michael Barone, "American Politics in the Networking Era," *National Journal,* February 25, 2005.

*Karl Rove's remarks:* Interview, May 2005, at the White House.

*Terry Nelson's remarks:* Interviews, May and November 2005, in Washington, D.C.

*Tim Kaine's strategies:* Interview with Mike Henry, January 2006, in Washington, D.C.

*President Bush's communication strategies:* Primary sources included interviews with Will Feltus in May 2005; and Katharine Q. Seelye, "How to Sell a Candidate to a Porsche-Driving Leno-Loving Nascar Fan," *The New York Times*, December 6, 2004.

*Ken Mehlman's remarks:* Interviews in May 2005 and January 2006, both in Washington, D.C.

*Bonnie Kohn's remarks:* Telephone interview in September 2004.

*Health insurance statistics:* "The Medical Reporter," an Internet-based nonprofit health magazine, 2005.

*Corruption polling:* The Associated Press–Ipsos poll, December 2005.


## 2: Business: Selling Community

Much of this chapter is based on a series of interviews with Applebee's executive team.

*David Goebel's remarks and recollections:* Interviews in January 2005 and January 2006, and supplemented by Laurie Ellison.

*Phil Crimmin's remarks:* Telephone interview, June 2005.

Jim Collins and Jerry I. Porras, *Built to Last: Successful Habits of Visionary Companies* (New York: Harper Collins, 2004).

*Starbucks details:* Interview with Howard Schultz in January 2006; Sosnik's notes on February 2006 shareholders meeting; also see Schultz and Dori Jones Yang, *Pour Your Heart into It: How Starbucks Built a Company One Cup at a Time* (New York: Hyperion, 1997).

*JetBlue background:* Barbara Peterson, *Inside jetBlue, the Upstart That Rocked an Industry* (New York: Penguin Books, 2004).

*Apple Computer background:* "Apple Emerges from the Pod," *BBC News Magazine*, December 16, 2003.

*McDonald's:* Shawn McCarthy, "Can a Leaner Menu Yield McTurnaround?," *The Globe and Mail* [Toronto], March 15, 2004; Kate MacArthur, "MTV and McDonald's in Global Deal," www.chicagobusiness.com, February 17, 2005.

*Applebee's retention strategies:* Erin White, "How to Reduce Turnover," *The Wall Street Journal*, November 21, 2005.

*Harrah's data-mining strategies:* Joe Saumarez Smith, "Why Harvard Lost Out to Vegas," *Financial Times*, April 8, 2005; Carol Pogash, "From Harvard Yard to Vegas Strip," October 7, 2002; "Harrah's Hits the Jackpot with CRM," *Stores*, June 2003; "Harrah's Survey '04: Profile of the American Casino Gambler."

*Businesses' use of religion:* Cathy Lynn Grossman, "Starbucks Stirs Things Up with a God Quote on Cups," *USA Today*, October 19, 2005; Damien Cave, "How Breweth Java with Jesus," *The New York Times*, October 23, 2005.

*Bob Buford remarks:* Telephone interview, September 2005.

*Home Depot details:* Paco Underhill, *Why We Buy: The Science of Shopping* (New York: Simon and Schuster, 1999); Bruce Upbin, "Merchant Princes,"

*Forbes*, January 20, 2003; Amy Tsao, "Retooling Home Improvement," February 14, 2005.

*George Heier remarks:* Interview, January 2005, at Applebee's in Kansas City, Kansas.

*W. R. Grace:* "The History of W. R. Grace & Co.," *Seattle Post-Intelligencer*, November 18, 1999.

*Abe Gustin remarks:* Telephone interview, April 2005.

*Wanda Cole remarks:* Telephone interview, April 2005.

*Weight Watchers program:* Focus group videotapes, August 27, 2003, in Wayne, New Jersey, and February 10, 2004, in Providence, Rhode Island.

*Hill address:* Remarks videotaped March 30, 2005, in Overland Park, Kansas.

*Dick DeVos remarks:* Interview, January 2005, in Washington, D.C.


## 3: Religion: A Cause Greater than Yourself

Principal sources included: Scott Thumma and John Vaughan, "Megachurches Today," Hartford Institute for Religion and Leadership Network, 2001; Scott Thumma, Dave Travis, and Warren Bird, "Megachurches Today 2005," released in January 2006; Adam Hamilton, *Selling Swimsuits in the Arctic: Seven Simple Keys to Growing Churches* (Nashville, Tenn.: Abingdon Press, 2005); Rick Warren, *The Purpose-Driven Church: Growth Without Compromising Your Message and Mission* (Grand Rapids, Mich.: Zondervan, 1995); Rick Warren, *The Purpose-Driven Life* (Grand Rapids, Mich.: Zondervan, 2002); Bob Buford, *Halftime: Changing Your Game Plan from Success to Significance* (Grand Rapids, Mich.: Zondervan, 1994); Bob Buford, *Finishing Well: What People Who Really Live Do Differently* (Brentwood, Tenn.: Integrity, 2004); "Jesus, CEO; Churches as Businesses," *The Economist*, December 24, 2005; James Twitchell, *Branded Nation* (New York: Simon and Schuster, 2004); Kendrick Blackwood, "Christmas Eve at Adam's House," *Kansas City Pitch Weekly*, December 19, 2002; Robert D. Putnam and Lewis M. Feldstein, *Better Together: Restoring the American Community* (New York: Simon and Schuster, 2003); James L. Kidd, "Megachurch Methods," *Christian Century*, May 14, 1997; Catherine Gabe, "Supersized Debate," *The Plain Dealer* [Cleveland], May 9, 2004; Kris Axtman, "The Rise of the American Megachurch," *The Christian Science Monitor*, December 30, 2003; Steven Ginsberg, "Rural Enclaves Resist Megachurches," *The Washington Post*, July 23, 2003; James B. Twitchell, "Jesus Christ Superflock," *Mother Jones*, April 2005; Waveney Ann Moore, "Big-Box Salvation," *St. Petersburg Times* [Florida], August 29, 2004; John Mahler, "The Soul of the Exurb," *The New York Times Magazine*, March 27, 2005; Malcolm Gladwell, "The Cellular Church," *The New Yorker*, September 12, 2005.

*McLean Bible Church:* David Cho, "A Pastor with a Drive to Convert," *The Washington Post*, June 27, 2004; church Web site and onsite literature; interview with Solomon in August 2005 at the church and telephone interview in December 2005.

*Thumma remarks:* Telephone interviews, August 2005 and January 2006.

*Joel Osteen and Lakewood Church:* William C. Symonds, "Earthly Empires," *Business Week*, May 23, 2005; John Leland, "A Church That Packs Them In," *The New York Times*, July 18, 2005; Osteen interview, *Larry King Live*, CNN, June 20, 2005.

*Bob Buford remarks:* Interview, June 2005.

*Warren background:* Principal sources include Howard Manly, "A Purpose-Driven Pastor," *Boston Herald,* March 13, 2005; Richard Vara, "Spiritual Quest Gets Under Way," *Houston Chronicle,* September 27, 2003; Bob von Sternberg, "Purpose of Life?" *Star Tribune* [Minneapolis], November 2, 2003; Tim Stafford, "A Regular Purpose-Driven Guy," *Christianity Today,* November 18, 2002; Sonja Steptoe, "The Man with the Purpose," *Time,* March 29, 2004.

*Willow Creek background:* Principal sources were Lyman A. Kellstedt and John C. Green, "The Politics of the Willow Creek Association of Pastors," *Journal for the Scientific Study of Religion,* 2003; Jim Mellado, "Willow Creek Community Church," Harvard Business School, 1991; David S. Luecke, "Is Willow Creek the Wave of the Future?" May 1, 1997, The Christian Century.

*Mellado remarks:* Interview, July 2005, in Barrington, Illinois.

*Robert Rizzo remarks on strategies:* Telephone interview, April 2005.

*Tom Hoyt remarks on Percept:* Telephone interview, January 2006.

*Mark Batterson remarks on technology:* Interview with Fournier, May 2005, in Washington, D.C.

*Twentieth-century churches:* Principal sources included Fredric Smoler, "The Fourth Great Awakening," *American Heritage,* July 2001; Anne C. Loveland and Otis B. Wheeler, *From Meetinghouse to Megachurch: A Material and Cultural History* (Columbia, Mo.: University of Missouri Press, 2003).

*Peter Drucker background:* Principal sources included Tim Stafford, "The Business of the Kingdom," *Christianity Today,* November 15, 1999; Rich Karlgaard, "Conversations with a Giant," *Forbes,* December 13, 2004; Peter Drucker, "Management's New Paradigms," *Forbes,* October 5, 1998; interviews with Buford.

*Robert Putnam remarks on communities:* Interview, February 2005, in Cambridge, Massachusetts.

*Andy Stern remarks on unions:* Interview, May 2005, in Washington, D.C.; Matt Bai, "The New Boss," *The Washington Post Magazine,* January 30, 2005.

*Robert Lewis remarks on future steps:* Telephone interview, January 2005.

*Dick DeVos remarks:* Interview, January 2005, in Washington, D.C.

## 4: Anxious Americans

Much of this chapter is based on interviews with average Americans from 2003 to 2005. Primary research sources include GfK NOP annual presentations to clients 2001–2006; Roper Reports, "Public Pulse," a product of GfK NOP; several interviews with Jon Berry, vice president of NOP World and coauthor of *The Influentials;* and various polls cited throughout.

*Dubuque scene:* Fournier, "Anxious America" series, The Associated Press, March 24, 2004.

*Trust polling:* Erin McClam, "Six Months After Katrina, AP-Ipsos Poll Finds Fading Confidence in Government," The Associated Press, February 22, 2006.

*Historical context:* William Strauss and Neil Howe, *The Fourth Turning: What the Cycles of History Tell Us About America's Next Rendezvous with Destiny* (New York: Broadway, 1997); telephone interview with Strauss, June 2005.

*Senator John McCain remarks:* Interview, August 2005, in Washington, D.C.

# Notes

*Public opinion on eavesdropping:* Associated Press–Ipsos poll, early February 2006.

*Clinton ratings:* John F. Harris, *The Survivor: Bill Clinton in the White House* (New York: Random House, 2005).

*Rick Linamen remarks:* Interview, August 2005, in Scottsdale, Arizona.

*Newsweek poll:* Jerry Alder, "Spirituality 2005," *Newsweek,* August 29, 2005.

*Scott Thumma remarks:* Telephone interview with Fournier, August 2005.

*Jim Mellado remarks:* Interview with Fournier, July 2005, in Barrington, Illinois.

*Background:* Pamela Paul, "True Believers," *American Demographics,* September 2002.

*Background:* Rebecca Gardyn, "Family Matters," *American Demographics,* September 2002.

## 5: The 3 Cs: Connections, Community, and Civic Engagement

*Jamie Ferrande:* Kim Curtis, "Katrina: It Takes a Network," The Associated Press, September 7, 2005.

*Background on community building:* Robert Putnam, *Bowling Alone: The Collapse and Revival of American Community* (New York: Simon and Schuster, 2000).

*McCain remarks:* Interview, August 2005, in Washington, D.C.

*Scott Heiferman remarks:* Interview, September 2005, in Washington, D.C.

*Background:* Annette Fuentes, "Won't You Be My Neighbor?" *American Demographics,* June 2000.

*Background:* Haya El Nasser, "Beyond Kiwanis: Internet Builds New Communities," *USA Today,* June 2, 2005.

*Bush supporters:* Interview with Terry Nelson, May 2005, in Washington, D.C.

*Atchley obit: The Times* [Shreveport, Los Angeles], October 2, 2005.

*Meetup details:* Interview with Heiferman; and Meetup Web site.

*"Diedre" remarks:* Telephone interview, December 2005.

*Census data:* Interview with John Bridgeland, August 2005, in Washington, D.C.

*Putnam remarks:* Interview, March 2005, in Cambridge, Massachusetts.

*Internet background:* "The Internet Improves American Capacity to Maintain Their Social Networks and Get Help," press release from Pew Internet & American Life Project, January 25, 2006; Jeffrey Boase et al., "The Strength of Internet Ties," Pew Internet & American Life Project, January 25, 2006.

*Netville:* Keith Hampton, "Grieving for a Lost Network: Collective Action in a Wired Suburb," Department of Urban Studies and Planning, Massachusetts Institute of Technology; telephone interview with Hampton, October 2005.

*Volleyball interviews:* Conducted October 2005, at an Arlington, Virginia, gym.

*Roberta Bailey remarks:* Telephone interview, September 2005.

*Philip Lutz remarks:* Telephone interview, October 2005.

*Cindy Seip remarks:* Telephone interview, November 2005.

*Adam Wolbaum remarks:* Telephone interview, November 2005.

*"Vanesti" remarks:* From Meetup Web site.

*IM conversation:* Provided to researcher Eric Lesser by the participants. Screen names charged for publication at their request.

*IM background:* Primary sources included Amanda Lenhart et al., "Teens and Technology," Pew Internet & American Life Project, July 27, 2005; Eulynn Shiu and Amanda Lenhart, "How Americans Use Instant Message," Pew, September 1, 2004.

*Diana Read remarks:* Fournier's interviews in Vienna, Virginia, bar and in Washington, D.C.

*Howard Dean remarks:* Interview, September 2005, in Washington, D.C.

*Karen Hicks remarks:* Telephone interview, January 2006.

*Dean critics:* E. J. Dionne Jr., "Dean Bubble Not a Complete Bust," *The Washington Post,* February 20, 2004.

*Dean background:* Hanna Rosin, "People-Powered: In New Hampshire, Howard Dean's Campaign Has Energized Voters," *The Washington Post,* December 9, 2003.

*Fantasy sports:* Primary sources include telephone interviews with Ilan Graff, Daniel Okrent, and Dan Epstein, October 2005; Devin Gordon, "A Healthy Fantasy Life," *Newsweek,* August 29, 2005; John Moore, "The Marketing Juju of Fantasy Football," www.marketingprofs.com, August 23, 2005; "It's Football, Friends and Fun," press release from Sports and Entertainment Academy, Kelley School of Business, Indiana University, August 29, 2000.

*Video games:* Primary sources include Kemp Peterson interview with researcher Eric Lesser; "Let the Games Begin," Pew Internet & American Life Project, July 6, 2003; subscriber numbers from PricewaterhouseCooper LLP, Wilkofsky Grue Associates.

*Battle lessons:* Dan Baum, "Battle Lessons," *The New Yorker,* January 17, 2005.

*Hurricane Katrina:* U.S. *News & World Report,* September 19, 2005; Gillian Flaccus, "Americans Open Their Wallets and Offer Their Skills to Help Hurricane Victims," The Associated Press, September 1, 2005; interview with Huckabee, September 2005; Kaye D. Trammell, "Slogging and Blogging Through Katrina," *The Washington Post,* September 3, 2005.

*Citizen journalists:* Dan Gillmor, *We the Media: Grassroots Journalism by the People for the People* (Sebastopol, Calif.: O'Reilly, 2004); David Kirkpatrick, "Why There's No Escaping the Blogs," *Fortune,* January 10, 2005; Theo Emery, "Widely Used Bike Lock Can Be Picked with a Ballpoint Pen," Associated Press, September 16, 2004; telephone interview with Donna Tocci, October 2005.

*Chris Kofinis remarks:* Interview, January 2006, in Washington, D.C.

## 6: Navigators

Primary sources for data on media fragmentation include "Fundamental Shifts in U.S. Media and Advertising Industries," New Politics Institute: A Think Tank for Politics, November 2005; "Changing Media Landscape," Echoditto fact sheet based on Nielsen Media Research and Forrester Research.

Primary sources on word-of-mouth marketing include Rob Walker, "The Hidden (in Plain Sight) Persuaders," *The New York Times,* December 5, 2004; Dave Godes of Harvard Business School and Dina Mayzlin of Yale University, "Firm-Created Word-of-Mouth Communication: A Field Based Quasi Experiment Executive Summary," Spring 2003; Dave Balter, "The Word of Word of Mouth," undated; Kara Kridler, "Procter & Gamble to Cut Its Television Advertising," The

Daily Record [Baltimore], June 14, 2005; Samar Farah, "Making Waves," www. cmomagazine.com, July 2005; Jeffrey Boase et al., "The Strength of Internet Ties," Pew Internet & American Life Project, January 25, 2006.

*Bonnie Kohn and Julian Sowa remarks:* Interview, July 2005, at Barington, Illinois, Applebee's.

*Mary Shull remarks:* Telephone interview, November 2005.

*Shannon Sullivan remarks:* Telephone interview, January 2006.

*Dave Balter remarks:* Telephone Interview, August 2004.

Michael Hill, "Old Brews Cool to Young Drinkers," The Associated Press, June 10, 2005.

*John Hayes remarks:* "Fundamental Shifts in U.S. Media and Advertising Industries," New Politics Institute: A Think Tank for Politics, November 2005.

*Joe Andrew remarks:* Text of keynote address, Politics and the Law Symposium, Duke Law School, October 18, 2005.

*La Esquina:* Frank Bruni, "A Secret Too Dark to Keep," *The New York Times,* August 31, 2005; telephone interviews with Jennifer Baum and James Gersten, September 2005; Denny Lee, "Remember, You Didn't Read It Here," *"The New York Times,* July 31, 2005.

*20Q.net: Patti Saitow remarks:* Telephone interview, August 2005; "Radica 20Q BzzCampaign summary," August 2005; Linda Tischler, "What's the Buzz?" *Fast Company,* May 2004.

*Malchow remarks:* Interview, June 2005, in Washington, D.C.

## 7: Americans on the Move

Much of this chapter is the result of several visits to Livingston County by Fournier during 2004 and 2005. Principal sources included David Brooks, *On Paradise Drive: How We Live (and Always Have) in the Future Tense* (New York: Simon & Schuster, 2004); Fred Barnes, "The Revolt in the Exurbs," *Weekly Standard,* November 21, 2005; Haya El Nasser, "For Political Trends, Think Micropolitan," *USA Today,* November 23, 2004; Robert E. Lang, Dawn Dhavale, and Kristin Haworth, "Micropolitics: The 2004 Vote in Small-Town America," Metropolitan Institute, Virginia Polytechnic Institute, November 2004; Mark Gersh, "Micro-Politics," New Democrats Online, March 15, 2005; Bruce Katz, "Small Growth: The Future of the American Metropolis?" London School of Economics, July 2002; Ben Brown, "Exurbs Flourish, But Is This What We Really Want?" *USA Today,* December 2, 2004; C. Kenneth Orski, "The Emerging Influence of the Micropolis," *Innovation Briefs,* January–February 2005; Robert E. Lang, "New Metropolis Counties: Suburbs of Suburbs," Metropolitan Institute, Virginia Polytechnic Institute, December 2003; Robert E. Lang, "Edgeless Cities: Exploring the Elusive Metropolis," Metropolitan Institute, Virginia Polytechnic Institute, 2002; Stephanie McCrummen, "Subdivisions Impose Social Divide," *The Washington Post,* May 1, 2005; Stephanie McCrummen, "A Subdivision Becomes a Home," *The Washington Post,* February 27, 2005; David Brooks, "A Nation of Villages," *The Washington Post,* January 19, 2006.

*Moving data:* Robert Putnam, *Bowling Alone: The Collapse and Revival of American Community* (New York: Simon and Schuster, 2000).

*New Sun Belt:* William H. Frey, "Regional Shifts in America's Voting Aged

Population: What Do They Mean for National Politics?" University of Michigan News Service, 2000.

*Minority trends:* Paul Overberg and Haya El Nasser, "Minority Groups Breaking Patterns," *USA Today*, August 11, 2005.

*Third wave:* Jim Taylor, "Manifest Destiny," *American Demographics*, September 2004.

*Lifestyle motivators:* Jennifer C. Kerr, "Americans Migrate to Cities in South, West," The Associated Press, June 30, 2005.

*First suburbs:* Stephen Ohlemacher, "Inner-Ring Suburbs Face Challenges Threatening Their Stability," The Associated Press, February 15, 2006.

*Population trends:* Census Bureau; www.americancity.org; Rutgers sociology professor Max Herman, "Riots-67" Web site; Witold Rybczynski, "Shrinking Cities," Wharton School, University of Pennsylvania, June 8, 1999; Larry Copeland and Barbara Hansen, "Out-Migration Cools Talk of Inner-City Resurgences," *USA Today*, June 30, 2005.

*Background:* Joel Kotkin, "Rule Suburbia: The Verdict's In, We Love It There," *The Washington Post*, February 6, 2005.

*Robert Block remarks:* Interview, March 2005, in Howell, Michigan.

*Livingston County data:* Block interview; county Web site; "2003 Livingston County DataBook & Community Profiles," Livingston County Department of Planning.

*Fastest-growing locales:* U.S. Census Bureau press release, February 15, 2006.

*Debbie Kromer remarks:* Interview, May 2005, at Howell, Michigan, Applebee's.

*Diversity in suburbs:* Bruce Katz, "Welcome to the 'Exit Ramp' Economy," *The Boston Globe*, May 13, 2001.

*Commutes:* Robert Tanner, "Stuck in Traffic," The Associated Press, June 11, 2005; Rick Lyman, "In Exurbs, Life Framed by Hours Spent in the Car," *The New York Times*, December 18, 2005; Brad Edmondson, "In the Driver's Seat," *American Demographics*, March 1996.

*Housing:* Primary sources included Livingston County data book; telephone interview with Gordon V. Hartman, October 2005; telephone interview with Marshall Gray, division president of K. B. Home, January 2006; interview with Steve Boone conducted by researcher Kelly Ward, September 2005; Mary Lynn Smith, "Porches Are Coming Back Front & Center," *Star Tribune* [Minneapolis], April 23, 2005; Tamara M. Freund, "Back to the Front Porch," Iowa State University Extension Service, June 24, 1996.

*Cindy Moran remarks:* Interview, March 2005, in Howell, Michigan.

*Election results:* Livingston County Web site; U.S. Census Bureau on micropolitan zones.

*Mike Brewster remarks:* Interview, May 2004, at Howell, Michigan, Applebee's.

*Mary Gillard remarks:* Interview, October 2004, at Tampa, Florida, Applebee's.

*Virginia election analysis:* ViaNovo, for Dowd.

*Minnesota:* Stan Greenberg, "The Changing Shape of Minnesota," www.greenbergresearch.com, December 14, 2004.

*Food:* Kristina Shevory, "You Made the Meatloaf. You Just Didn't Make It at Home," *The New York Times*, August 28, 2005.

*Land use:* Robert J. Samuelson, "America by the Numbers," *The Washington Post*, January 18, 2006.

## 8: Generation 9/11

We are indebted to Kelly Ward, a graduate student at the Kennedy School of Government, who worked with Sosnik to research this chapter.

*George Heier remarks:* Interview, January 2005, at Kansas City, Kansas, Applebee's.

*Diversity and technology:* "Generation Y: The New Global Citizen," Merrill Associates Topic of the Month, June 2004; "Like Most Americans, College Students Rate President Bush Near Historic Lows," Harvard University Institute of Politics press release, November 16, 2005.

*Women and work–life balance:* Interview with Robert Strauss, *The Exchange with Laura Knoy*, New Hampshire NPR, January 1, 2004.

*Institutions:* Pamela Price, "Community: Next Generation Civic Groups," *The Next American City*, January 2005.

*Spiritual:* Kurt Thiel, *The Millennial Generation*, Fuller Seminary, Spring 2000; William Strauss and Neil Howe, *Millenials Rising: The Next Great Generation* (New York: Vintage Books: 2000); Strauss's NPR interview is a source throughout the chapter.

Fall 2005 Survey of Student Opinions, Harvard University Institute of Politics, press release, November 16, 2005.

*Voting:* U.S. Census Bureau; Fournier and Stephen Ohlemacher, "Youngsters Led Voter Turnout Surges in Presidential Elections," The Associated Press, November 16, 2005; Center for Information and Research on Civic Learning and Engagement, "Quick Facts about Young Voters 2004"; exit polls.

*Statistics on college students:* Harvard IOP "Young Voters Guide," 2005.

*Graduation rates:* Jay Greene, "High School Graduation Rates in the United States," Manhattan Institute for Policy Research, April 2002.

*Education gap:* Michael Dobbs, "School Achievement Gap Is Narrowing," *The Washington Post*, July 15, 2005.

*Spirituality:* "A Brookings Brief: Faith and Youth in the iPod Era," Brookings Institute, April 5, 2005.

*Majority minority data:* Census Bureau press release, "Texas Becomes Nation's Newest Majority-Minority State," August 11, 2005.

*Diplomas by gender:* National Center for Education Statistics, 2004–2005; U.S. National Center for Education Statistics, Digest of Education Statistics.

*Third party:* Howard Fineman, "Generation Ys First Vote," *Newsweek*, July 17, 2000.

*Youth spirituality:* Greenberg, Quinlan, and Rosner: "OMG! How Generation Y Is Redefining Faith in the iPod Era," www.greenbergresearch.com, April 2005; "Huricanes, Earthquakes, Tsunamis and Terrorism: The end of the world? Not according to Generation Y," www.greenbergresearch.com, December 2005.

# Index

# About the Authors

RON FOURNIER, formerly chief political writer for The Associated Press, is co-founder and editor-in-chief of HOTSOUP.com, an online community of Navigators (also called Opinion Drivers). The winner of major awards for his coverage of the 2000 and 2004 presidential elections, he lives in Arlington, Virginia.

MATTHEW DOWD was chief campaign strategist for President George W. Bush in 2004. Founding partner of Vianovo, a corporate brand and positioning firm, Dowd is an adviser to California Governor Arnold Schwarzenegger and Michigan gubernatorial candidate Dick DeVos. He also is a HOTSOUP.com co-founder.

DOUGLAS B. SOSNIK was for six years a senior adviser to President Bill Clinton. In the second Clinton term, he served as senior adviser for policy and strategy. He now advises Fortune 500 companies, the National Basketball Association, as well as Democratic governors and senators.